Philosophy and Literature in Latin America

SUNY Series in Latin American and Iberian Thought and Culture
Jorge J. E. Gracia, EDITOR

PHILOSOPHY AND LITERATURE IN LATIN AMERICA

A Critical Assessment of the Current Situation

Jorge J.E. Gracia and Mireya Camurati

editors

STATE UNIVERSITY OF NEW YORK PRESS

Published by
State University of New York Press, Albany

© 1989 State University of New York

Printed in the United States of America

For information, address State University of New York
Press, State University Plaza, Albany, NY 12246

Library of Congress Cataloging-in Publication Data

Philosophy and literature in Latin America : a critical assessment of
    the current situation / edited by Jorge J. E. Gracia and Mireya
    Camurati.
        p. cm. — (SUNY series in Latin American and Iberian thought
    and culture)
    Bibliography: p.
    Includes index.
    ISBN 0-7914-0038-7. — ISBN 0-7914-0039-5 (pbk.)
    1. Latin American literature – 20th century – History and criticism.
    2. Philosophy, Latin American – History – 20th century.
    3. Bibliography – Latin America.   I. Gracia, Jorge J. E.
    II. Camurati, Mireya.   III. Series.
    PQ7081.P47   1989
    860'.9'98 – dc19   88-31670
                                                                          CIP

10 9 8 7 6 5 4 3 2 1

Contents

PART II. LITERATURE

WRITERS

Preface

It can no longer be doubted that Latin American literature is one of the great world literatures. Indeed, the list of Latin American literary figures of first order goes back several centuries and includes some of the world's most important poets, novelists and playwrights. Moreover, it is in Latin America that Western philosophy has been more clearly faced with the challenges posed by the moral and conceptual issues that arise from Third World societies, and it is in Latin America that philosophy has responded to such challenges more explicitly.

Yet, when one looks at the field of Latin American studies, particularly to the way these studies are carried out in the United States, one is struck by the comparatively little importance that is placed upon literature and philosophy. It cannot be denied that Latin American literature receives considerable attention on the whole, but such attention is largely paid by departments of Spanish and Portuguese and by journals that concentrate on those languages. The situation with philosophy is much worse, for Latin American philosophy is not only ignored by Latin Americanists in general, but is regarded as non-existent by professional philosophers in this country. Indeed, in the United States there are only a few teaching positions at the college level available to individuals who specialize in the field.

Centers, departments, and journals of so-called "Latin-American studies" pay little attention to literature and/or philosophy. Their bias is clearly in favor of the social sciences: anthropology, economics, geography, history, political science, and sociology. This bias, of course, may be in part the result of an old prejudice that sees the humanities as of only marginal interest in the so-called "scientific" study of peoples. And it may be in part a result of a well-intentioned regard for disciplines that have a direct bearing on what appear to be the most pressing needs of Latin American societies: food, shelter, and political stability. Unfortunately, this bias neglects to take into account that the humanities have often played a significant role in Latin American society that goes well beyond their intellectual and cultural dimensions, affecting also the functioning of government and the formulation of policy. This should be evident to anyone who knows any of the history of Latin America, for many of its philosophers, authors, and other intellectuals of note have occupied positions of leadership in government and have chartered the course of development of Latin American societies for decades. One needs only to refer to how positivist thinkers and ideologues were able to introduce their views into the fabric of Latin American society in the nineteenth century to realize the importance of the study and understanding of the humanities and the need to integrate them into the general field of Latin American studies.

Needless to say, not all programs and journals devoted to Latin American studies suffer from a bias in favor of the social sciences and against the humanities; many of them are trying to strike a balance among the various disciplines that constitute the field. For example, the Latin American Studies Association makes room in its program for sessions and discussions organized by societies devoted to the study of the humanities, and the *Latin American Research Review* and the *Inter-American Review of Bibliography* often take into account published research in literary and other humanistic studies related to Latin America. But these efforts are exceptions and often fail to do justice to the complexity of the fields involved. There is, therefore, considerable room for improvement.

It is with that improvement in mind that we publish this volume. Its aim, as the title indicates, is to present an overall, although necessarily incomplete, view of two disciplines that are at the core of the humanities and in which cross-fertilization is common in Latin America. Indeed, the work of Samuel Ramos, Octavio Paz, and Jorge Luis Borges, among others, testifies to these points. The volume is divided into two parts, which are devoted respectively to each of the mentioned disciplines. The section on philosophy contains five papers. Four of these aim to illustrate the current state of the discipline in three leading countries: Argentina, Brazil, and Mexico. The fifth paper presents, in a very schematic fashion, the situation in other countries. The literature section has been divided into two parts. The first contains papers dealing with poetry, narrative and drama. The second adds a dimension of particular importance to Latin Americanists working in the United States: It deals with the awarding of literary prizes to Spanish writers, the publication of inter-American journals, and the presence of Latin American books in the libraries of this country. These are areas in which very little research has been carried out and which, for that reason, should add an interesting new dimension to the field of Latin American studies.

All but two of the papers contained in the volume were presented at the 3rd Congress of the Federación Internacional de Estudios sobre América Latina y el Caribe that took place in Buffalo, New York, September 23–26, 1987. The congress papers have been appropriately revised for publication, but their main thrust has been left unchanged. The papers especially written for the volume are Hugo Biagini's "Contemporary Argentinian Philosophy" and Jorge J. E. Gracia's "Philosophy in Other Countries of Latin America." The general theme of the congress was "A Critical Assessment of Latin American Studies" and it is within that context that the papers contained in this book should be read. The papers do not aim to provide an exhaustive description of past gains in a particular discipline, nor do they claim to be the last word on a particular topic. Rather, they are meant as tentative charts of what is happening now in various areas of humanistic activity and are intended to help those who need an introduction to them.

Finally, we would like to express our appreciation to all those who in one way or another have helped make this book a reality. First of all are the authors themselves who cooperated willingly and patiently with the editors in the preparation of the book. Second, we would like to thank the various institutions and organizations that functioned as sponsors of the Congress of the FIEALC, thus indirectly contributing to the realization of this project. A complete list of all the organizations would be too long to be reproduced here, but we would like to recognize at least those without whose help the event would not have taken place: State University of New York at Buffalo, New York Council for the Humanities, Roswell Park Memorial Institute, Los Buenos Vecinos, Puerto Rican American Community Association and the International Institute of Buffalo. Also we would like to thank Barry Luby for his permission to reprint José Kozer's poems "You Remember, Sylvia" and "Franz Kafka's Sprout," whose English translation appeared in his *Anthology of Contemporary Latin American Literature* (New Jersey: Farleigh Dickinson University Press, 1985). Finally, we would like to thank Marie Fleischauer for her willing cooperation in the technical aspects involved in the preparation of the manuscript.

Jorge J. E. Gracia
Mireya Camurati

PART I

PHILOSOPHY

Introduction

JORGE J. E. GRACIA

Latin American philosophy did not become well established as an independent and professional discipline until the fifth decade of this century, a period that Francisco Romero called "período de normalidad filosófica." Risieri Frondizi's description of Latin American philosophy before 1940 speaks for itself:

> There is no Latin American philosophy in the sense we give to the term when we speak of a British philosophy, or of a German or French and Italian, or modern and contemporary, or North American philosophy beginning with Peirce, Royce and James. In other words, there has not been in Latin America any original philosophy which may be the genuine expression of the spiritual characteristics of Latin Americans. The so called Latin American philosophy is nothing more than the reformulation of philosophical problems originated in Europe. Hence, to be concerned about its history is to deal with the influence that European philosophy had on it.[1]

It does not take much research into the history of Latin American philosophy to realize that Frondizi's words are true. The development of philosophy in Latin America before 1940 can be characterized in two ways: Prior to 1910, it can be described largely as ideological; from 1910 to 1940, it may be characterized as a reaction against positivism. During the first period, the ideas used and the dialectic in which philosophers engaged generally responded to needs external to philosophy. This is true of the three movements that dominated Latin American philosophy at the time: scholasticism, liberalism, and positivism. The use of philosophy for nonphilosophical purposes, however, became most explicit with the third. In positivism, ideas were

1

Between 1910 and 1940 the ideological character of Latin American philosophy diminished considerably. There were still influential ideological currents, but on the whole Latin American philosophers were concerned rather with the rejection of positivism. Many of their ideas, however, were borrowed from European thinkers, such as Bergson and Boutroux, and as a result their originality was limited. Moreover, although the ideas they borrowed and the end they pursued were fundamentally philosophical, they often failed to internalize the problems that had given rise to those ideas or to develop original solutions to those problems, and they faced additional obstacles related to the lack of proper institutional support. Consequently, in most instances they were unable to enter fully in the philosophical mainstream of the West, to develop new issues, and to achieve recognition outside of Latin America.

The task of internalizing problems, rather than simply borrowing ideas, and of following the inner dialectic of these problems was left to a great extent to the next generation — the generation of normalcy. This period, as mentioned earlier, began around 1940 and some of its participants, like Romero, made original contributions to philosophy. Nonetheless, at this time there is no Latin American philosophy in the sense of Latin America's developing and maintaining an autochthonous philosophical tradition based on problems arising from its own inner dialectic. Even today Latin American philosophy still moves to a large extent due to external stimuli: it reacts instead of acting by itself. The changes that take place within it periodically are still largely the result of the impact of European and North American ideas on Latin American philosophers. A trip abroad, the translation of a book, the visit of a European or North American philosopher, a congress with international participants and similar events, give Latin Americans the opportunity to enter into dialogue with new ideas, imported from outside of Latin America. On the other hand, the situation of Latin American philosophy today is different from the one described by Frondizi in that Latin American philosophers have been able, particularly since 1960, to make many and regular original contributions to philosophy. Frondizi himself is one of the first examples of this new development in Latin American thought. His work is known both in Latin America and in the United States, where it has been introduced and studied.[2]

The present situation of Latin American philosophy, therefore, is not so desperate as it was forty years ago. Latin American Philosophers have superseded the stage of what one might call *uncritical absorption* that characterized their first philosophical steps and are moving from a period of *critical interaction* into a period of *maturity*.[3]

Obviously, the level of development is not the same in every country of Latin America. In some, such as Argentina, Brazil, and Mexico, philosophical reflection has gone well beyond the initial stages of development, having acquired a respectable level of sophistication. But there are other countries where, properly speaking, philosophical investigation does not exist. In those countries, philosophy remains a subject in the university or secondary school curriculum that has not gone beyond an elementary pedagogical level. In fact, in some of those countries the development of the discipline does not even reach the level of uncritical absorption that was common in many other Latin American countries before 1940.

The first thirty years of this period, from 1940 to 1970, have been fairly well studied. Books such as Francisco Miró Quesada's *Despertar y proyecto del filosofar latinoamericano* (Fondo de Cultura Económica, 1974), Sergio Sarti's *Panorama della filosofia ispanoamericana contemporanea* (Cisalpino-Golliardica, 1976), and others have given us a good picture of the history and development of philosophical ideas in Latin America at the time. There are also several fairly good studies of twentieth-century Latin American philosophy in Spanish that explore these years. In English there are some general studies of the period, such as H. E. Davis's *Latin American Thought: A Historical Introduction* (Louisiana, 1972) and W. R. Crawford's *A Century of Latin American Thought* (Harvard, 1944). There are also works limited to particular countries and some that concentrate on the more idiosyncratically nationalistic and regionalistic viewpoints. An example of the first type is M. Weinstein's *The Polarity of Mexican Thought* (Penn State, 1976), which deals exclusively with Mexico. Perhaps the best example of the second is Martin S. Stabb's *In Quest of Identity: Patterns in the Spanish American Essay of Ideas. 1890–1960* (Chapel Hill, 1967).

Various collections of texts complement these studies. There are many anthologies in Spanish and at least three English ones that should be mentioned. Aníbal Sánchez Reulet's general compilation *Contemporary Latin American Philosophy* (New Mexico, 1954) ends with a selection from Francisco Romero (1891–1962). *Philosophical Analysis in Latin American* (Dordrecht, Holland, 1984), edited by E. Rabossi, E. Villanueva, M. Dascal, and J. J. E. Gracia is a specialized text that pays attention to only one philosophical current in Latin America. Of the fourteen authors included in my most recent text, *Latin American Philosophy in the Twentieth Century* (Buffalo, 1986), only four are living.

From all this it should be clear that at least for the English-speaking public there is still no general source of information on recent Latin American philosophy. There is adequate material for the frequently used not only to further economic and technological development, but even, as in the case of the government of Porfirio Díaz in Mexico, to support political regimes.

period that ends in 1940 and there is some material that covers the period between 1940 and 1975. But there is practically nothing on what has been happening to Latin American philosophy in the last ten years. Indeed, a survey of the periodical literature shows that the number of articles being published in the United States dealing with recent philosophical developments in Latin America is insignificant.[4]

Yet the productivity and sophistication of Latin American philosophers recently has dramatically increased. For example, there are now in Latin America more than half a dozen journals of philosophy with an international reputation that publish articles of excellent quality: *Revista Latinoamericana de Filosofía* (Buenos Aires), *Análisis Filosófico* (Buenos Aires), *Crítica* (Mexico), *Diánoia* (Mexico), *Manuscrito* (Campinas, Brazil), *Discurso* (São Paulo), and *Diálogos* (Puerto Rico). The three major centers of philosophical activity, Buenos Aires, Mexico City and São Paulo-Campinas, have impressive institutes devoted to research in philosophy. True, all of this has to do with the infrastructure of the discipline, but much could be said as well concerning the sophistication of philosophical discourse that is now taking place in Latin America.

There is, therefore, a clear need to provide an introductory chart to the recent development of philosophy in Latin America and this is what the five philosophy papers included in this part aim to do. Three papers concentrate on the three countries that have the most active philosophical life in Latin America. It is well known that Argentina, perhaps because of its close ties to Europe, has always been a leader in this area and, although recent political and economic events have interfered with the proper development of the discipline, Buenos Aires is still the most important philosophical center of Latin America. Moreover, since the recent return to democracy in the country, there has been a resurgence of philosophical activity that promises to bear important fruits in the near future. But Mexico and Brazil are not far behind. The sheer size and resources of Brazil have resulted in the creation of large universities, and this has opened unusual opportunities for philosophers. Finally, Mexico has a long and well established tradition of philosophical excellence that is finding unusual new outlets in recent years. Mexico has become a haven for philosophers from all over Latin America who, owing to political persecution, have had to leave their own countries. This influx has created an interesting situation that merits special attention.

By looking at what is happening in philosophy in these three countries one can get a pretty good idea of what is occurring philosophically in Latin America. Still, philosophical activity is not confined to the three countries mentioned. In spite of the limited philosophical development of other Latin American countries there are important figures and landmarks that need to be taken into account in an overview of the whole area. There are signs of change and progress even in some of the most philosophically backward countries. For this reason we have added a fifth, brief paper, dealing with the philosophical situation of other countries in Latin America. We hope that the overview we present provides a balanced introduction to recent Latin American philosophy and serves as the basis for comparison of its situation with that of literature, the other discipline discussed in this book.

CHAPTER 1

Contemporary Argentinian Philosophy*

HUGO E. BIAGINI

We are going to cover a relatively conventional span in Argentinian philosophy, namely, the last thirty years (1958–87). During that span of time our society — indeed, the whole Southern cone of South America — was subjected to lengthy military autocracies (with some scattered democratic interregnums), which, however, lacked the necessary stamina to undermine the entrenched power of oligarchic factions and were constantly under the threat of destabilization. During every one of the dictatorships, these oligarchic factions took hold of the nation, initiating processes of denationalization and privatization, which put severe constraints on social justice and civil rights.

Obviously, philosophy too went through a period of great deterioration. At the beginning of that period, philosophers formerly connected with Peronism were ousted from their posts at national universities by the so-called "Revolución Libertadora" (1955–58). They were fortunate enough, however, to find employment in private universities. But by 1966, as a result of the further erosion of the constitutional order, they began emigrating from Argentina, in small numbers at first. Ten years later, however, a sustained exodus could be observed, resulting from work limitations, ideological taboos, and the very physical insecurity with which people were threatened under the state-run terrorism of the period that goes from 1976 to 1983.

Happily enough, favorable opportunities allowed an important cluster of Argentine philosophers to move to other countries where they found work. In many cases they were able to achieve a level of development and proficiency unattainable to those who were forced into "internal exile," so to speak.

---

*Translated by Jorge J. E. Gracia.

Thus, the panorama of contemporary Argentinian philosophy that developed is quite complex. On the one hand, there are many individuals who for personal reasons decided to move out of the country or who have collaborated in one way or another in courses, publications, and events originating outside of Argentina. To these must be added those who found themselves in a kind of political-intellectual exile, which, although not historically new, has acquired in recent times some peculiar characteristics. On the other hand, there are some foreign thinkers and philosophers who have established themselves in Argentina and have done significant work, although their numbers have diminished considerably in recent times.

For these reasons we shall use very broad criteria to refer to Argentinian philosophy. We shall include in it both the work of Argentinians who practice philosophy inside and outside of Argentina, as well as the work of all those who have settled among us and have contributed to philosophical reflection in our country. Obviously, we will not include any kind of foreign philosophical work, even if it has been published in Argentina, although the importance of such materials for Latin America should not be underestimated.

We shall restrict, however, our understanding of 'philosophy' to its most academic sense, leaving out many other connotations the term has in Latin America.[1] It should also be noted that several important figures died before the period that concerns us and several others had ceased to make important contributions to philosophy. I refer in particular to Luis Juan Guerrero, Vicente Fatone, Francisco Romero, Carlos Cossio, Angel Vasallo and many other representative figures of Argentinian philosophy.

Between Technification and Problematization: Definition

From a certain perspective, Argentina seemed to have been destined to be something like the United States of South America, to the point that by the end of the nineteenth century it had received the most varied world immigration in relation to the number of inhabitants. Moreover, Buenos Aires, the capital, came to be perceived as the South American Paris or the Athens of the River Plate for its receptivity to new ideas and its ability to adapt them to its own situation.

The deep institutional and economic misfortunes that Argentina has been suffering for many years do not seem to have blunted in a similar proportion the cultural gains it had achieved even during times when its geographical isolation had been an obstacle to cultural prominence. In the philosophical sphere it is possible to show how Argentina has achieved a clear intellectual maturity, as conceived traditionally. In addition to an acceptable academic level in the practice and teaching of philosophy in Argentina, there are many examples of progress. Among these indicators stand out the existence of numerous professional centers and associations, the growing appearance of *ad hoc* journals and the organizing of all sorts of meetings. Some of these centers, journals, and meetings have a general perspective, but others are highly specialized; today, for example, there are almost ten nuclei of philosophical activity in Buenos Aires alone, apart from university centers and institutes.[2] Besides the many periodicals with a long history,[3] in the last few years several journals that take a somewhat circumscribed approach[4] have appeared in various parts of the country. And finally, several meetings of every possible scope and orientation have recently taken place,[5] including the first World Congress of Philosophy. The 12th Inter American Congress of Philosophy is planned for 1989, the second of its kind to be held in Argentina (the other was the 6th Congress, held in 1959).

Moreover, there is practically no philosophical subdiscipline that lacks Argentinian practitioners − inside and outside Argentina − with international profiles. All main philosophical orientations include substantial numbers of representative figures in spite of the counterproductive efforts of interfering government officials. Apart from the lack of major philosophical figures all over the world, there is no shortage in our mileu of individuals who keep up with the latest developments in the discipline. In short, Argentina is an example of progressive and important philosophical thought.

Exegesis

Even if we restrict our examination to the exposition of European thought carried out by Argentinians, we find that these exegeses can be favorably compared with those carried out in other countries.

The study of Greek philosophy has reached a high level of excellence thanks to the influence of Rodolfo Mondolfo, who settled in Argentina in 1939. In the last few decades ambitious studies on various aspects of the work of several thinkers of classical antiquity, such as Parmenides, Plato, Aristotle, Plotinus, Philo and others, have been published. One of the most active authors in this area is Angel Cappelletti, who has also worked on anarchist thought as well as on many other areas of the history of philosophy.

In the area of Oriental philosophy, a difficult field with limited antecedents in Argentina, the most important exponents are Fernando Tola and Carmen Dragonetti who have worked on Buddhist philosophy in India. They publish in specialized journals and their major work on Yoga has been translated into English.

Although during this period few substantial works on modern philosophers were produced, there are, however, some respectable surveys as well as introductions. These works have been published by Rodolfo Agoglia, Emilio Estiú, Angel Vasallo and Francisco Romero, among others. Indeed, one of Romero's books has been called "the best exposition in this period of European thought written in Spanish."[6]

Various exponents of Western contemporary philosophy have also been carefully and critically studied. There are entire volumes devoted to the analysis of the thought of Althusser, Blondel, Buber, Croce, Dworkin, Foucault, Frege, Freud, Hartmann, Heidegger, Husserl, Jaspers, Levinas, Lévi-Strauss, Merleau-Ponty, Nietzsche, Ortega, Piaget, Ricoeur, Sartre, Scheler, Unamuno and Zubiri.

Indeed, the study of Latin American philosophy has gained breadth, rigour and depth. Both general works on different periods as well as those dealing with schools, individuals or special topics are updated regularly. Arturo Andrés Roig has played a leading role, inside and outside the country, in the exploration of unsuspected doctrinal trends and in the elaboration of new theoretical and historiographical categories. The impact of Roig's work has been felt beyond the purely national level, within which, with few exceptions (such as the work of José Luis Romero), most works in the history of ideas have been confined, failing to achieve an international profile. Thanks to Roig's indefatigable spirit, similar to that of the Uruguayan Arturo Ardao, we have become aware of the leading role played by eclecticism in the structuring of the Argentinian nation from 1852 onwards, and of Krausism, in the difficult road toward democracy.[7]

We turn now to relevant publications concerning some classic works of our thought: the anthologies of previously unedited colonial sources composed by Celina Lértora Mendoza and of nineteenth-century spiritualist trends by Roig himself, the compilation of Alberini's works by Diego Pró and of texts from Alfredo Franceschi by Armando Asti Vera, the *Obras completas* of Aníbal Ponce edited by Héctor Agosti, the first critical edition of Alberdi's *Bases* under the editorship of Jorge Mayer, and the selection on Latin American philosophical anthropology and axiology carried out by Risieri Frondizi and Jorge Gracia, which includes a substantial number of Argentinian philosophers.[8]

Nor is there a lack of valuable contributions in other disciplines during the period in question. We may mention, among others, the following: the work of Rodolfo Agoglia to the theory of history, of Florencio González Asenjo to epistemology, of Eugenio Pucciarelli to metaphysics, of Miguel Angel Virasoro to philosophical anthropology, of Genaro Carrió and Enrique Marí to the philosophy of law, of Néstor García Canclini and Rosa María Ravera to aesthetics, of Osvaldo Guariglia, Ricardo Maliandi and Eliseo Verón to action theory and of Severino Croatto, Luis Farré and Víctor Massuh to the philosophy of religion.

In the area of the philosophy of language an essay by Roberto Rojo on the conflicting aspects of language stands out, along with the disagreements of Eduardo Rabossi with Bertrand Russell's theory of signs, and the works of Ricardo Pochtar anticipating the criticism of transformational theory as presented by Mario Bunge, a born critic, to the founder of the theory himself, Noam Chomsky.

Perspectives

Philosophy of Liberation

Although those who have raised the flag of liberation from a theological standpoint are primarily linked with Peru and Brazil, it is in Argentina that the first significant *philosophical* nucleus dealing with liberation is to be found. It is in Argentina, in the 1970s that a group of young thinkers came together to work out the principles of this perspective. It happened during the advances made by the Right in the government and the universities after the death of President Perón, whose heterogeneous political backers became powerfully attractive to the group in question.

As in the case of neopositivism, a representative section of this current rejected the existing philosophical tradition and attributed to itself enormous substitutive powers. In contrast to logical empiricists, however, they assigned to philosophy a saving character, while at the same time despising rationality, scientific knowledge and liberal thought. Opposed to the Marxist view of social classes and alienation, this group concerned itself with ambiguous praise of the people, the nation and the State.

Some liberationists adopted fascist-like positions similar to those favored by supporters of army-led coups, while others suffered ostracism or were killed by repressive forces. The former ended up facilitating the ouster of former colleagues and comrades from their posts, collaborating in Castrist publications, or helping the intellectual meeting of minorities organized by the military establishment. Rodolfo Kusch may be considered one of the principal local leaders of the nationalist-populist group.

Another spokesman for liberation, Carlos Cullen,[9] returned to the line espoused by Hegel's *Phenomenology of the Spirit*, without neglecting "ethical-religious" experience, geopolitical considerations and the national character itself. He proclaims as well the "law of the land" and the pristine wisdom of peoples, even though the people will achieve sovereignty only through "the leader's" guidance. Poverty appears almost as a theological virtue, since thanks to it "universal equilibrium, in accordance with the gods" is restored.

Enrique Dussel, a widely read author and victim of persecution, has synthesized his basic views in *Introducción a la filosofía de la liberación*.[10] In this book Dussel insists on the need to establish a type of situational thought, while opposing ontologizing conceptions that, from an irreducibly totalizing perspective, would prevent the recognition of differences and of "the other as other": the poor, the oppressed, whose destiny and reality ought to be exposed by the philosophy of liberation. The philosophy of liberation turns to the rescue of otherness and to the denunciation of the abuse and subjection in which both Hispanic America and the Third World exist. Under a certain eschatological pretense, and prescinding from careful distinctions between the government and the governed, it is affirmed that "the evil" is the result of the world domination by Europe and the United States of peripheral countries, while omitting reference to the subjugation exercised by local elites. Considered apart from concrete circumstances, domination seems to be interpreted as an inevitable negative foundation that undermines every existing project or system, a negativism against which the philosopher should always be ready to direct "liberating criticism." On the one hand, poverty is condemned insofar as it is a sign of human exploitation; but on the other hand, is glorified as sacrosanct. Meanwhile, even a minimum of historical relevance is denied to the bourgeoisie and "being-right" is denounced as alienating.

The strongest, and not unoriginal, critical attack on the basic ideas of this view was made by another of the protagonists of the movement, Horacio Cerutti-Guldberg, in *Filosofía de la liberación latinoamericana* (México: Fondo de Cultura Económica, 1983), adapted from his 1977 doctoral dissertation. Dussel, among others, has tried to answer Cerutti's objections, but Cerutti has continued to add further dimensions to his original arguments.[11]

Analytic Philosophy

The doctrinal complex composed of neopositivism, logical empiricism, philosophical analysis and the so-called "scientific" or "exact" philosophy began to acquire academic status after the end of the first Peronist period (1955), when a group of individuals including Mario Bunge and Gregorio Klimovsky began to teach and work with unusual eagerness within this perspective at the University of Buenos Aires. Fifteen years later, around 1972, the Sociedad de Análisis Filosófico (SADAF) was founded, during a period in which, according to Jorge Gracia, this philosophical current became stabilized.

The active participation of analytic philosophers in congresses of philosophy began in 1980 (Buenos Aires, 3rd National Congress of Philosophy) and played a leading role in 1983 (Salta, 4th National Congress), 1986 (La Plata, 5th National Congress) and 1987 (Córdoba, Extraordinary International Congress). In the last one, relatively prominent figures like Georg von Wright, Donald Davidson, Ernesto Sosa and Mario Bunge participated in plenary sessions, although other expected important spokesmen of the perspective (Ayer, Searle) did not attend in the end.

With the recent electoral victory of the *Partido Radical*,[12] a party supported by a well-defined analytical group, neopositivism spread to various universities. Thus we can see that by this time the dominant philosophical atmosphere in the 1960s had changed considerably. It was in the 1960s that the Agrupación Rioplatense de Lógica y Filosofía Científica had been founded, according to Mario Bunge, "to support enlightened philosophy in a medium where any obscurity translated from German or French enjoyed greater prestige than conceptual analysis."[13]

Not everyone agrees to assign substantial value to neopositivism. The comments in a dialogue among Spanish philosophers who attended the mentioned meeting in Córdoba, reflect such disparity of opinion:

CEREZO: The predominance of the analytic school [at the congress] was evident: it looks as if the Left is of no consequence and Marxism has no prestige (although one can see the influence of the Frankfurt School). Analysts seem to have academic power.

ABELLÁN: The situation is similar to that of Spain. During Franco's time, many thinkers favored analytic views, because these views were politically safe. Later on these views became institutionalized.

SUBIRATS: But analysis has become today a new scholasticism, far from the original anti-establishment positions of Bertrand Russell, Wittgenstein, and Popper. Now it is formal and academic.

CEREZO: That doesn't mean that it is bound to sterility in Argentina. It allows criticism within the boundaries imposed by tolerance.[14]

Argentinian analysts themselves have made repeated efforts to clarify their position, revealing the various currents of thought and ideas operating within the movement, in order to defend themselves against the caricatures of which they are objects. Mario Bunge, for example, rejects the label of "positivist," leaning instead toward a systematic methodology, pluralist monism, and what he calls "critical realism." He accepts, however, being classified as scientific, a position from which he has fought not only futurology, parapsychology, and dialectics but also economics, Marxism, and psychoanalysis. Indeed, in spite of the enormous development of psychoanalysis in Argentina, Bunge has compared it with spiritualism and astrology.[15]

In spite of Bunge's leanings toward epistemology and the physical and mathematical sciences to the detriment of the human sciences, he displays greater acquaintance with bibliographical sources of various philosophical schools than other authors who hold opinions similar to his. Such is the case with Carlos Nino, who, speaking vaguely about "our civilization" in *Etica y derechos humanos* (Paidós, 1984), undermines his framework by limiting it to analytic sources and omitting consideration of the crucial literature produced by other philosophical perspectives.

One of the most important texts produced by the Argentinian analytic school, *Normative Systems*, was published by Carlos Alchourrón and Eugenio Bulygin, in which they explored the application of an axiomatic system and of deontic logic to normative jurisprudence.

The objections against neopositivism have been formulated in various ways, beginning with the initial criticism by Risieri Frondizi in *El punto de partida del filosofar* (1945) to more recent criticisms from more hostile groups.[16] Thus, partly inspired by Husserl's *Philosophical Investigations*, Jorge Saltor questioned the conception of truth in authors like Wittgenstein, Schlick, Russell, Tarski, Carnap, and Hempel. In an entirely different style and from diverse Marxist perspectives, Carlos Astrada and Enrique Marí also criticized this position. Marí, moreover, besides attacking international exponents of the position, also rejected various local manifestations of current positivism.

Other Perspectives

Even though *phenomenology* has not had the agglutinative and organic profile imparted by analysts and liberationists to their activities, it does not lack results worthy of mention, particularly in the areas of law, education, anthropology and psychology. One need only refer to the works listed in the bibliography by José Vilanova, Gustavo Cirigliano, José Mainetti, Aida Aisenson, Roberto Yáñez Cortés or Carlos Ceriotto. The last one, incidentally, contributed to the introduction of Paul Ricoeur in Argentina.

With respect to the rebirth of Marxism – from dogmatic and Stalinist versions to Gramscian positions – the original conduits have been the journals *Cuadernos de Cultura*, edited by the Argentinian Communist Party, and above all *Pasado y Presente*, published in Córdoba between 1963 and 1965. Structuralism, on the other hand, has spread very specifically through an *ad hoc* series directed by José Sazbón for the publishing house Nueva Visión toward the end of the same decade. This was the moment in which other "critical theories" also arrived: French neo-Marxism, the Frankfurt School, as well as other border areas of human knowledge such as American radical sociology, Freudian Marxism, genetic epistemology and Lacanism.

The picture presented by Roman Catholic thought in Argentina today is uneven in quality, notoriously diverse, and at times indecisive. There are those who follow in the footsteps of the greater part of the Argentinian hierarchy and continue to be faithful to traditional orthodoxy: Julio Meinvielle, Bruno Genta, Octavio Derisi, José María de Estrada, and Alberto Caturelli. There are also those who evolved from Thomism to a greater doctrinal *aggiornamento* or to a profound radicalization such as Nimio de Anquín, Arturo Sampay, and Manuel Gonzalo Casas. Finally, there are some that have displayed a generally open attitude such as Ismael Quiles and Juan Sepich. As it has happened with the Marxists, some of these Catholic authors have much less theoretical importance than their practical impact would lead one to believe.

International Presence

According to the professional conception of Latin American philosophy, one of the most effective criteria of intellectual caliber is visibility in advanced foreign philosophical centers. As a result, Argentinian thought has acquired some visibility outside Argentina. For example, there is still interest in a figure like José Ingenieros, who in his time enjoyed considerable attention. The same is true of Alejandro Korn and Francisco Romero, about whom much has been written outside Argentina. Likewise interest has been rising on the Marxist stage of Aníbal Ponce's thought.

There are as well more recent cases of individuals who enjoy a growing recognition, for example, Mario Bunge, who is a member of the International Institute of Philosophy and the International Academy of the Philosophy of Science; or Enrique Dussel, doctor *honoris causa* of Freiburg University, whose work has been translated into other languages and whose thought has been the subject of doctoral dissertations outside the Hispanic world. A look at the references at the end of this chapter will substantiate the points made.

In short, there is today a host of Argentinian philosophers who figure regularly in the most prestigious circles and publications. In addition, significant numbers have received temporary or permanent contracts in important foreign teaching or research institutions.[17]

Conclusion

In spite of the worsening instability in the teaching profession, ideological discrimination and scarcity of research resources during the period covered by this article, the picture drawn above indicates the existence of an appreciable philosophical professionalization. Nevertheless, there seems still to be a need, pointed out by many of those who came before us, for a deeper philosophical meditation that would allow disentangling our national problems, questioning recessive factors, and proposing attainable goals. The issue then is the relation among ideas and actual reality, the players involved in it, and the medium where they act, as well as the possibility of formulating alternative plans.

In order to carry out such a program it will be necessary, in addition, to pay attention to the trends and specializations current in Latin America and elsewhere, to lay the foundations for philosophical activity that, arising from the regional context itself, will analyze it, leading to greater development.[18] Such a program will be difficult to carry out unless profound social changes occur that lead to the establishment of a genuine atmosphere of freedom and equality, devoid of bureaucratic pseudoevaluations.

Present-day Argentina seems to offer better possibilities of moving in the aforementioned direction for three reasons: First, the repressive doctrine of national security has been buried; second, its perpetrators have been brought to trial; and finally, there is free cultural and political activity devoid of established parameters. We seem to have left behind the sinister period in our history when thousands of teachers were fired because they were judged to be "potentially subversive." This was a time in which the Ministry of Education went so far as to ban the teaching of modern mathematics on the grounds that it contained views that could undermine the public order. Such events allow us to understand the following excerpt:

> The range of theories, disciplines and perspectives considered "subversive" [included]: Marxism, psychoanalysis, third-world ideologies, populism, existentialism, Paulo Freire's psychology, alternative psychiatric theories, liberation theology, structuralism, sociology, human rights, the theory of dependence; in short, not even the tango, [José Hernández's] *Martín Fierro*,[19] or [Saint-Exupéry's] *The Little Prince* escaped the State cannibalism advocated by those who portrayed themselves as defenders of Western Christian culture.[20]

The blacklists of forbidden publications reached enormous proportions, leading to absurd situations. In some parts of the country, while books like Unamuno's *La agonía del cristianismo* – and even some books written by high officials, whose titles sounded suspicious – were burned, it was thought appropriate to preserve a Marxist classic because its Spanish title was *The Holy Family*.

Even though the situation has improved markedly, the bad habits of political parochialism and favoritism still persist. One of them has to do with the manipulation of presumably open contests to fill university teaching posts, in order to exclude recognized philosophical figures. Meanwhile, an institute founded during the military dictatorship, completely lacking academic substance and having as director a man whose only credentials were a background in international McCarthyism, was reactivated. There is also the case of an important and recent congress, where, owing to ideological differences, no reference was made to the centenary of the birth of a distinguished Argentinian thinker. Moreover, many philosophers, like Oward Ferrari (at present at the University of Toulouse), who had to leave the country, are still unable to return to their former posts.

On a more general plane, although closely related to the problems indicated in these concluding remarks, it is necessary for Argentina to unburden itself from the weight of so many unpopular measures. A careful plan to eliminate the essential causes of underdevelopment and dependency is required. We must supersede the conservative project of modernization insulated from the people and the nation that has been oppressing us from the nineteenth century and reaches paroxysmal proportions during dictatorial regimes. Modernization even in the best of cases, implies an increase in productivity, but always without social distribution of produced goods.

In contrast to the turn-of-the-century model of development, which was never discussed or formulated by representative sectors of the population of Argentina, it is imperative that a wide-ranging national plan be established. Such a plan, after appropriate consultation with the people, must establish the goals and expectations of Argentinians with respect to health, housing, science and technology, the foreign debt, foreign companies and capital, the operation of the judicial system, the process and rules governing congressional investigations, and others. At the same time, both intellectuals and political leaders, instead of simply seeking power in academia or the government, should work toward our incipient democracy's becoming entrenched in all aspects of Argentinian reality.

CHAPTER 2

On the Diversity of Brazilian Philosophical Expression[1]

ONÉSIMO TEOTÓNIO ALMEIDA

Any attempt at assessing Brazilian philosophy cannot avoid dealing, at some point, with the issue of national thought, if only to demarcate boundaries of what *is* and what is *not*, and why it is not national philosophy, Brazilian philosophy, or simply philosophy in Brazil.

Since the Romantic nationalism of the last century, national philosophies have been a controversial issue. After generalizing that British philosophy was empiricist, German philosophy idealist, and French philosophy rationalist, philosophers in various countries decided that philosophy could not be universal. They reached the conclusion, therefore, that in each culture philosophy could and should pursue its own path. A culture should develop its own philosophical themes and explore them. Such themes would be dictated by the specific and typical characteristics of the culture in question. Thus, the identification of the value structure, the cultural system, or the patterns of behavior of a people was essential in order to identify its deep-seated philosophical problems. Among the key philosophical issues were questions regarding the global direction of the culture or nation, its most problematic facet. Topics such as national psychology, cultural identity, cultural tradition, national character, and national identity were seen to be intertwined with topics of intellectual and cultural history, and even political theory. Some argue that it is appropriate to refer to these traditions, often subsumed under "philosophy of history," as "national philosophies."

Iberian scholars are all too familiar with the recurrent debates on whether or not there is a Spanish or a Portuguese philosophy (as opposed to philosophy *in* Portugal or Spain), and Latin Americanists know very well how heated any conversation on Latin American philosophy or thought can become.[2]

Brazil is seldom included in this debate, for "Latin American philosophy" is taken to mean "Spanish-American." But the issue of Brazilian philosophy is a recurrent one in Brazil, even though it does not recur so frequently nor with the same intensity it receives in some of the Spanish-American countries. Brazil has witnessed much philosophical activity in the traditional sense, but the general agreement among historians of philosophy is that imitation and eclectic assimilation of European and North American currents are the characterizing features of Brazilian thought. The most influential European intellectual tradition is not even philosophical but sociological-positivism. Of the movements that are, strictly speaking, philosophical, there seems to be an agreement that it is Neo-Thomism that has had, at least until recently, the strongest influence in Brazilian intellectual life. Obviously, the above distinctions presuppose traditional nomenclature, which reserves the classification of "philosophy" for a set of specific areas and problems, i.e., those traditionally studied in the discipline. These areas and problems do not incorporate global interpretations of cultural history within its domain.

Actually, in Brazil, where there is probably the richest series of attempts at understanding national history and culture of any Latin American country, such efforts have not claimed the status of philosophy. They present themselves as explanations of the Brazilian idiosyncrasy, its cultural (behavioral) patterns, generally as tools for understanding the Brazilian developmental gap in regard to Europe until the beginning of the century, and to North America for most of this century.

Dante Moreira Leite, who wrote the most critical and comprehensive analysis of this tradition of meditation on national *Weltanschauung* as a means of explaining Brazilian history, goes so far as to state that "the idea of a *Brazilian national character*, or as it is usually referred to, a psychology of the Brazilian people, can be considered as axle of our historical and intellectual tradition." This statement is found on the back cover of Dante Moreira Leite's *o caracter nacional brasileiro* (São Paulo: Livraria Pioneira Editora, 1976).

Silvio Romero locates the beginning of the tradition in the second half of the nineteenth century, the period of "the most profound commotion in the national soul" (preface to Tobias Barreto's *Vários escritos* [Rio de Janeiro, 1900], p. xxiii). He himself is one of the leading figures on a list that includes, among so many, the names of de Farias Brito (whose works were used by the Integralist movement, a Brazilian soft version of fascism), Graça Aranha (who even proposed a Brazilian metaphysics), Euclides da Cunha, Gilberto Freyre, Sérgio Buarque de Hollanda, Paulo Prado, Vianna Moog, Cruz Costa, and Caio Prado Junior. Their political views, however, differ widely. Mention should be made also of two significant collective attempts at interpreting and guiding action as carried out by those in the 1930s, the first now known as the "authoritarian thought group" with Oliveira Vianna as the leading figure, and the second associated with the Institute of Brazilian Studies (ISEB) in the 1950s, which included Nelson Werneck Sodré and Alvaro Vieira Pinto.

Dante Moreira Leite was the most accomplished critic of such a tradition, as well as its best exponent. In his book, *O carácter nacional brasileiro: História de una ideologia*, he identified the underlying prejudices, values, ideologies, and points of view of each of the cultural historians who attempted a portrait of the Brazilian people. Interestingly enough, as often happens with critics of ideology and ideologies, he thought that his criticism was beyond ideology (the last chapter of the book is entitled "A superação das ideologias" ("The overcoming of ideologies"). Nevertheless, the book exercised a powerful influence and put a temporary stop to the tradition of Brazilian self-analysis in terms of collective psychological character.[3] Recently, however, the tradition was continued in the works of several people, among them the anthropologist Roberto da Matta, particularly with his book *Carnaval, malandros e heróis*, and Darcy Ribeiro, with his *Teoria do Brasil*. Da Matta even had a TV program called "Os Brasileiros" ("The Brazilians").[4]

This sort of study, however, though now back in full swing, is to be classified under anthropology or the social sciences, not as philosophy or even philosophy of history.

The issue of Brazilian philosophy, however, did not resurface until a few years ago. A series of attempts have been made to survey the history of philosophy in Brazil, but the titles of these studies and surveys have all given a clear indication that the issue of national philosophy has somehow been resolved. The authors speak of *philosophy in Brazil* and not *Brazilian philosophy*,[5] the main exception being Antônio Paim, who, in spite of what he says in his voluminous *História das ideias filosóficas no Brasil*,[6] has said, in a smaller volume, *O estudo do pensamento filosófico brasileiro*[7]:

One verifies that the Brazilian meditation reaches for its own path, maintaining an equidistance from unreasonable revindication of a national philosophy as well as the hypothesis, equally improper, that a philosophy could be ready and finalized and only needing to be trans-

planted. While building its own path, the Brazilian meditation constitutes an original segment of universal philosophy. This originality
consists in favoring the theme of the person understood in the beginning as freedom and, later, as conscience, which led it to confront
itself with the great questions resulting from the deepening of the
Western philosophical conscience though a very particular access
path.[8]

In a more recent article, Antônio Paim returns to this view of the
original and unique path of Brazilian philosophy as distinct from mere
philosophy done in Brazil, as well as from Brazilian national thought.
He supports Francisco Martins de Souza's position, according to
which, in the dialogue among equals, Brazilian thinkers accept some
ideas from foreign authors, but take care to adapt them to the unique
context of their cultural meditation.[9] Paim restates his view that "the
nuclear problem of Brazilian philosophy has been the question of
Man." He adds, though: "Brazilian philosophy is radically different
from all other national philosophies which appeared in the Modern
Age."[10]

The issue of Brazilian "national" philosophy, however, was resur-
rected recently by Roberto Gomes in a small but incisively critical
book, *Crítica da razão tupiniquim*.[11] Since its publication in 1977, it has
gone into at least eight editions. Gomes analyzes the views of the
major Brazilian thinkers who have engaged in the "national meditation
of Brazil" and chastizes all of them, sometimes with wit, for being
"prisoners of European models and ends" disconnected from Brazilian
reality.[12] Brazilian thinkers have indeed made a path of their own, he
claims, but it is one of pure rhetoric without content, one concerned
merely with the aesthetic dimension of discourse. He coins the expression "Razão ornamental" ("Ornamental reason") to describe Brazilian
thought.

Elsewhere I have analyzed in some detail Gomes's thesis.[13] Here,
I will state simply that Gomes's book reads more like a critical manifesto that, while rejecting the work of his predecessors, does not lay
out any suggestion about the possible directions a "Brazilian
philosophy" might take. One of his final pleas vaguely urges a rupture
from the foreign dominant world of ideas (Europe and North
America): "It is urgent to be what we are – discover ourselves *in*
Brazil, *in* Latin America. Without attaching ourselves to some "other"
thing. Only solitude generates thought – only in tragedy is philosophy
born."[14]

In spite of the apparent popularity of *Crítica da razão tupiniquim* – judging at least by the number of editions it has enjoyed –
I have not come across any discussion of the book in philosophy

journals. The impression one gathers from journals is that the present national mood is one of optimism about the state of philosophy in Brazil and that all sorts of philosophical tends participate in this rejuvenating spirit.

The "cultural" newspaper *Leia* published last May a special section on philosophy in Brazil, with articles by some of the most respected of the young Brazilian philosophers. The general picture inspires optimism. *Leia* refers to an existing "intense philosophical thinking, open to life and serenely committed" (engajada). The stress is on the diversity of trends, taking place in a variety of places (meaning "universities") where philosophy is done, e.g. (Universidade de São Paulo), (Universidade Estadual de Campinas) and (Pontifícia Universidade Católica) in São Paulo, (Universidade Federal do Rio de Janeiro) in Rio de Janeiro, (Universidade Federal de Minas Gerais) in Belo Horizonte, and (Universidade do Rio Grande Sul) in Porto Alegre.[15]

Writing for a Portuguese audience in the Lisbon newspaper *Expresso*, João Paulo Monteiro, chairman of the philosophy department of the University of São Paulo, characterized the present scenario of Brazilian philosophical activity as "pluralist and cosmopolitan."[16] Monteiro expresses his satisfaction with the fact that Brazilian philosophy did not follow the path of a "national tradition" initiated by Tobias Barreto and Farias de Brito. He considers the issue a dead one and advocates the development of a philosophy emanating from Brazil. In his words,

> the trademark of Brazilian philosophical production is, on one hand, pluralism and diversity and, on the other hand, what can be referred to by a somewhat wornout and devaluated term: cosmopolitanism, i.e., there is not in Brasil a philosophical school and not even two or three of them fighting each other. Besides, philosophical creativity did not in any case take form through the illusory search for "national roots." Philosophical writing followed paths dictated by each individual's itinerary and not by the concentration of research groups. Moreover, neither group nor individuals concentrate their efforts on the search for a philosophical thought which in any way could express a national identity. . . . Brazilian philosophy has followed the paths of French structuralism, phenomenology, analytical philosophy, and a thousand others, without one ever being perceived as dominant. Nowadays, of course, there are those more inclined to the exploration of the so-called "analytical rationality," and others are turned to "dialectical rationality." There are those attracted by hermeneutics, and there are those who make out of the history of philosophy a path for a personal and contemporary meditation. There are those whose area could be defined as either political problems, philosophy of science, or

philosophy of language. There are also those who search for more personal roads, always in a "cosmopolitan" fashion, however. They take off from the thought of Marx, Quine, Aristotle, Gadamer or Popper, but never of Brazilian thought (or the meditation on Brazil), much less do they attempt to prolong the almost inexistent national tradition of people such as Tobias Barreto and de Farias Brito.[17]

But this picture of the state of the art of Brazilian philosophy should not end without a reference to the three Brazilian philosophers best known abroad, more precisely, in the English-speaking world. One of them is the *enfant terrible*, José Guilherme Merquior, who has written extensively on a variety of subjects, ranging from structuralism and literature to sociology and political philosophy. Among his books, mention should be made of *The Veil and the Mask: Essays on Culture and Ideology*,[18] *Rousseau and Weber: Two Studies in the Theory of Legitimacy*,[19] and, most recently, *Michel Foucault, ou o niilismo da cátedra*.[20] The other is Roberto Mangabeira Unger, the leading theorist of the "critical school" of legal philosophy at the Harvard Law School. His books, well known among legal theorists, have started to attract the attention of philosophers, particularly in philosophy of law and political philosophy. Besides his two books, *Knowledge and politics*[21] and *Law in Modern Society*,[22] he has published, recently, *Passion*[23] and a trilogy under the general title of *Politics, A Work in Constructive Social Theory*.[24] A reference should here be made also to Paulo Freire and his widely known works on philosophy of education, particularly *Pedagogy of the Oppressed*.[25]

But here we have already crossed a boundary: Is Unger a Brazilian philosopher just because he was born in Brazil, even when his writings are strictly North American and in English?[26] But Unger has now returned to his native country. What will he write? and will it matter? We have here a wonderful paradigm case to shake up the debate on national boundaries. Even though many philosophers may reflect, in a lesser or higher degree, the traits of their cultural (national) tradition, in the case of Unger that is not visible. He happens to be a Brazilian whose philosophical work lies outside any particular tradition of his native country and belongs totally in the European and North American world.

Philosophy is alive and well in Brazil, it seems. And may philosophers make an impact in Brazilian society that perhaps no contemporary American philosopher can claim to have on the United States, even though little of that impact may be due to philosophy *per se*. As for the tradition of "national meditation" discussed above, it is also alive and well in the particular form of the search for "national character." Those who engage in it, however, do not call such activity "philosophy."[27]

In the more strictly defined area of philosophy, a pluralistic coexistence of practically all European and North American trends obtains. Some of them, however, have attempted a particular grasp of Brazilian realities. Once again, they come both from the conservative and the most politicized traditions: Miguel Reale and Antônio Paim, for the first, and, for the latter, J. Arthur Giannotti, Bento Prado Júnior and Marilena Chauí.

If some Brazilians have claimed that the philosophical spirit is alien to their national character, all their philosophical production notwithstanding, the European tradition of the intellectual concerned with the realities and the destinies of his nation has been and is still alive and well in Brazil. However, unlike as in some other Latin American countries, the association between the questions of national character and philosophical thought seems to have died out long ago, almost at its very inception.

As for the present state of diversity, well, such is the predicament of contemporary philosophy in open societies. There seems to be more than one legitimate way of doing what is traditionally referred to as philosophy. "Let them all come to the fore," seems to be the prevailing mood in Brazil. Not an original solution, one might add. Once again, Brazil imitates Europe and the United States. Granted, but if we take a close look at the philosophical work being produced by contemporary Brazilian thinkers, we get a clear impression that some sort of liberation process has occurred, for the dependence complex is almost alien to it. Quite a few Brazilian philosophers – even though still looking to Europe and North America – are decidedly thinking by themselves and about themselves.

CHAPTER 3

Philosophy in Brazil Today

FRED GILLETTE STURM

A year ago Leônidas Hegenberg, professor of philosophy at ITA, the Brazilian Technological Institute of Aeronautics, published a report of the Eighth *Encontro Brasileiro de Lógica*, entitled: "E como vai a Lógica no Brasil?" ("And How Goes Logic in Brazil?"). At the end of his eight-page report he responded to the question: "A lógica vai muito bem, obrigado." ("Logic is going very well, thanks."). Were my topic to be put in the form of a question – "And how goes philosophy in Brazil today?" – I would respond just as Leônidas: "Philosophy in Brazil is going very well, thanks!"

I have been in touch with Brazilian philosophy since 1950, and I am convinced that the status of philosophical studies and research in Brazil has never been livelier or healthier. One merely has to browse through a bookstore in Brazil, or to glance at the annual "Brazilian Philosophical Bibliography" which has been prepared by Antônio Paim since 1967 and published in the *Revista Brasileira de Filosofia*, to appreciate the great interest taken in philosophical ideas by the Brazilian reading public. There appear regularly translations into Portuguese of not only the classical works of Western philosophy, but contemporary works as well, along with original works by Brazilian authors across the entire range of philosophy from mathematical logic to the history of philosophy, from aesthetics to the philosophy of science.

There are two principal reasons for this great activity and interest in philosophy: first, the rapid growth of university education over the past half century; second, the successful functioning of the Instituto Brasileiro de Filosofia as a truly inclusive national association, and its journal, the *Revista Brasileira de Filosofia*. Portugal had refused to permit the establishment of a university on Brazilian soil during the colonial period, and it was not until 1932 that there existed in Brazil a comprehensive center of higher education. Prior to the Francisco Campos Educational Reform Act of 1931 there were only separate faculties for the training of professionals, and the teaching of philosophy occurred almost exclusively within the curricula of those schools – the faculties of law, medicine, engineering, etc. – or as part of the secondary curriculum of preparatory schools, such as Colégio Dom Pedro II in Rio de Janeiro. With the creation of universities came departments of philosophy. By 1959 there were 20 universities with programs leading to a diploma in philosophy.[1] That number more than doubled in the next decade, and there were 48 in 1969. By 1979 there were 65, with 5000 students enrolled. Most of the 700 students graduated each year were employed by secondary schools to teach a course in philosophy which, until the late seventies, was required during the last two years of *colégio*, and which is about to be reinstituted.

In February 1969 the Conselho Federal de Educação formulated norms to govern graduate programs in philosophy leading to the degrees of master of arts and doctor of philosophy. In 1971 the University of São Paulo became the first institution to introduce graduate work in philosophy. By 1982 it had awarded 44 master's degrees and 2l Ph.D.'s. The Catholic University of Rio de Janeiro followed suit in 1972, and by 1982 had awarded 68 master's degrees. At present seven federal universities, four Catholic universities, one state university, and one private university offer graduate work in philosophy. Of the 26l master's degrees awarded by 1982, 60 were in History of Philosophy, 46 in Brazilian Thought, 37 in Logic and the Philosophy of Science, and 118 in either Aesthetics, Ethics, Philosophical Anthropology, or Political Philosophy. Twenty-nine doctoral degrees had been awarded by 1982. Complete figures for graduate degrees awarded in the last four years or about to be granted this December are not available to me. However, the existence of graduate centers for the study of philosophy at 13 universities throughout the country has led to a decided maturation of philosophical discussion and writing. The Federal University of Minas Gerais has founded its own Society of Philosophical Studies and Activities (SEAF) which sponsors a weeklong seminar annually, focusing each time on a different figure such as Hegel and Marx, with publication of the presented papers. The Federal University of Paraíba has sponsored a National Week of Philosophy in Brazil, inviting philosophers from other universities and publishing the proceedings.

The Instituto Brasileiro de Filosofia (the Brazilian Institute of Philosophy), founded in 1949, and its highly successful quarterly journal, *Revista Brasileira de Filosofia*, which has enjoyed uninterrupted publication since it was launched in 1951, have provided a national infrastructure for the expansion of philosophical work within the universities. The institute, from its inception, has managed to attract into its membership both academic and nonacademic philosophers of virtually every type – Catholics and Marxists, existentialists and logical positivists, phenomenologists and analysts – and through the National Congresses of Philosophy, which it has sponsored, it has fostered genuine face-to-face philosophical dialogue, a dialogue that continues through the pages of the *Revista*, where a policy favoring philosophical pluralism has been espoused since its inception. State and local branches of the institute sponsor adult education courses in philosophy and hold local and regional philosophical conferences.

The Instituto Brasileiro de Filosofia and the *Revista Brasileira de Filosofia* cannot be mentioned without making reference to Miguel Reale who was not only instrumental in their founding, but responsible for much of their continued success. Now 77, he remains active and alert, still engaging in polemic, and still publishing work that cannot be ignored. Aquiles Côtes Guimarães was not exaggerating when he wrote five years ago in his book *O tema da consciência na filosofia brasileira*: "Miguel Reale (1910–) represents the most significant phase of the entire history of Brasilian thought."[2] A firm defender of pluralism within both political and intellectual spheres, Reale has made significant contributions in philosophy of law and jurisprudence with his tridimensional model for the understanding of the nature and function of law; in philosophical foundations, with his elaboration of onto-gnoseological dialectics; and in the history of Brazilian thought with a good number of monographs reporting original research into hitherto neglected or forgotten eighteenth- and nineteenth-century texts. It is not surprising that the University of Brasília in 1981 devoted one of its "Weeks of Study of Representative Figures in Brasilian Intellectual Life" to Miguel Reale.

Two other journals of national circulation, both edited by members of the institute, that provide opportunity for the publication of philosophical writings should be mentioned: *Convívium*, edited by Adolpho Crippa for the Sociedade de Cultura Convívio, published regularly since 1962; *ITA Humanidades*, edited by Leônidas Hegenberg at the Instituto Tecnológico de Aeronaútica, published continuously since 1965. The vast majority of articles in each of these two journals deal with philosophical issues and represent a broad variety of approaches and viewpoints. For ten years *Manuscrito*, a semiannual "international journal of philosophy" with a distinguished advisory board from several countries in Europe and the Americas, has been published by the State University of Campinas. It features articles in the fields of logic, philosophy of science, philosophy of language, most of which appear in English. *Kriterion*, a publication of the Federal University of Minas Gerais, often carries philosophical essays and enjoys a national readership.

The vitality of philosophical activity in Brazil is nowhere more evident than in the fields of symbolic logic, philosophy of science, and foundations of mathematics. Interest in these areas was first sparked during W. Quine's Fulbright lectureship at São Paulo's old Escola Livre de Sociologia e Política in 1942 and the book he published in Portuguese the following year, *O sentido da nova lógica*. It continued with the books published by Euralyo Cannabrava on "scientific philosophy" in the mid-1950s, introducing the thought of Bertrand Russell, A. J. Ayer, Alfred Tarski, Ernest Nagel, and Nelson Goodman, along with the courses in modern logic offered at the University of São Paulo during the same period by the French logician, Gilles Gaston Granger, who published a book in Portuguese entitled *Lógica e filosofia de ciência*. It was toward the end of the 1950s and the beginning of the 1960s that what Leônidas Hegenberg calls the "era of the pioneers" began,[3] with a seminar on logic directed by Edson Farah of the University of São Paulo's Department of Mathematics, and a similar seminar led by Jorge Emmanuel Ferreira Barbosa at the Federal Fluminense University in Niteroi.

Two members of the São Paulo seminar have gone on to make what surely has been the greatest contributions toward the study and practice of logic, philosophy of mathematics, and philosophy of science in contemporary Brazil. Leônidas Hegenberg continued graduate work in logic at Berkeley and then joined the faculty at the Technological Institute of Aeronautics. Under his leadership ITA has become a center for work in philosophy of science and logic. Work in logic is underway in the Division of Computational Analysis, and investigations into artificial intelligence and "fuzzy" logic (diffuse or nebulous logic) have been undertaken in ITA's affiliated Institute for Space Research. Leônidas has written three advanced texts in logic: (1) *Symbolization and Deduction*, (2) *Sentenial Calculus*, (3) *Calculus of Predicables*, and three major works in philosophy of science: (1) *Scientific Explanations*, (2) *Meaning and Knowledge*, (3) the two-volume *Stages of Scientific Investigation*. In addition he has translated into Portuguese over fifty books in logic, philosophy of science, and foundations of mathematics. He publishes regularly in the *Revista*

Brasileira de Filosofia, Convívium, and his own *ITA Humanidades,* and is in great demand as a lecturer throughout the country. Despite his background in physics, he is concerned with the philosophy of the biological, social, and historical sciences as well. An example of this far-reaching concern: in 1981 he conducted an "Intensive Course in the Philosophy of Medicine" cosponsored by the São Paulo Academy of Medicine and the Instituto Brasileiro de Filosofia, analyzing the medical use of the term "normality," and comparing classic and modern uses of the concept "illness."

The other member of the old São Paulo seminar who has made a great contribution in logic and the foundations of mathematics is Newton Carneiro Alfonso da Costa. In 1962 he published an *Introduction to the Foundations of Mathematics* in Portuguese. Shortly thereafter he told me that this was an elementary text, used only in the classrooms of Brazilian universities, and that henceforth he would publish only in English, French, and German, because otherwise he would have no audience and no opportunity to enter into communication with scholars at the forefront of symbolic logic and the foundations of mathematics. Until seven years ago he kept that vow. Approximately seventy articles have appeared in European and United States journals giving him an international reputation. He has been a visiting professor at Berkeley (1972–73) and at San Marcos in Lima, Peru (1975), and has hosted the first Latin American Conference on Mathematical Logic. Although most of his teaching has been at the University of São Paulo, he did serve on the faculty of the Federal University of Campinas from 1968 to 1970, and continues to collaborate there with his colleagues, many of whom were his former students, a collaboration that has resulted in the formation of the well-known Center of Logic, Epistemology, and History of Science. It was from this base that the Sociedade Brasileira de Lógica was launched in 1978 with its annual "Encontros Nacionais de Lógica" with proceedings published by the center. Last year the center initiated publication of the English-language *Journal of Non-Classical Logic* with an international board of editors. Newton now, however, finds a Brazilian audience for his work and has published two books in Portuguese: *Ensaio sôbre os fundamentos da lógica* (1980), and *Lógica indutiva e probabilidade* (1981). Leônidas has reported a recent conversation in which Newton playfully expressed the desire "to abandon logic, to devote himself to philosophy and, at the end of his life, to become a religious leader."[4] He continues to dedicate his attention, however, to questions of inductive logic and probability, and is at work on developing a means for measuring the degree of the "quasi-truth" of inductive generalizations.

Universities in Brazil are indeed innovators in philosophic studies. The Federal University of Campinas (UNICAMP), through its Center for Logic, Epistemology, and History of Science, has established a reputation in the United States, Canada, and several European nations, through its policy of recruiting visiting professors from abroad to foster dialogue at the forefront of these fields of philosophic study. Brazilian philosophy also manifests great vitality in the fields of philosophy of law and sociopolitical philosophy. Law is the area that characterized much of Brazilian philosophy during the nineteenth century and the first three decades of the present century. The old faculties of law were centers of philosophical debate. The renowned "Escola do Recife" centered around the figure of Tobias Barreto, a professor of Recife's Faculty of Law, and Farias Brito spent the early half of his academic career as a professor of law. Miguel Reale held the chair in Philosophy of Law at the University of São Paulo for years before his retirement and established his international reputation through his two-volume *Filosofia do direito*, which has been translated into several languages including Spanish, French, and Italian, and is now in its ninth Portuguese-language edition.

When the International Association for Philosophy of Law and Social Philosophy, with headquarters in Helsinki, Finland, was founded a decade ago at a conference held in the United States, Miguel Reale was elected vice president. He immediately organized a Brazilian affiliate, the Associação Brasileira de Filosofia Social e Jurídica (BRASIUS). BRASIUS held its first annual Encontro Nacional de Filosofia do Direito in 1980, and its first annual Congresso Brasileiro de Filosofia Jurídica e Social in 1985.

Because of the "Abertura," a return of government to civilian control, and the convocation of a constituent assembly, questions of judicial and political philosophy have captured a wide audience. I am reminded of the years when the Instituto Superior de Estudos Brasileiros (ISEB) functioned, and Roland Cobisier, Hélio Jaguaribe, and Vieira Pinto, wrote about the need to articulate an authentic ideology to serve as a basis for Brazilian development, an ideology that could appeal to mass support, and that would take into consideration Brazil's cultural and intellectual heritage and resources on the one hand, and her problems on the other. *Convivium* has devoted an entire issue to a debate over constitutional issues. Miguel Reale published a volume entitled *Por uma constituição brasileira* in which he argues for a "democracia social" that would preserve the values of both the socialist and the liberal traditions, incorporating them into a juridical synthesis. Several volumes have appeared that trace the history of political ideas in Brasil with a view toward informing the Brasilian public of its political and juridical heritage.

The philosophy of art and aesthetics is another field in which Brazilian philosophy has exhibited considerable activity. The Centro Brasileiro de Estudos Estéticos was founded in March 1982. With headquarters in Salvador, Baía, it has begun to sponsor conferences of an interdisciplinary nature involving artists and critics as well as philosophers of art and aestheticians, and has embarked on a program of publication. The center's president, Romano Galeffi, has been an active member of the Instituto Brasileiro de Filosofia and a regular contributor to the *Revista Brasileira de Filosofia*. He is by far the best known of Brasil's philosophers of art. His two-volume work, *Investigações de estética*, has been translated into Italian, German, and modern Greek. Other works include *Fundamentos da criação artística* and *Fundamentos da crítica de arte*.

In listing philosophical disciplines in which there has been considerable activity in Brazil the philosophy of education cannot be overlooked. The work of Paulo Freire is known, discussed, and put into practice throughout the world. In 1980 a São Paulo publisher, Edições Loyola, initiated the publication of seven volumes designed to provide expositions of, and commentaries on, the educational philosophy of Freire, written and edited by three specialists in Freirean pedagogy: Alberto Torres Novoa, Simões Gorge, and Brian Wren.

Great vitality is manifest in yet another of the philosophical disciplines: the History of Philosophy, and most specifically the History of Brazilian Philosophy. Sílvio Romero had initiated the study in the last century, and João Cruz Costa is probably the best known historian of Brazilian thought in this century. The *Revista Brasileira de Filosofia*, under the leadership of Miguel Reale and the late Luis Washington Vita, from its inception began to print classic texts and commentaries in Brazilian philosophic thought. *Convivium* encouraged studies in Brazilian intellectual history and last year devoted an entire issue to "Philosophy in Brazil."

A series of seventeen volumes of critical editions of classic texts and commentaries was issued between 1967 and 1977 under the heading "Estante do Pensamento Brasileiro," edited by Miguel Reale and published by the now-defunct Editôra Grijalbo. Adolpho Crippa's Editôra Convívio picked up the series and is continuing it as "Biblioteca do Pensamento Brasileiro," including not only texts and commentaries, but also essays on aspects of the history of Brasilian thought. During the 1970s the Department of Philosophy of the Catholic University in Rio de Janeiro published a nine-volume series, "Textos

Didáticos do Pensamento Brasileiro."

In 1983 the Bahian anthropologist, Vivaldo da Costa Lima, established in Salvador the Centro de Documentação do Pensamento Brasileiro, featuring a library of books, periodicals, and archival materials pertaining to Brazilian philosophy and Brazilian anthropology, and an ambitious publication agenda, including cumulative indices of journals, exhaustive bibliographies, and bibliographic essays.

In 1979 the Universidade Gama Filho in Rio de Janeiro hired the philosophers who had lost their positions at PUC-Rio over a question of censorship of textbooks, and initiated a successful program of graduate studies in Brazilian thought that has been producing both master's theses and doctoral dissertations of real value for the understanding of Brazilian intellectual history.

One name stands out distinctly among those who are working in the field of Brazilian philosophic history. Antônio Paim has been associated with many of the aforementioned projects, has been a careful researcher and a prolific author of books and articles, and has written the standard work in the field: *História das idéias filosóficas no Brasil* which is now in its third revised and greatly augmented edition of 615 pages.

A word concerning Catholic philosophy in Brazil is now in order. With the passing from the scene of Alceu Amoroso Lima and his strong leadership of the Centro Dom Vital, the Neo-Thomism of Jacques Maritain no longer can be said to dominate the thought of Brazilian Catholic philosophers. The scene is now one of flux with a variety of positions being espoused. Under the leadership of the Jesuit philosopher Stanislavs Ladusāns, however, opportunities have been afforded for a pluralistic exchange of views. In 1970 he established COMPEFIL (Centro Católico de Filosofia de São Paulo) and the Sociedade Brasileira de Filósofos Católicos. Soon regular conferences were being held on state and national levels. In 1978 Ladusāns organized ACIP (Associação Católica Interamericana de Filosofia) with twenty-four national affiliates. The following year a World Congress of Christian Philosophy was sponsored by ACIF and hosted by its affiliate, La Sociedad Católica Argentina de Filosofía.

Of greater interest, perhaps, is the activity that has been taking place in Brazilian theological circles. The challenge addressed to Catholic theologians in Brazil to enter into dialogue with philosophical Marxism was first issued by Pe. Henrique C. de Lima Vaz, S.J., at the end of the 1950s and the first half of the 60s. Lima Vaz suggested the time was propitious for considering seriously the possibility of articulating the Christian faith using Marxist terminology and concepts in much the same way that St. Thomas Aquinas used the terms and concepts of Aristotelian philosophy to formulate a theological system in the thirteenth century. More recently Catholic theologians such as Leonardo Boff, Hugo Assman, and Dom Helder Câmara, and Protestant theologians like Richard Schaull and Rubem Álves have contributed to the revolutionary new way of approaching the theological task known as Liberation Theology, which has spread far beyond Latin America to countries of the Third World in Africa, Southeast Asia, and East Asia. The interpretation of the faith and the mission of the Church as articulated by Leonardo Boff has been perceived by the Vatican to constitute a threat both intellectual and political to the ecclesiastical establishment and for a long time Boff was silenced. When accused of abandoning traditional Catholic theological tenets in favor of Marxist principles, Boff responded that Liberationists use Marxist tools of analysis for understanding the structures and process of socioeconomic history, and that the motivation of transforming human society and the social ideals toward which such transformation is directed stem directly from the Gospel and not from Marxist ideology.

There is a presence of Marxists within Brazilian philosophical circles today, but they have failed to make contributions as significant and substantial as those produced by the previous generation, which included Leôncio Basbaum with his masterly work on historiography, *O processo evolutivo da historia* (1963); and Caio Prado Júnior with his analyses of Marxist epistemology and logic, *Dialética do conhecimento* (2nd. rev. ed., 1965) and *Notas introdutórias à lógica dialética* (1959).

During the 80s a group of heterodox Marxist intellectuals have been collaborating through the pages of a journal *Ensaio: Revista de Filosofia, Política, e Ciência da História* to restore Marxism from its status of static and dogmatic ideology to an effective philosophy of thought and action within Brazilian society. The movement is led by the editor of *Ensaio*, J. Chasin, Professor of Philosophy at the Federal University of Minas Gerais, who is calling for a rediscovery of Marx through a "post-political and post-epistemological" reading of the texts to serve as a basis for creating a "new or original form of thinking and doing politics of the left."[5] Other members of the group include Ricardo Antunes, Professor of Sociology at the University of Campinas; Floristan Fernandes, Professor in the Graduate Program in Social Sciences of the Catholic University of São Paulo; Cesare Giuseppe Galván, Professor of Economics at the Federal University of Pernambuco; Ernildo Stein, Professor of Philosophy at the Federal University of Rio Grande do Sul; and Maurício Tragtenberg, Professor of Social Sciences at FGV of São Paulo. A Week of Studies commemorating the centennial of the death of Karl Marx was held in Belo

Horizonte with Henrique Lima Vaz giving the opening address on the philosophical roots of Marx's thought. The papers presented during the Week were published in a special double number (N°s 11/12) of *Ensaio*, and have been reissued in a two-volume book, *Marx hoje* (1st ed. 1987; 2nd ed. 1988) which inaugurates a new series, "Cadernos Ensaio", which will include translations of classical Marxist works and contemporary Marxist discussion.

Other philosophical movements might be mentioned briefly. Since 1977 Comtean Positivists have held annual meetings at a national level. Most delegates hail from Paraná, Rio de Janeiro, Rio Grande do Sul, Santa Catarina, and São Paulo. The proceedings of each annual conference are published and reveal not merely an interest in the history of positivism's influence on Brazilian thought and society, but an effort to interpret contemporary problems of Brazilian life from the standpoint of Comteanism.

Phenomenology continues to be employed in the work of many Brazilian philosophers, and there is a Society for Phenomenology. Perhaps the most outstanding recent work of this genre has been done by Gerd Bornheim of Pôrto Alegre, an independent thinker who was profoundly influenced by Heidegger, and whose greatest study is entitled *Dialética: Teoria, praxis; Ensaio para uma crítica da fundamentação ontológica da dialética*, in which he addresses the question of the relation between theory and praxis, drawing critically upon Hegelian and Marxist dialectic on the one hand, and Heideggerian historical ontology on the other. Students and colleagues of Bornheim, all of whom have concerned themselves with questions of hermeneutics rather than the utilization of phenomenological methodology in the sciences, following a Heideggerian rather than a Husserlian lead, include Ernildo Stein and João Alberto Leivas Job (Federal University of Rio Grande do Sul), Urbano Zilles (Catholic University of Rio Grande do Sul), Emanuel Carneiro Leão and Gilvan Fogel (Federal University of Rio de Janeiro), Zanilda Lopes de Siqueira (State University of Rio de Janeiro), and Maria da Conceição Miranda (Federal University of Pernambuco). Brazilian phenomenologists working in the fields of psychology and sociology include João de Souza Ferrar (*Compreesão fenomenológica das emoções*), Isaias Paim (*Fenomenologia da atividade representativa*), and Creusa Capalho (*Fenomenologia e ciências humanas; Fenomenologia e ciências sociais*).[6]

Miguel Reale takes up a similar problematic in what he considers to be his most important philosophical work, *Existência e realidade*, where both Marxist and Hegelian dialectics on the one hand, and Husserlian and Heideggerian phenomenology on the other, are subjected to careful criticism; a synthesis is articulated which goes well beyond the two positions. Mention should be made as well of the late Machado Neto's effort to follow Husserl's methodology in sociological investigations, expressed in the posthumous volume: *Para uma eidética sociológica* (1977); and of Creusa Capalho's analysis of phenomenological methodology in the social sciences: *Fenomenologia e ciências humanas* (1973). Beneval de Oliveira provides a survey of Brazilian phenomenological activity in *A fenomenologia no Brasil* (1983).

Commemorative dates are celebrated regularly with special symposia or colloquia such as the Hegel Colloquium in Pôrto Alegre, Rio Grande do Sul, in August, 1983, and the Habermas Colloquium in Novo Friburgo, State of Rio de Janeiro, in November, 1985. The most fruitful of these in terms of lasting impact have been the Kant conferences. In 1981, to celebrate the 200th anniversary of the publication of the *Critique of Pure Reason*, two colloquia were held, one at the Federal University of Rio Grande do Sul, and the other at the University of Campinas. An informal group of graduate students in philosophy began to meet to discuss Kantian thought as the result of those conferences. In 1986 they became organized formally as the "Grupo Kant" of the National Association of Graduate Students in Philosophy. The end of August, 1988, the group helped to sponsor a four-day First Kant Congress at the Federal University of Rio de Janeiro in celebration of the 200th anniversary of the publication of the *Critique of Practical Reason* with the presence of five Kant specialists from Europe and thirty Brasilian professors of philosophy. The Congress was coordinated by Zeljko Loparić, Professor of Philosophy at the University of Campinas. A Kant Society was organized at the Congress which will function as a national section of the Kant-Gesellschaft. The publication of a journal, *Revista de Filosofia Kantiana*, was announced as a project of the new Society.

I began this discussion of present-day philosophical studies in Brasil with Leônidas Hegenberg's question concerning the state of health of studies in logic in Brasil today. Were the question to be put: "And how goes Philosophy in Brasil today?", I should respond "Philosophy is indeed alive and healthy and goes very well in Brasil today, thanks!"

CHAPTER 4

Mexican Philosophy in the 1980s: Possibilities and Limits[1]

OSCAR R. MARTÍ

This essay is an introduction to Mexican philosophy during the decade of the 1980s. It seeks to fulfill the needs of English-speaking scholars who face the field for the first time, and who find, instead of the expected beliefs and trends, a bewildering array of opinions and interests that go by the name of philosophy. To understand this literally foreign landscape, newcomers usually turn to their more knowledgeable brethren from other fields.[2] Unfortunately, crossing disciplinary borders does not help, in part because of some presuppositions about the nature of philosophy, in part because of philosophy's insularity. To remedy the latter I shall give a historical background of Mexican philosophy, describe some features of the economic landscape, and construct an intellectual map by outlining contemporary philosophical activity and listing the main published works. To remedy the former, I must first make some remarks on the nature and function of philosophy.

Philosophy can mean many things: a state of mind, the writings of someone called a philosopher, a world-view, folk tales, and so on. Professional philosophers agree that it is a method or technique for resolving some special problems, or the reading of a universally recognized corpus of writings — a doing and a knowing. This distinction hangs on the deeper one of philosophy as a vocation, as a profession, and as a discipline. The *vocation* is the philosophical attitude of questioning, a desire to know reality, timeless Truth, Beauty, and Goodness. It evokes the image of the sage, the saint, the hermit so alien to contemporary philosophy. Philosophy as a *profession* emerges from teaching the tools for exercising the vocation. The corresponding image of the college professor is more familiar. The *discipline* is the philosophical vocation taught by the professional at a fixed time and in a given educational system. Its embodiments are the text and the curriculum. In spite of the adage that those who can't, teach, the profession is still central, for in its task of dissemination and education it shapes the discipline, the educational system, and the vocation itself.

In writing about Mexican philosophy during the 1980s, I shall perforce deal with the profession and the discipline, as it makes no sense to qualify the vocation as Mexican.[3] Focusing on the educational context has some pluses: I do not have to take a philosophical position as academia is the natural bearer of philosophical traditions and has been for centuries the source of the most intense activity of philosophers.[4]

My task is not to evaluate the vocation or opt for one or another side of the controversies that naturally arise in the course of practicing the profession. I do not want or dare to evaluate it. Neither will I speak of its development or evolution for they, again, imply an evaluation – the opposite of development is degeneration and of evolution atavism. And, since I cannot foresee the future, I shall try not to predict trends.[5] I speak of change, and seek only to establish the possibilities and limits of the profession and the discipline in Mexico during the 1980s. By *possibilities* I mean the potential, the permissible, what can be done given the abilities of the practitioners and the evidence of prior changes; by *limits* the political, economic, and social barriers that restrict possibilities.

Possibilities

Historical Background

Though outside Anglo-European currents, philosophy in Mexico has not lacked merit or vision throughout its long and varied career.[6] Brought to New Spain by the Catholic church during the sixteenth century, philosophy made a home in the cloister and the school, where it was used first to justify and afterwards to recreate the medieval world, regardless of whatever changes the discovery of the *Orbis novo* had brought upon the European mind. The earliest themes dealt with the nature, rights, and place of the conquered in the conqueror's scheme of things. Among its most distinguished philosophers were Alonzo de la Veracruz (see Gómez Robledo, *El magisterio filosófico y jurídico de Alonzo de la Veracruz*),[7] Antonio Rubio, and Tomás Mercado (*Comentarios lucidísimos al texto de Pedro Hispano*).

During the seventeenth century, philosophical energies were wasted in upholding the medieval system against political and social changes. Some of the tasks set were ridding Aristotle of scholastic frivolities, and the justification of faith against Protestantism, science, novelty, or anything that threatened the established order. Hence, the best-known figures, the poetess Sor Juana Inés de la Cruz[8] and the astronomer and mathematician Carlos Sigüenza y Góngora (*Libra astronómica y filosófica*), turn out not to be professional philosophers.

The philosophical calm of the first half of the eighteenth century was disturbed at mid-century by the innovative interests of a generation of scholars, mostly Jesuits and including Francisco Clavijero, Diego José Abad, Francisco Javier Alegre, and Benito Díaz de Gamarra (*Elementos de la filosofía moderna*). Aware of Italian and French philosophy since the Renaissance, this new generation tried to break with Aristotelian thought and to bring Mexican philosophy into "modernity" (Méndez Plancarte, *Humanistas del Siglo XVIII*). Their expulsion from the Spanish-speaking world in 1767 was a setback to the introduction of European academic philosophy into Mexico. Nevertheless, some of these ideas made an impact outside the university, and toward the end of the century views of the Enlightenment, the American and the French Revolutions appeared in social and political discourse, mainly in pamphlets and newspapers.[9]

The wars of independence, the anarchy, the civil and foreign wars, the sporadic closing of the Universidad Real y Pontíficia and of other important centers of learning, put a stop to the spread of academic learning during the first half of the nineteenth century. Yet philosophic ideas continued to show up in political arguments over the moral obligation of the metropolis, the difficulties in formulating political autonomy, the foundations of constitutional governments, even the ideas of nation, sovereignty, progress, modernity and their means of attainment.[10] The writings of José María Luis Mora are good examples of this amalgam of philosophy and politics (*Obras*, especially volume 1). The best introduction to the period is still Luis Villoro's *Proceso ideológico de la Revolución de Independencia*.

After the French intervention and the liberals' victory in 1867, positivism became popular.[11] Comtian ideas appeared first, promising to bring the nation into the nineteenth century through educational and political reforms. Under that plan, the Escuela Nacional Preparatoria was founded, and philosophy as a career moved into the lay classrooms. Intellectuals were encouraged to study science and its philosophy — particularly the social sciences — to improve social conditions. During the *Porfiriato*, from the 1880s on, Spencerian positivism and evolutionism grew in popularity and stifled differing views, but by the first decade of the twentieth century, new currents had surfaced, some markedly anti-positivistic, and people began to discuss idealism, vitalism, pragmatism, something of Krausism, and various movements nowadays subsumed under socialism.

In contrast to the past, the aftermath of the Mexican Revolution proved to be a stimulating environment for intellectual and philosophical production, and positivism became a convenient ghost against which to rebel. And that is just what the Ateneo de la Juventud did, a group that had met in 1910, and to which José Vasconcelos, Antonio Caso, Pedro Henríquez Ureña and others belonged — intellectuals of the first order who sought methods of investigation or modes of expression other than those sanctioned by the then-prevailing scientism. Their speeches are collected in the useful *Conferencias del Ateneo de la Juventud* (Caso et al., 1984). For them the proper study of philosophy was Man. After the Revolution, Caso and Vasconcelos, redefined the sources and direction of philosophy in Mexico — a program that extended well into the 1930s and 1940s. Caso, aware of European currents, introduced contemporary French thought, but also returned to classical system building to formulate a universal philosophy that still spoke of man's values and needs (*La existencia como economía, como desinterés y como caridad*). Vasconcelos, rather than using European sources, wanted a reconstruction of Mexican and Latin American philosophy and culture on the basis of its indigenous past (*La raza cósmica*).[12]

The vernacular influence of the generation of the Ateneo began to wane in the 1940s and 1950s when they shared the limelight with the Spanish philosophers exiled after the fall of Republican Spain. The ranks of the "transterrados" included José María Gallegos Rocafull, José Gaos, Eduardo Nicol, Wenceslao Roces, Adolfo Sánchez Vásquez, and Joaquín Xirau. Some were students of the Spanish philosopher José Ortega y Gasset; some had brought with them the influence of German writers such as Husserl, Hartmann, Jaspers, Dilthey, etc., whom they had translated into Spanish (Gaos's translation of Hartmann's *Ontología* and Husserl's *Ideas relativas a una fenomenología pura y una filosofía fenomenológica* or Xirau's translation of Jaeger's *Paideia* and *Aristóteles*, for instance). Others found a congenial and cultured audience tested by the fires of the Revolution and sympathetic to the philosophies of the left.[13]

As a result, there are conflicting tendencies in the works of Samuel Ramos, Emilio Uranga, Vicente Lombardo Toledano, and others. On the one hand, they re-approach contemporary European —

especially French — thought. On the other, they demand that philosophy express Mexican reality and concerns, and be based on the circumstances of the individual doing philosophy.[14] That requirement was not easy, and Lombardo Toledano, for instance, was caught between the particularism prevalent at the time and the universalism predicated by Marxist dogma.[15] The result was the construction of the concept of the "filosofía de lo mexicano," and the search for a national identity, activities that characterized the 1950s and 1960s. Perhaps the best-known writers are the historian Edmundo O'Gorman, the philosopher Leopoldo Zea, and the Hiperión group, of which Luis Villoro, Fernando Salmerón, and Joaquín Sánchez McGregor are the most visible. The amount and quality of their philosophic output made them the most influential writers of the 1970s and the 1980s.

During the 1960s and 1970s, other tendencies began to impose themselves and challenge the influences of the vernacular and the transterrados. Several traditional European trends are recognizable: Neo-Thomism, Marxism, phenomenology, and historicism. Neo-Thomism had its best exponents in José Sánchez Villaseñor[16] and Oswaldo Robles,[17] figures of the 1950s and 1960s. Though it is perhaps the oldest of the mentioned trends, as a Catholic philosophy it did not find fertile soil in the Mexico of the *Reforma* and the revolution. Neo-Thomism still has its defenders in the 1980s, particularly at the Universidad Iberoamericana, and among some legal realists. Faced with the challenges of the Cuban and Nicaraguan revolutions, and with internal crises, Marxism changed from an earlier pamphleteering activity and was made more precise: the acerbic analysis of Lombardo Toledano, the careful refinements of Adolfo Sánchez Vázquez[18] to accommodate aesthetic problems, and Elí de Gortari's groundwork to allow for the spread of scientific philosophies (*Ensayos filosóficos sobre la ciencia moderna, Método materialista dialéctico*). The introduction and vigor of phenomenological thinking was due, for the most part, to the influence of Gaos and his disciples, but may now be in the wane.[19] Finally, and perhaps the trend best noted outside Mexico for its originality and fruitfulness, is historicism. Stemming from Caso and Ramos, and influenced by Gaos, it has had its best-known exponent in Zea,[20] whose enormous production ranges from the study of positivism in Mexico[21] to that of formulating a philosophy of history[22] and of identity, not just Mexican but Latin American (*Latinoamérica en la encrucijada de la historia*).

Newer forms of philosophical argumentation have also appeared in Mexico, among them analytical philosophy and the philosophy of liberation. The first, of Anglo-American origin, has intrigued many members of the previous generation (Villoro, *Creer, saber, y conocer,* and Salmerón, *La filosofía y las actitudes morales*). It recognizes the advantages of logic and the philosophy of science in the clarification of many traditional problems of ethics or epistemology. Analytical philosophy, however, has been criticized as a philosophy of the dominant nations, even a return to nineteenth-century positivism.

The philosophy of liberation, of Argentinian origin, wants to remedy many of the social and political ills that affect Latin America. Its main exponents in Mexico are Enrique Dussel[23] (*La producción teórica de Marx*) and Horacio Cerutti Guldberg (see his important *Filosofía de la liberación*). The philosophy of liberation has been criticized as oriented toward the left, as theology, or as a grassroots populism, more political rhetoric than philosophy. And curiously, because of its interest in changing social realities through philosophic methods, its objective is probably closer to nineteenth-century positivism than that of analytical philosophy.

Philosophy as an Academic Profession

From its inception, Mexican philosophy has been intimately linked to academia.[24] It has been, more than a vocation, a profession. Its career has been described as follows:

> The study of philosophy prepares the specialist in the scientific method for questioning the basis, sense, and meaning of man and his reality. The task of this science is to transmit philosophic knowledge through teaching and systematic investigation of each of its branches (metaphysics, theory of knowledge, axiology, logic). As a teacher, the *licenciado* in philosophy can work in secondary or higher institutions of learning. Research can be carried out in specialized institutions.[25]

The discipline was taught in seminaries and universities not only as preparation for missionary work but to create future teachers. In times of academic activity the profession grew and suffered when the schools were weakened or closed because of internal struggles or civil wars. From the *Reforma* onwards its relative prosperity and prominence were due partly to the establishment of the Escuela Nacional Preparatoria (1867) and the Universidad Nacional (1910).

Statistics tend to back the claims to professionalism of contemporary Mexican philosophy.[26] In Mexico, of over 250 institutions of higher learning, 42 are universities (1980),[27] with a total of over 1,200,000 students and 106,000 teachers. (See Table 4.1). Of these, 23 offer a "licenciatura" (bachelor's degree) in philosophy, and 5 the master's degree, though only 2 offer a doctorate (see Tables 4.2 and

4.3).[28] These figures become meaningful only when they are compared with those of countries of similar size, culture, or industrial development.

The number of philosophy majors nationwide is about 1,900 undergraduates and 130 graduate students (see Tables 4.4 and 4.5). Out of over 100,000 teachers at all educational levels, about 1,100 are philosophy and humanity teachers (see table 4.6). The number of doctorates in philosophy is between 40 and 50, less than 1% of all Mexican Ph.D.'s. Most are employed in education. There are two major philosophical societies, the Asociación Filosófica de México, and the Sociedad Mexicana de Filosofía, and several philosophy research centers.[29] A study of their ranks show again the predominance of careers in education.

Economic analysis is often used to assess the health of a discipline in any given country. It is a truism that philosophy flourishes where it is economically rewarded and does not where it is persecuted. But in the case of Mexico, economic indicators are not always trustworthy for reasons that I shall discuss later. Nevertheless, in Mexico, where the minimum salary in mid-1987 was 120,000 pesos a month, a low-level bureaucrat earns 350,000 pesos and a university professor between 360,000 and 890,000 pesos a month. A half-time teacher at the higher ranks earns between 260,000 and 350,000 pesos a month, and those employed hourly, between 12,000 and 14,600 pesos an hour. (A fall 1987 across-the-board salary increase has raised these figures by 25%). These figures are meaningful only if one takes into account the acquisitive power of professional salaries, and if they are compared with those of countries in similar circumstances.

Higher education in Mexico is free and thus available to all. The government (primarily the federal government) subsidizes the university system, earmarking for higher education a comparatively high (but decreasing) percentage of the national budget (3.4% in 1974, 2.9% in 1982, and 2.2% in 1987). The main administrative organ is the Secretaría de Educación Pública (SEP) which sets budgets, priorities, national standards, and curricula up to the secondary level. Because of the heavy subsidy, economic aid to students is limited to cover subsistence, study, and research. An important annex is the Consejo Nacional de Ciencia y Tecnología (CONACYT), which awards fellowships to students and researchers. For example, the CONACYT sabbatical fellowships consist of twelve monthly installments of 400,000 pesos, transportation and insurance costs for research in Mexican institutions outside the metropolitan area of Mexico City. Also, the Sistema Nacional de Investigadores gives stipends to deserving professionals. Fellowships are available for study abroad from the

U.S.–funded Benito Juárez and Fulbright programs, and Latin American Scholarship Programs for American Universities (LASPAU). Research fellowships are available to outstanding scholars from several private foundations such as Ford, MacArthur, Guggenheim, and Hewlitt-Packard, and from public entities such as UNESCO, the Organization of American States, the German government's Humboldt Foundation, etc.

The Philosophic Expression

I shall now examine the expression of the vocation. One does philosophy in many ways: written, in books, academic journals, newspapers, even popular magazines; orally, in the classroom, in conferences, on radio and television. Mexico is no exception: During the 1980s, it kept up an impressive philosophic production as evidenced by an extensive list of publications, congresses, and public events. For a partial list of books published since 1980, consult the selected bibliography at the end of this chapter.[30]

The principal means of philosophic expression is the essay, appearing in journals, anthologies, and newspapers. Journals can be classified as multidisciplinary or philosophical.[31] Many multidisciplinary journals publish essays with philosophical content. *Cuadernos Americanos*, in a new editorial period and dedicated to the cultural, political, and literary problems of Latin America is a good example; so are *Quipu*, dedicated to the history of science and technology in America; *Siglo XIX*, of multidisciplinary focus but devoted to a specific historical period; and *Estudios: Filosofía/Historia/Letras*. Among the philosophy journals, many are written for the general public, *Diánoia*, for instance, while others opt for particular philosophical points of view: *Dialéctica* (Marxism), *Crítica* (analytic philosophy), *Prometeo* (Latin American history and philosophy), *Revista de Filosofía* (Neo-Thomism). Journals often play an anthological role when they publish the proceedings or papers from a congress, or when they publish special volumes: *Contrafuerte* dedicated a number to Berkeley, *Cuadernos de Filosofía* (Universidad Iberoamericana) to Freud, and each issue of *Nuestra América*, of the Centro Coordinador y Difusor de Estudios Latinoamericanos, is devoted to a specific topic – the philosophy of liberation, the Latin American baroque, etc.

Of the written philosophical production, books are the most important. It must be said that Mexico, with Argentina and Spain, is a leader in the publication of books in Spanish, especially in philosophy. This labor has been carried out by editorial houses like Grijalbo, the Fondo de Cultura Económica, Porrúa, Siglo XXI, Trillas, etc. and the university presses, of which the Universidad Nacional Autónoma de México has a distinguished record.

Philosophy books can be classified as collective works (anthologies) and monographs. (I shall ignore textbooks.) Among the most recently published anthologies I must mention the valuable editorial efforts of Jorge J. E. Gracia (*El análisis filosófico en América Latina*, edited by Gracia *et al.*, and Frondizi and Gracia, *El hombre y los valores en la filosofía latinoamericana del siglo XX*)[32] both containing writings of Mexican philosophers, classic and contemporary; *Etica y análisis*, edited by Fernando Salmerón and Eduardo Rabossi, which has translated Anglo-American analytic classics into Spanish. Reprinted and updated is the de la Cueva anthology, *Estudios de historia de la filosofía en México*, a series of essays on philosophy in Mexico ranging from the pre-Hispanic period to the impact of the Spanish exiles — still the best introduction to the topic.[33]

Of the monographs, a large number of titles have appeared since 1980, dealing with the history of philosophy, be it ancient (Beuchot, *Ensayos marginales sobre Aristóteles*; Gómez Robledo, *Platón: los seis grandes temas de su filosofía*); medieval (Beuchot's *La filosofía del lenguaje en la Edad Media* and Gracia's *Introducción al problema de la individuación en la alta edad media*); modern (García de Oteyza, *La identidad personal de Hume*; the classic by Rovira, *Eclécticos portugueses del siglo XVIII*); or contemporary (Cerutti Guldberg, *Ideologías políticas contemporáneas*).

Several monographs deal with topics on Latin American philosophy by thinkers of the highest order such as Miró Quesada's *Proyecto y realización del filosofar latinoamericano*;[34] Roig's collections of essays *Teoría y crítica del pensamiento latinoamericano*, and *Filosofía, universidad y filósofos en América Latina*; or Cerutti Guldberg's groundbreaking *Hacia una metodología de la historia de las ideas (filosóficas) en América Latina*.

Others deal with Mexican philosophy and its figures (Vera y Cuspines, *El pensamiento de Vasconcelos*; Yamuni, *José Gaos*); especially Antonio Caso (Cardiel Reyes, *Retorno a Caso*; Rosa Krauze, *La filosofía de Antonio Caso*). For an account of the intellectual life of Mexico during this century, and its relation to politics, certainly Abelardo Villegas's *Autognosis: El pensamiento mexicano en el siglo XX* is the best.

On the history of logic, especially in Mexico, there is the learned yet very readable introduction by Redmond and Beuchot to the logical works of Veracruz, Rubio, and Mercado, *La Lógica mexicana en el siglo de oro*. Several methodologies are represented, most prominently historicism (Zea, *Simón Bolívar*; Escobar, *La Ilustración en la filosofía latinoamericana*); Marxism (Sánchez Vázquez, *Filosofía de la praxis*; Terán, *Discutir Mariátegui*); and philosophical analysis, with its stress on the philosophy of science – the historical (Navarrete *et al.*, *Matemáticas y realidad*); the social (Yturbe, *La explicación en la historia*; Olivé, ed., *La explicación social del conocimiento*); physical (Flematti, *Reconstrucción lógica de teorías empíricas*); or the formal sciences (Salazar Resines, *Introducción a la lógica deductiva y teoría de conjuntos*).

A variety of philosophical investigations have appeared on topics such as the nature of philosophical inquiry (Nicol, *La reforma de la filosofía*); psychoanalysis (Conde, *Las ideas estéticas de Freud*); ethics (Escobar, *Etica*); philosophy of religion (Xirau, *Cuatro filósofos y lo sagrado*); social and political philosophies (Olivé, *Estado, legitimación y crisis*; or the anthology by Aguilar and Yturbe, *Filosofía política: Razón y poder*); legal philosophy (Basave, *Filosofía del derecho internacional*, and García Máynez, *Ensayos filosófico-jurídicos*); aesthetics (Palazón Mayoral, *Reflexiones sobre estética a partir de André Bretón*); feminism (Hierro, *Etica y feminismo*); ideology (Villoro, *El concepto de ideología*; Gómez Pérez, *Polémica en ideología*); and several studies of contemporary figures: on the Argentinian Alejandro Korn (Torchia Estrada, *Alejandro Korn: Profesión y vocación*); on José Ortega y Gasset (the classic by Salmerón, *Las mocedades de Ortega*; Durán, *Ortega hoy*); on Russell and Wittgenstein (Tomasini, *Los atomismos lógicos de Russell y Wittgenstein*); on Adolfo Sánchez Vázquez (González, Pereyra, and Vargas, *Praxis y filosofía, Ensayos en homenaje a Adolfo Sánchez Vázquez*; González Rojo, *Epistemología y socialismo: La crítica de Sánchez a Althuser*, both highly recommended); on Ramón Xirau (González, *Presencia de Ramón Xirau*); on Leopoldo Zea (Medin, *Leopoldo Zea: Ideología, historia y filosofía de América Latina*), to mention a few.

In addition to the already mentioned translations by Gaos and Xirau, other translations of important works have been published: classical (Galeno, *Iniciación a la dialéctica*; Rousseau, *El contrato social*); colonial (Pedro Hispano, *Tractatus, llamados después Summule logicales*; Juan de Santo Tomás, *Compendio de lógica*; both excellent editions by Mauricio Beuchot); and recent (Derrida, *De la gramatología*; Wittgenstein, *Diario filosófico*); on logic (Copi, *Lógica simbólica*; Quine, *Lógica elemental*); philosophy of science (Poincaré, *Filosofía de la ciencia*). Also published are new editions or reprints of the works of many Mexican thinkers including Díaz de Gamarra (*Máximas de educación*); Caso (*Antología filosófica*); Reyes (*Universidad, política y pueblo*); and Gaos (*Historia de nuestra idea del mundo*).

The problems Mexican philosophers set out to solve stand out not only for their similarity to those of other philosophers, but also for their differences. Of note are the issues of the Latin American identity (Zea, *Sentido de la difusión cultural latinoamericana*), colonial history and logic (Benítez, *La idea de la historia en Carlos Sigüenza y Góngora*), liberation philosophy and theology (Dussel, *De Medellín a Puebla*), utopian thought (Velázquez, *Pensamiento utópico: revolución o contrarrevolución*), and so on. The past few years have witnessed a decrease in interest on the problem formulated by Ramos of "mexicanidad," "imitation," and the "inferiority complex" (of interest to anthropologists, sociologists, and psychiatrists, but not to many philosophers).

Other philosophical expressions can be found in theses written to fulfill degree requirements. To obtain a degree, the student must not only take the prescribed courses but offer a substantial work and defend it in a public exam. This requirement applies not only to master's and doctoral theses but to the *licenciatura*. In addition to fulfilling requirements, these works usually offer careful analyses of the topic under investigation and are frequently of sufficient quality to be published as monographs.

The most natural philosophical expression remains, however, oral — in classrooms, congresses and conferences. In any university that offers a *licenciatura* in philosophy, there is a variety of philosophy courses.[35]

As for professional meetings, during the 1980s many philosophy congresses were held in Mexico. I attended the 2nd Coloquio de Filosofía (Puebla, December 1979), the 1st Congreso Nacional (Guanajuato, November 1981), the 3rd Congreso (Guadalajara, 1985), and in November 1987, the 4th Congreso Nacional, in Toluca. Of an international character, the 9th Congreso Interamericano de Filosofía was also held in Guadalajara in 1985. Of lesser size, but still of major importance, are the meetings organized by the institutes. Worthy of mention are those organized by the Centro Coordinador y Difusor de Estudios Latinoamericanos (CCYDEL) on Latinity, Bolívar, the Discovery of America, etc. These meetings brought together Mexican and foreign scholars to carry out joint projects of international scope. Unfortunately, few proceedings of the colloquia or congresses have been published, thus diminishing the diffusion of many important investigations. The prominent exceptions are Leopoldo Zea, ed., *La latinidad y su sentido en América Latina*: Graciela Hierro, ed., *La naturaleza femenina*: issues 2 and 3 of *Teoría* that present the 1980 Symposium "Problemas Filosóficos del Conocimiento Sociohistórico," and the 1981 Kant Congress held at UNAM respectively; and the 1979 Puebla logic symposium *Hacía una Explicación de las Entidades Lógicas*.

Another important parameter is the academic exchanges between philosophers.[36] The aim of these exchanges, and of transnational relations in general, is as much to widen the audience as to gain international recognition for philosophical labor. In Mexico, the push toward cosmopolitanism has many causes, among them Mexico's lack of acknowledgment of its own cultural contribution, and the need to discover its own philosophical style (both stimulated by the search for identity). Equally important are the contacts between Mexican and foreign philosophers within and outside Mexico. To Mexico have migrated the Spanish "transterrados" and other European and Latin American exiles, and many Mexican philosophers have studied or done research outside the country.[37] These relations have born fruit during the 1980s, as evidenced by the diffusion and translation of works written by Mexicans, and the invitations, prizes, honorary doctorates, etc., that Mexican philosophers have received abroad.

What can be concluded from this sketch? That there is a diversity of philosophies in Mexico, that it is up-to-date on philosophical developments in the rest of the world, that a series of problems have been formulated that are considered important, and that there is interest in these problems. There is everything: philosophical progressives and conservatives, atavists and visionaries, pragmatists and idealists, exalted materialists and crass spiritualists. And no movement dominates. This is the closest to philosophical normalcy that can be desired: A multifaceted and active profession with sufficient means for diffusion, an interested public, and a government that continually reasserts the importance of education in the development of the nation.

Limits

Economic Limitations

Even though the most important events in Mexico during the 1980s have been external to philosophy, they have had a savage impact on the development of the profession and will continue to influence the discipline for years to come.[38] I am speaking of the economic crisis that began in 1982. This crisis has overwhelmed the nation and the university. The lacks, the "¡No hay!" ("There isn't any!") extend as much to the university as to the marketplace. On one side, inflation has decimated the acquisitive power of salaries and educational budgets. On the other, the imposed austerity has not kept salaries and budgets at equitable levels. To understand the situation it is not necessary to make invidious comparisons with the salaries of other professions or of professors in other countries. It is enough to remember the economic life of Mexico in 1979.

University salaries are not up to par with a professor's education, responsibility, or intellectual demands. When measured in terms of dollars, an academic's salary has decreased an average of 35% a year since 1982. And in 1987 the inflation grew at an annual rate of 157 percent. According to Banco de México estimates, 2,212 pesos were needed to buy at the end of 1987 what was bought with 100 pesos in 1980. Under these conditions, it is not possible to speak of dedication to the profession, training, growth, or university development. To make ends meet, the academic is forced to moonlight at other institutions, sell books or clothes, give up the university for more lucrative areas or abandon his career and follow the route of the emigrants, legal or illegal, to the United States. If the philosophy professor's economic situation does not improve, his ranks will diminish, followed by a decrease in students interested in philosophy. Finally, in a not-too-distant future, the discipline will suffer irreparable damage. Though these predictions may not affect the vocation, they will have, nonetheless, a negative impact on the influence and prestige of all philosophers.

Economic aid, public or private, is not enough either. The Sistema Nacional de Investigadores was developed to help a limited number of qualified professionals, not to subsidize every academic. Help from the private sector is minimal and is infected with a mutual mistrust. The academic fears that the private sector lacks the civic virtue of giving unconditionally for research, and that it has tried to and will continue to meddle in, and profit from, research.[39]

Funds for travel to conferences, congresses, or symposia, especially the international ones, are scarce and insufficient. Mexican cosmopolitanism and international recognition, won after so much effort, will soon be seriously hampered. Equally curtailed is the acquisition of foreign books, given their increasingly higher cost after each devaluation. The result is an even-greater limitation on communication with the rest of the world.

Other lacks can be cited: the lack of statistics about the profession, and of complete bibliographies of philosophy books or essays published in Mexico. Also, many libraries do not have up-to-date catalogues. Exceptions are the Archivo General de la Nación, specialized libraries like the Simón Bolívar, the Eduardo García Máynez, or those of private universities. The rest leave much to be desired.

Some measures have been taken. The Instituto de Investigaciones Filosóficas plans to renew the bibliographic series discontinued in 1976. In the meantime, several journals, both commercial (*Libros de México*) and academic (*Prometeo*), have published annual bibliographies. To this end, the use of high technology is more promising, though few data banks now operate in Mexico. Outstanding are those at the Centre Scientifique et Technique (a bibliographic bank on France and Latin America) and at the Biblioteca Benjamín Franklyn (tapping the DIALOG network). The Universidad Nacional Autónoma de México plans to complete an electronic catalogue of its libraries, similar to the one in place at the Universidad Iberoamericana. The Centro Coordinador y Difusor de Estudios Latinoamericanos and the Instituto de Investigaciones Jurídicas are in the process of compiling their own. The use of computers has, in addition, had a positive impact on philosophy – in epistemology, logic, ethics, and the history of ideas (such as the fascinating monograph by Negrete, *Popper vs. Bayes vs. Hempel: un diálogo entre robots*. Yet a more efficient use demands a defeat of technological illiteracy through quality technical instruction and sufficient hardware. The warnings are clear: Clinging to pre-technological modes of information can retard the growth of a discipline, a delay comparable perhaps to the one caused by the insistence on Latin as the scientific language of the sixteenth and seventeenth centuries.

Another limit to the diffusion of philosophy, also remediable, is the insufficient use of radio and television. Cost and technical knowledge are obstacles. Videocassettes or films on philosophical themes are beyond budgetary allocations. But this does not mean that local talent cannot be used for creating programs in which philosophical problems are discussed, instead of those devoted to other themes.[40] Obviously, the biggest obstacle is to convince mass media producers of the value of these ideas. How difficult this is, is evident from the quality of daily television programming.

The economic factor re-emerges. Not only does it limit professional ambitions, but also many disciplinary and vocational ones – the possibility of normalcy, cosmopolitanism, international recognition, adequate facilities, or books. The hardest blow is the realization of the vulnerability of the profession and the discipline. Philosophers are neither seriously listened to, nor, with rare exceptions, do they participate in decision-making dialogues outside academia. Some bureaucrats remind us that in times of crisis philosophy is worth very little. It is easier to cut budgets for philosophy departments than for those of economics, political science, or sociology. The national debt, they claim, cannot be paid with culture.

Political Limitations

Perhaps the best-known limitations to the development of learning in Latin America are the periodic strikes that plague the university. In

general, Latin American students and faculty are an elite that safe-
guards its class interests and often the *status quo* by recourse precisely
to that discourse that attacks inequities, to non-negotiable demands,
even refusing to talk lest such dialogue lead to legitimation of the
governmental structures that need change. If some strikes are motivated by less than disinterested reasons masked by a rhetoric of idealism, brotherhood of man, or populism, others are expressions of
genuine frustration at a situation beyond their control or desires.

In the past, strikes by Mexican university students have had vio-
lent outcomes – Tlatelolco is a sad reminder. To avoid them, the
physical layout of the university has changed drastically since the
1960s. New universities lack a central campus and are often spread
over a city, with a well-bastioned administrative center separated from
the rest. There are no cafeterias, student centers, few bookstores and
almost no cafés near the instruction centers. The rationale is to prevent students from meeting and talking. The guiding belief is that
such activities will certainly lead to expressions of civil disorder.

The UNAM strikes and demands for university reform late in
1987, brought to the fore perceptions of closing doors, of lack of
opportunities, of social disasters, of governmental dishonesty, and
double standards toward higher education. If the strike was pre-
cipitated by fear of the university reform called for by the rector's plan
for strengthening academic standards, and perceived as threatening
academically weak and economically poor students, it was taken up
by the very people most affected by change, who felt that they had not
even been consulted. The resulting resolution of the conflict was a
university council. The elections of student and faculty representatives, and the political and educational ramifications of the 1988
presidential elections are not within the scope of this easy. It should
be added, however, that philosophers took a very active part in the
many sides of the debate.

Projections

Finally, the unavoidable question: What is the future of philosophy as
a profession and a discipline in Mexico? On the negative side, fewer
students and professors, more ideologies of hard times. On the
positive side, less philosophical and cultural dependence, greater
introspection and interest in the critical problems of politics such as
a questioning of the value of development, the role of the university,
and that of the philosopher in a society in crisis. Much is going to
change.

To conclude, I will now touch on the marginal problem of whether philosophy can be achieved in economically depressed environments. It has been argued elsewhere that philosophy cannot be carried out in anything but an environment of freedom and economic well-being.[41] Though this assertion has been challenged, it has some value. Economic well-being and freedom are always helpful to the philosophical task. But they are not enough. There have been many peoples who, although economically well-off, lacked a philosophical vocation (Imperial Rome, Persia, sixth-century China, much of Africa). I am not criticizing them, only observing that they have not had philosophies. A taste for raw fish, circumcision, a bone in the nose to accentuate beauty, or philosophy are not universal cultural phenomena. And if not every era of economic prosperity has resulted in a philosophy, neither have those of crisis. It can be affirmed, however, that times of peace result in a renewal of philosophy, and that those of crisis give forth new ones. Crisis does not renew philosophies, it changes them.

I would venture to guess that philosophy in Mexico will not perish but continue in spite of the imposed limitations. I expect not a philosophical renaissance but new philosophies. Other conditions are present, for example, the intelligence or courage of its practitioners, or the enormous variety of philosophical views generated in the past. I do not speak of achieving philosophical normalcy for I do not know what that means in a field that, in principle, is abnormal. On the contrary, it is desirable that philosophy be abnormal. Normal men and normal philosophers adapt to circumstances, and, contrary to the laws of evolution, are swallowed by the environment. The abnormal try to change that environment and, in times of crisis, those who adapt are already half-dead. But these are sophisms and not critical analyses, quixotisms. And quixotisms, of necessity, abound in Mexico today.

TABLE 4.1
Comparative Demographic/Educational Figures

	Mexico	Argentina	Brazil	USA
Population	75,870,000	30,097,000	132,580,000	236,600,000
Number of Universities	42	61	63	3,095
	(1980)	(1981)	(1976)	(1977)
Students*	1,280,300	550,500	1,377,200	12,372,000
Professors**	103,400	53,100	109,800	395,992
	(1983–84)	(1982)	(1980)	(1980)
Libraries	2,435	1,559	10,508	99,707
Volumes	13,735,000	11,412,000	25,999,000	1,636,600,000
	(1978–79)	(1977)	(1978)	(1977–79)
Educational Budget	13.1%	6.2%	4.6%	2.1%
(National %)	(1982)	(1982)	(1982)	(1982)

*Includes students from all post-secondary programs.
**Includes full time, half-time and hourly instructors from all postsecondary programs.

Sources: UNESCO; *Statistical Yearbook, 1984; Almanaque Mundial, 1987; Estadísticas Básicas del Sistema Educacional Nacional*; James Wilkie and Adam Perkal, *Statistical Abstracts of Latin America*, vol. 23.

TABLE 4.2
Master's Degree Students By School (1986)

	Entering	Total (Men/Women)	1986 Grads
Universidad Nacional Autónoma de México	4	59 (33/26)	0
Iberoamericana	6	24 (16/8)	0
Universidad Autónoma Metropolitana, Iztapalapa (MA Philo of Science)	0	19 (16/3)	0
Universidad Autónoma de Nuevo León	0	0 (0/0)	0
Universidad Autónoma del Estado de México	0	6 (1/5)	0

Sources: *Anuario Estadístico, 1987: Postgrado*

TABLE 4.3
Doctoral Students By School (1986)

	Entering	Total (Men/Women)	1986 Grads
Universidad Nacional Autónoma de México	2	14 (5/9)	0
Universidad Iberoamericana	1	3 (3/0)	0

Sources: *Anuario Estadístico, 1987: Postgrado*

TABLE 4.4
Philosophy Students: Nationwide Figures (1986)

	Entering	Total (Men/Women)	1986 Grads
Licenciaturas	560	1,934 (1,278/656)	190
M.A.	10	89 (50/39)	0
M.A. (philosophy of science)	0	19 (16/3)	0
Ph.D.'s	3	17 (8/9)	0

Sources: *Anuario Estadístico, 1987: Postgrado.*
  Anuario Estadístico, 1987: Licenciatura

TABLE 4.5
Total Student Figures (1986)

	Entering	Total (Men/Women)	1985 Grads
Licenciaturas	224,321	989,414 (620,625/368,789)	106,693
M.A. students	8,502	23,751 (16,528/7223)	3,074
Ph.D. students	294	1,379 (824/555)	156
Special Studies	6,535	13,084 (9,323/3,761)	3,035

Sources: *Anuario Estadístico, 1987: Postgrado.*
  Anuario Estadístico, 1987: Licenciatura

TABLE 4.6
Faculty Population: Graduate and Undergraduate (Academic Year 1986)

	Full time	Half-time	Hourly	Total Positions
Graduate	2,410	549	6,086	9,045
Undergraduate	20,174	7,287	63,731	91,183

Sources: *Anuario Estadístico, 1986: Licenciatura*
  Anuario Estadístico, 1986: Postgrado

Selected Bibliography of Books Published During the 1980s

Monographs

Basave Fernández del Valle, Agustín. *Metafísica de muerte*. México: Editorial Limusa, 1983.

_____. *Filosofía del derecho internacional. Iusfilosofía y politosofía de la sociedad mundial*. México: Universidad Nacional Autónoma de México, 1985.

Benítez Grobet, Laura. *La idea de historia en Carlos Sigüenza y Góngora*. México: Universidad Nacional Autónoma de México, 1982.

Beuchot, Mauricio. *La filosofía del lenguaje en la Edad Media*. Cuadernos 32. Instituto de Investigaciones Filosóficas. México: Universidad Nacional Autónoma de México, 1981.

_____. *Ensayos marginales sobre Aristóteles*. México: Universidad Nacional Autónoma de México, 1985.

Cardiel Reyes, Raúl. *Retorno a Caso*. México: Universidad Nacional Autónoma de México, 1986.

Caso, Antonio. *El concepto de la historia universal*. In *Obras completas*. Vol. 10. México: Universidad Nacional Autónoma de México, 1985.

Cerutti Guldberg, Horacio. *Filosofía de la liberación*. México: Fondo de Cultura Económica, 1983.

_____. *Ideologías políticas contemporáneas*. Grandes Tendencias Políticas Contemporáneas. Coordinación de Humanidades. México: Universidad Nacional Autónoma de México, 1986.

_____. *Hacia una metodología de la historia de las ideas (filosóficas) en América Latina*. Guadalajara: Universidad de Guadalajara, 1986.

Conde, Teresa del. *Las ideas estéticas de Freud*. México: Grijalbo, 1986.

Cortés del Moral, Rodolfo. *El método dialéctico*. México: Trillas, 1985.

Durán, Manuel. *Ortega hoy*. Xalapa, Veracruz: Universidad Veracruzana, 1985.

Dussel, Enrique. *La producción teórica de Marx*. México: Siglo XXI, 1985.

_____. *De Medellín a Puebla*. México: Edicol, 1979 (1980).

Escobar Valenzuela, Gustavo. *Etica. Introducción a su problemática y su historia*. México: McGraw Hill de México, 1985.

_____. *La ilustración en la filosofía latinoamericana.* Temas Básicos 1. México: Trillas, 1980.

García de Oteyza, Mercedes. *La identidad personal de Hume.* México: Universidad Nacional Autónoma de México, 1985.

García Máynez, Eduardo. *Ensayos filosófico-jurídicos.* 2nd ed. corrected and augmented. Facultad de Derecho. Textos Universitarios. México: Universidad Nacional Autónoma de México, 1984.

Gómez Pérez, Germán. *Polémica e ideología.* México: Universidad Nacional Autónoma de México, 1985.

Gómez Robledo, Antonio. *Platón: los seis grades temas de su filosofía.* México: Fondo de Cultura Económica, 1986.

González, Juliana. *El malestar en la moral.* México: Joaquín Moritz, 1986.

González Rojo, Enrique. *Epistemología y socialismo: La crítica de Sánchez a Louis Althusser.* México: Diógenes, 1982.

Hierro, Graciela. *Etica y feminismo.* México: Universidad Nacional Autónoma de México, 1983.

Krauze, Enrique. *Por una democracia sin adjetivos.* México: Joaquín Moritz, Editorial Planeta, 1986.

Krauze de Kolteniuk, Rosa. *La filosofía de Antonio Caso.* 2nd ed. México: Universidad Nacional Autónoma de México, 1986.

Kolteniuk, Miguel. *Cultura e individuo.* México: Grijalbo, 1986.

Labastida, Horacio. *Filosofía y política.* México: Miguel Angel Porrúa, 1986.

Medin, Tziv. *Leopoldo Zea: Ideología, historia y filosofía de América Latina.* México: Universidad Nacional Autónoma de México, 1983.

Miró Quesada, Francisco. *Proyecto y realizatión del filosofar latinoamericano.* México: Fondo de Cultura Económica, 1981.

Nicol, Eduardo. *La reforma de la filosofía.* México: Fondo de Cultura Económica, 1980.

_____. *El porvenir de la filosofía.* México: Fondo de Cultura Económica, 1985.

Olivé, León. *Estado, legitimación y crisis.* México: Siglo XXI, 1985.

Palazón de Mayoral, María Rosa. *Reflexiones sobre estética a partir de André Breton.* México: Universidad Nacional Autónoma de México, 1986.

Redmond, Walter and Mauricio Beuchot. *La lógica mexicana en el siglo de oro.* Cuadernos 41. Instituto de Investigaciones Filosóficas. México: Universidad Nacional Autónoma de México, 1985.

Roig, Arturo Andrés. *Teoría y crítica del pensamiento latinoamericano.* México: Fondo de Cultura Económica, 1982.

_____. *Filosofía, universidad y filósofos en América Latina.* México: Universidad Nacional Autónoma de México, 1981.

Rovira, María del Carmen. *Eclécticos portugueses del siglo XVIII y algunas de sus influencias en América.* México: Universidad Nacional Autónoma de México, 1979, 1980.

Salmerón, Fernando. *Cuestiones educativas y páginas sobre México.* Prologue by José Gaos. 2nd ed. Xalapa: Universidad Veracruzana, 1980.

_____. *Las mocedades de Ortega.* 3rd ed. México: Universidad Nacional Autónoma de México, 1983.

_____. *La filosofía y las actividades morales.* 3rd ed. México: Sigo XXI, 1986.

Sánchez Vázquez, Adolfo. *Filosofía de la praxis.* México: Grijalbo, 1985.

Terán, Oscar. *Discutir Mariátegui.* Puebla: Universidad Autónoma de Puebla, 1985.

Tomasini, Alejandro B. *Los atomismos lógicos de Russell y Wittgenstein.* México: Universidad Nacional Autónoma de México, 1985.

Torchia Estrada, Juan Carlos. *Alejandro Korn: Profesión y vocación.* Nuestra América 14. México: Centro Coordinador y Difusor de Estudios Latinoamericanos, Universidad Nacional Autónoma de México, 1986.

Vera y Cuspines, Margarita. *El pensamiento filosófico de Vasconcelos.* México: Extemporáneos, 1979, 1985.

Villegas, Abelardo. *México en el horizonte liberal.* México: Fondo de Cultura Económica, 1983.

_____. *Autognosis: El pensamiento mexicano en el siglo XX.* México: Instituto Panamericano de Geografía e Historia, 1985.

_____. *El Liberalismo.* México: Universidad Nacional Autónoma de México, 1986.

_____. *Violencia y racionalidad.* México: Universidad Autónoma Metropolitana, 1985.

Villoro, Luis. *Creer, saber, conocer*. México: Siglo XXI, 1982.

_____. *El concepto de ideología*. México: Fondo de Cultura Económica, 1985.

Xirau, Ramón. *Tiempo vivido: acerca de "estar"*. México: Siglo XXI, 1986.

_____. *Cuatro filósofos y lo sagrado*. México: Joaquín Mortiz, 1986.

Yamuni, Vera. *José Gaos. El hombre y su pensamiento*. México: Universidad Nacional Autónoma de México, 1980.

Yturbe, Corina. *La explicación de la historia*. México: Universidad Nacional Autónoma de México, 1981.

Zea, Leopoldo. *Simón Bolívar*. México: Edicol, 1980.

_____. *Latinoamérica en la encrucijada de la historia*. México: Universidad Nacional Autónoma de México, 1981.

_____. *Sentido de la difusión cultural latinoamericana*. Centro de Estudios Sobre la Universidad. México: Universidad Nacional Autónoma de México, 1981.

Anthologies

Aguilar, Luis and Corina Yturbe, eds. *Filosofía y política: Razón y poder*. México: Universidad Nacional Autónoma de México, 1987.

Caso, Antonio, *et al. Conferencias del Ateneo de la Juventud*. Prologue and notes by Juán Fernández Luna. México: Universidad Nacional Autónoma de México, 1984.

Cueva, Mario de la, *et al. Estudios de historia de la filosofía en México*. 3rd and 4th ed. México: Universidad Nacional Autónoma de México, 1980, 1985.

Frondizi, Risieri and Jorge J. E. Gracia, eds. *El hombre y los valores en la filosofía latinoamericana del siglo XX*. México: Fondo de Cultura Económica, 1974, 1981.

Gómez Robledo, Antonio. *El magisterio filosófico y jurídico de Alonso de la Vera Cruz*. México: Porrúa, 1984.

González, Juliana, *et al. Presencia de Ramón Xirau*. México: Universidad Nacional Autónoma de México, 1986.

González, Juliana, Carlos Pereyra, and Gabriel Vargas Lozano, eds. *Praxis y filosofía: Ensayos en homenaje a Adolfo Sánchez Vázquez*. México: Grijalbo, 1987.

Gracia, Jorge, J. E., Eduardo Rabossi, Enrique Villanueva, and Marcelo Dascal, eds. *El análisis filosófico en América Latina*. México: Fondo de Cultura Económica, 1985.

Mora, José María Luis. *Obras*. 5 vols. México: Secretaría de Educación Pública, 1986.

Olivé, León, ed. *La explicación social del conocimiento*. México: Universidad Nacional Autónoma de México, 1985.

Rabossi, E. and Fernando Salmerón, eds. *Ética y análisis*. Vol. I. México: Universidad Nacional Autónoma de México, 1986.

Velázquez Mejía, Manuel. *Revolución o contrarevolución*. Toluca: Centro de Investigación en Ciencias Sociales y Humanidades, Universidad Autónoma del Estado de Toluca, 1988.

Zarco, M. A., ed. *En torno al proyecto de Freud. Cuadernos de Filosofía*. México: Universidad Iberoamericana, 1985.

Zea, Leopoldo, ed. *América Latina en sus ideas*. México: UNESCO–Siglo XXI, 1986.

Translations

Copi, I. M. *Lógica simbólica*. 2nd printing. México: Compañía Editorial Continental, S.A., 1981.

Derridá, Jacques. *De la gramatología*. 4th ed. México: Siglo XXI, 1986.

Foucault, Michel. *Las palabras y las cosas*. 17th ed. México: Siglo XXI, 1986.

Frondizi, Risieri. *Ensayos filosóficos*. Ed. Jorge J. E. Gracia. Trans. Josefina Barbat. México: Fondo de Cultura Económica, 1986.

Galeno. *Iniciación a la dialéctica*. Trans. by Arturo Ramírez Trejo. With a prologue by Mario Otero. Instituto de Investigaciones Filológicas. México: Universidad Nacional Autónoma de México, 1982.

Gracia, Jorge J. E. *Introducción al problema de la individuación en la alta Edad Media*. Trans. into Spanish by B. Valdivia, rev. by M. Beuchot. Colección Estudios Clásicos, Instituto de Investigaciones Filosóficas. México: Universidad Nacional Autónoma de México, 1987.

Grisoni, Dominique. *Políticas de la filosofía*. Breviarios. México: Fondo de Cultura Económica, 1982.

Hartmann, Nicolai. *Ontología*. 6 vols. 2nd ed. Trans. José Gaos. México: Fondo de Cultura Económica, 1986.

Husserl, Edmund. *Ideas relativas a una fenomenología pura y una filosofía fenomenológica*. 2nd ed. Translated by José Gaos. México: Fondo de Cultura Económica, 1986.

Jaeger, Werner. *Aristóteles*. México: Fondo de Cultura Económica, 1982.

Juan de Santo Tomás. *Compendio de lógica*. Translated with an introduction and notes by Mauricio Beuchot. México: Universidad Nacional Autónoma de México, 1986.

Kant, Manuel. *Lógica: Intorducción al estudio de la filosofía*. México: Editora Nacional, 1981.

Locke, John. *Ensayo sobre el gobierno civil*. Translated, with an introduction and notes by Ernesto Ponce. México: Nuevomar, 1984.

_____. *Ensayo sobre el entendimiento humano*. México: Fondo de Cultura Económica, 1983.

Mercado, Tomás. *Comentarios lucidísimos al texto de Pedro Hispano*. Translated, with an introduction by Mauricio Beuchot. México: Universidad Nacional Autónoma de México, 1986.

Pedro Hispano. *Tractatus, llamados después Summule logicales*. Trans. Mauricio Beuchot. México: Universidad Nacional Autónoma de México, 1983.

Poincairé, Henri. *Filosofía de la ciencia*. Nuestros Clásicos 32. México: Universidad Nacional Autónoma de México, 1984.

Quine, W. *Lógica elemental*. México: Grijalbo, 1981.

_____. *Teorías y cosas*. México: Universidad Nacional Autónoma de México, 1986.

Rawls, John. *Teoría de la justicia*. México: Fondo de Cultura Económica, 1979, 1985.

Rousseau, Juan Jacobo. *El contrato social*. Nuestros Clásicos 23. México: Universidad Nacional Autónoma de México, 1984.

Santayana, Jorge. *Los reinos del ser*. México: Fondo de Cultura Económica, 1985.

Wittgenstein, Ludwig. *Diario filosófico*. Obras Maestras del Pensamiento Contemporáneo 46. México: Origen/Planeta, 1986.

Reissues

Caso, Antonio. *Antología filosófica*. 3rd ed. Biblioteca del Estudiante Universitario 80. México: Universidad Nacional Autónoma de México, 1985.

_____. *La existencia como economía, como desinterés y como caridad*. México: Universidad Nacional Autónoma de México, 1987.

Díaz de Gamarra Dávalos, Juan Benito. *Máximas de Educación: Academias de Filosofía. Academias de Educación*. Zamora, Michoacán: El Colegio de Michoacán, 1983.

_____. *Filosofía moderna*. Prologue by Barnabé Navarro. México: Universidad Nacional Autónoma de México, 1984.

Gaos, José. *Historia de nuestra idea del mundo*. 2nd printing. México: Fondo de Cultura Económica, 1983.

Jaeger, Werner. *Paideia: Los ideales de la cultura griega*. Trans. and ed. Joaquín Xirau. México: Fondo de Cultura Económica, 1980, 1986.

Las Casas, Bartolomé. *Doctrina*. Biblioteca del Estudiante Universitario 22. México: Universidad Nacional Autónoma de México, 1982.

Mendez Plancarte, Gabriel, ed. *Humanistas del siglo XVIII*. 2nd ed. México: Universidad Nacional Autónoma de México, 1982.

Ramírez, Ignacio. *México en pos de la libertad*. México: PRI, 1986.

Reyes, Alfonso. *Universidad, política y pueblo*. Prologue by Margarita Vera. 2nd ed. México: Universidad Nacional Autónoma de México, 1985.

Schaff, Adam. *Introducción a la semántica*. 4th printing. México: Fondo de Cultura Económica, 1983.

Sigüenza y Góngora, Carlos. *Libra astronómica y filosófica*. Edited by Bernabé Navarro. Prologue by José Gaos. México: Universidad Nacional Autónoma de México, 1984.

Vasconcelos, José. *La raza cósmica*. 6th ed. México: Espasa-Calpe, 1981.

Villoro, Luis. *Proceso ideológico de la Revolución de Independencia*. México: Dirección General de Publicaciones y Medios, 1986.

Academic Journals

Anuario Latinoamérica. Universidad Nacional Autónoma de México, México.

Contrafuerte. Universidad Nacional Autónoma de México, México.

Crítica. Instituto de Investigaciones Filosóficas. Universidad Nacional Autónoma de México, México.

Cuadernos Americanos. Segunda Epoca. Universidad Nacional Autónoma de México, México.

Cuadernos de Filosofía. Universidad Iberoamericana. México.

Dialéctica. Universidad Autónoma de Puebla, Puebla.

Diánoia. Anuario del Instituto de Investigaciones Filosóficas. Universidad Nacional Autónoma de México, México.

Diógenes. Universidad Nacional Autónoma de México, México.

Espacios. Universidad Autónoma de Puebla, Puebla.

Estudios: Filosofía/Historia/Letras. Instituto Tecnológico Autónomo de México, México.

Investigación Humanística. Universidad Autónoma Metropolitana, Iztapalapa, México.

Logos. Universidad de LaSalle, México.

Nuestra América. Centro Coordinador y Difusor de Estudios Latinoamericanos, Universidad Nacional Autónoma de México, México.

Omnia. Revista de la Secretaría Ejecutiva del Consejo de Estudios de Postgrado. Universidad Nacional Autónoma de México, México.

Prometeo. Universidad de Guadalajara, Guadalajara.

Quipu. Sociedad Latinoamericana de Historia de las Ciencias y la Tecnología, México.

Revista de Filosofía. Universidad Iberoamericana, México.

Siglo XIX. Revista de Historia. Universidad Autónoma de Nuevo León, Monterrey.

Signos. Departamento de Filosofía. Universidad Autónoma Metropolitana, Iztapalapa.

Teoría. Universidad Nacional Autónoma de México, México.

Congress Papers

Primer Simposio Internacional de Filosofía. Vol. 1. México: Universidad Nacional Autónoma de México, 1987.

Hacia una explicació de las entidades lógicas. México: Universidad Nacional Autónoma de México, 1984.

Hierro, Graciela, *et al. La naturaleza femenina.* Tercer Coloquio Nacional de Filosofía. México: Universidad Nacional Autónoma de México, 1985.

Zea, Leopoldo, *et al. La latinidad y su sentido en América Latina. Simposio.* México: Centro Coordinador y Difusor de Estudios Latinoamericanos, Universidad Nacional Autónoma de México, 1986.

Logic and Philosophy of Science

Flematti Alcalde, Jorge Gabriel. *Reconstrucción lógica de teorías empíricas. El caso de la hidrodinámica de fluidos.* México: Universidad Nacional Autónoma de México, 1985.

Gómez Calderón, Javier. *Lógica simbólica: Una breve introducción.* México: Continental, 1982.

Gortari, Elí. *Ciencia de la lógica.* México: Grijalbo, 1985.

_____. *Ensayos filosóficos sobre la ciencia moderna.* México: Grijalbo, 1985.

_____. *Método materialista dialéctico.* México: Grijalbo, 1986.

Mardoñes, J. M., and N. Ursúa. *Filosofía de las ciencias humanas y sociales.* México: Fontamara, 1986.

Méndez, Luz del Carmen. *Lógica, Curso 1.* México: Editorial Trillas, 1982.

Navarrete, Manuel, *et al. Matemáticas y realidad.* 2nd printing. México: Sep-Setentas/Diana, 1982.

Salazar Resines, Jaime. *Introducción a la lógica deductiva y teoría de conjuntos.* México: Universidad Nacional Autónoma de México, 1981.

Yurén Camarena, María Teresa. *Leyes, teorías y modelos.* 2nd ed. Temas Básicos: Metodología de la Ciencia. México: Trillas, 1978, reprinted 1979–84.

Mexican Philosophy and History

Bagú, S., *et al. De la historia e historiadores: Homenaje a José Luis Romero.* México: Siglo XXI, 1982.

Kaplan, Marcos. *Ciencia, sociedad y desarrollo.* México: Instituto de Investigaciones Jurídicas. Universidad Nacional Autónoma de México, 1987.

Moreno de los Arcos, Roberto. *La polémica del darwinismo en México: Siglo XIX. Testimonios.* Serie Historia de la Ciencia y Tecnología 2. Primera Serie. Instituto de Investigationes Históricas. México: Universidad Nacional Autónoma de México, 1984.

Moreno de los Arcos, Roberto. *Ensayos de historia de la ciencia y la tecnología en México.* Serie Historia de la Ciencia y Tecnología 2. Primera Serie. Instituto de Investigationes Históricas. México: Universidad Nacional Autónoma de México, 1986.

Negrete, José. *Popper vs. Bayes vs. Hempel: un diálogo entre robots.* Instituto de Investigationes Biomédicas Biomatemáticas. México: Universidad Nacional Autónoma de México, n.d. (1982).

Paz, Octavio. *Sor Juana o las trampas de la fe.* 3rd ed. México: Fondo de Cultura Económica, 1983.

Trabulse, Elías. *El círculo roto.* Lecturas Mexicanas 54. México: Secretaría de Educación Pública. Fondo de Cultura Económica, 1984.

CHAPTER 5

Philosophy in Other Countries
of Latin America

JORGE J. E. GRACIA

To write a comprehensive article on the recent philosophical development of Latin American countries, even if the three philosophically
most important ones (Argentina, Brazil, and Mexico) are excluded, is
too ambitious a project for an article of this size. There are simply too
many countries involved, several of which present a rather complex
philosophical situation. Besides, the sources of information on such
development are widely scattered and difficult to access, particularly
in recent times. This article, then, is to be considered only a very
schematic and provisional map of the complicated recent history of
philosophical ideas of the countries in question.[1]

In order to make the discussion easier, I have divided these countries into three groups, depending on the general geographical area to
which they belong. In the first group I have placed the Andean countries: Bolivia, Chile, Colombia, Ecuador, Peru, and Venezuela. The
second group includes countries from Central America. The third
group deals with Caribbean countries, particularly Cuba, Puerto Rico,
and the Dominican Republic. Paraguay is not discussed because there
is no evidence of any sustained philosophical activity in the country.[2]
Uruguay is discussed at the end, just before some general concluding
remarks, because it is a country whose philosophical development is
closely related to that of Argentina.

Andean Countries

As should be expected, it is in the Andean countries where we find greater philosophical activity, although even here there are some countries where philosophy is not studied or practiced much. Such is the case of Bolivia and Ecuador, where relatively little serious philosophical thinking and research has been done and what has been done is the product of the efforts of a handful of individuals. Let me begin with Bolivia.

Bolivia[3]

With the exception of Guillermo Francovich (b. 1901) and Manfredo Mercado Kempff, well-known historians of philosophy, the work of Bolivian philosophers has had little impact outside the country. Bolivia has remained at the margins of international philosophical activity and there have never been important philosophical meetings or congresses celebrated in the country. Needless to say, Bolivia produces no specialized philosophical journal.

Apart from the two individuals mentioned, another name that stands out in the history of philosophical ideas in Bolivia is that of Augusto Pescador (b. 1910). Pescador is one of the Spanish émigrés who settled in South America as a result of the Spanish Civil War. He moved to Bolivia in 1938 and taught logic and ethics at the Universidad Mayor de San Andrés until 1953, when he moved to Chile. He is important in Bolivia because he introduced the thought of N. Hartmann in the country and with it the phenomenological method.

The most important university in the country, the Universidad Mayor de San Andrés, founded in 1830, has approximately twenty thousand students. This university has a department of philosophy that offers a Licentiate in Philosophy and has a faculty of about twenty-five members. Most of them, however, work in law. Working in philosophy, properly speaking, there are fewer than ten faculty. The existence of the Instituto de Filosofía Jurídica y Social, located in the Universidad Mayor San Francisco Xavier de Chuquisaca, indicates the primarily law-oriented interests of Bolivian philosophers. The institute is directed by Rafael García Rosquellas, who also holds the chair of philosophy of law in the same university.

The current philosophical orientation of Bolivian philosophers is quite traditional: philosophy of Franco-German origin, Catholic traditional thought, and Marxism. There is also a kind of autochthonous mysticism that finds expression in various, primarily literary, outlets. Philosophical analysis and the philosophy of liberation have not had a serious impact on Bolivia as far as I have been able to determine, a fact that indicates Bolivia's reluctance to join in the most recent philosophical currents affecting Latin America. In short, the philosophical situation of Bolivia has not gone beyond an initial stage, in which the main business of the philosophical community is to absorb ideas worked out elsewhere and to transfer those ideas to new generations of students. There are, of course, exceptions to this rule, but even as exceptions go, they are not many. Moreover, it does not look as if the Bolivian philosophical community has established strong relations with philosophical communities outside the country.

Chile[4]

In contrast to Bolivia, Chile has an important philosophical tradition within the Latin American philosophical panorama. It gave us Enrique Molina (1871–1964), one of the so-called "founders" of Latin American philosophy, and in subsequent generations there have always been distinguished representatives of philosophy in the country. It suffices to mention Félix Schwartzmann (b. 1913), Jorge Millas (1919–84), Humberto Giannini (b. 1927), Roberto Torretti (b. 1930), and Gerold Stahl (b. 1926), among others.

In the *Directory of Latin American Philosophers*, 11 percent of all philosophers included are from Chile, placing the country in third place, after Argentina and Mexico. This is a significant indication of Chile's philosophical position in Latin America and of the widespread interest in philosophy in the country, particularly when one considers that Chile's total population (ca. 12,500,000) is one tenth that of Brazil and about a third of Colombia's.

The normalization of philosophical activity in Chile begins around 1950. The Sociedad Chilena de Filosofía, founded in 1948, began the publication of a purely philosophical journal of philosophy in 1949. This journal, entitled *Revista de Filosofía*, was one of the first of its type in Latin America. Owing to the internal political conflicts in the country, the journal has ceased publication on several occasions. These interruptions, however, prompted the publication of other journals, such as *Teoría* and *Escritos de Teoría*, both results of Giannini's efforts. Another important factor in the postwar philosophical development of Chile was the arrival of several European immigrants in the 1940s. Among them were José Ferrater Mora (b. 1912), Ernesto Grassi, Bogumil Jasinowski (Polish, 1882–1969) and Raimundo Kupareo (Dalmatian, b. 1915).

Chilean philosophy follows the general pattern of development of philosophy elsewhere in Latin America, although the influence of positivism lasted longer in Chile than in most other Latin American countries, preparing the ground for an early interest in logic, the philosophy of science, and the analytic movement. The earliest and most forceful opponent of positivism was Molina, who adhered to the vitalist ideas popular in Latin America during the first quarter of this century. He also opposed existentialism and its antitheistic stance. Indeed, theistic, Christian, and in particular Neo-Thomistic, ideas have played and continue to play an important role in Chilean philosophy. The presence of strong Catholic teaching institutions have insured the permanence of these ideas in spite of many attacks. Part of the survival of Christian and Catholic ideas can be explained because some of their adherents have successfully blended them with other popular philosophical positions. This was the case, for example, of Clarence Finlayson (1913–54), who integrated ideas taken from Bergson, Scheler, and some existentialists into his Neo-Thomistic framework. Among more recent proponents of Catholic thinking are Hernán Larraín (1921–74) and Arturo Gaete (b. 1924).

The second-most important figure in Chilean philosophy, Jorge Millas, was also influenced by the vitalists, particularly Bergson and Ortega, but like Ortega he borrowed from Hartmann and Scheler as well. Also important is Félix Schwartzmann, although he does not fall easily into any single philosophical tradition. His most important work is anthropological in character: *El sentimiento de lo humano en América* (1950 and 1952) tries to examine what is characteristic of Latin Americans through an analysis of the common features displayed by their cultural expressions. Likewise, the work of Juan Rivano defies classification. Interested in logic, the philosophy of science, and social philosophy, his work has found inspiration in Hegel, Marx, and recent developments in mathematical logic. His most controversial book is *El punto de vista de la miseria* (1965), where he attacks the possibility of any authentic Latin American philosophy as long as current socioeconomic conditions remain. He lives in Sweden at present.

The influence of Husserl is more recent, but it is clearly evident in the work of Félix Martínez Bonati, Carla Cordua, and Luis Flores. And the impact of Heidegger can be detected clearly in Francisco Soler's *Apuntes acerca del pensar de Heidegger* (1983) and in a slightly less evident fashion in Humberto Giannini's *La "reflexión" cotidiana: Hacia una arqueología de la experiencia* (1987). Giannini works within a Christian context.

From all this it should be clear that the vitalism characteristic of most Latin American thought in the first quarter of the twentieth century lingered in Chile until quite late, thanks to the influence first of Molina and later of Millas. However, phenomenology and existentialism asserted themselves in the 1960s and continue to be strong at present.

Another current whose influence in Chile should not be underestimated is analysis. As already pointed out, the long positivistic tradition in Chilean thought may have prepared the ground for its acceptance. As I have provided elsewhere a sketch of the development of analysis in Chile, I shall not dwell on it here.[5] Suffice it to say that there have been several philosophers interested in analysis working in Chile. Among them are the Pole Gerold Stalh, and the Chileans R. Chuaqui, Roberto Torretti, and Alfonso Gómez Lobo (b. 1940). The first and last two, however, left the country and have settled in France, Puerto Rico, and the United States respectively.

The main problem with the development of philosophy in Chile has not been the lack of tradition, as is the case in so many other Latin American countries, but the intolerable and repeated interference of successive governments, from both the left and the right, in the day-to-day business of doing philosophy. Present conditions continue to stand in the way of the normalization of philosophical activities in Chile.

Colombia[6]

Colombia, like Chile, belongs to the group of countries where philosophy has had some importance, but its development has never reached the level obtained in Chile, even though in many ways one would have expected similar or greater results. After all, Colombia was a reasonably well-developed colonial center and its present population is about three times that of Chile. The limitations of its philosophical development are in part due to the generally conservative spirit of Colombian society and the serious political problems that the country has experienced. Nevertheless, there are signs of progress in recent years and Sierra Mejía believes that philosophical activity has become "normalized" due to three factors: 1) the development of the publishing industry, 2) the growing professional practice of science, and 3) the growth of a political awareness and the need to provide theoretical principles to substantiate political action.[7] An important landmark in this development was the celebration of the first philosophical congress in the country, which took place in 1974.

Several institutionally related facts have affected the history of Colombian philosophy. The Instituto de Filosofía y Letras of the Universidad Nacional de Colombia was founded in 1945 as part of the Faculty of Law and became the Facultad de Filosofía y Letras in 1952; from 1965 it became a department of a larger unit, the Facultad de Ciencias Humanas. It is an important center of philosophical activity in the country, but there are also foci of philosophical activity in other universities. Among them Catholic universities stand out: The Universidad Pontificia Javeriana has a department of philosophy with more than twenty members. And there are a dozen universities where philosophy is taught in faculties or departments of philosophy. Overall, Colombia has more than one hundred professors who teach philosophy at the university level, a considerable number if compared with other Latin American countries. Indeed, Colombia accounts for 9 percent of all philosophers included in the *Directory of Latin American Philosophers*, behind Argentina, Mexico, Chile, and Brazil.

The Asociación Colombiana para la Investigación Filosófica was founded in 1975. A specialized philosophy journal, the short-lived *Revista Colombiana de Filosofía* was the official publication of the extinct Sociedad Colombiana de Filosofía. Fortunately, a more lasting philosophy journal, *Ideas y Valores*, had been founded in 1950 in the philosophy department of the National University. It ceased publication between 1954 and 1962, but it is currently active. There are other journals that publish philosophical articles, but are not devoted exclusively to philosophy. Among them are *Escritos*, founded in 1974 and edited by Gonzalo Soto Posada, and *Franciscanum*, founded in 1959 and currently edited by Jairo Muñoz. We see then that professional philosophical activity in Colombia begins late and keeps a limited pace. Moreover, the restrictions on the freedom of expression imposed by successive governments and the emphasis on a conservative attitude identified with the narrow Spanish Catholic tradition are constant obstacles to the free development of philosophy in the country.

From what has been said it should be clear that the attempts to integrate Colombia into the mainstream of modern, nonscholastic, professional philosophy date from the 1940s. The influence of three foreign thinkers is evident: José Ortega y Gasset, Max Scheler and Hans Kelsen. Among the driving force behind the interest in Ortega and Scheler at the time were Rafael Carrillo (b. 1901) and Danilo Cruz Vélez (b. 1920). The interest in phenomenology prepared the way for subsequent developments in existentialism and related schools. The works of Husserl, Heidegger, Jaspers, and others of the same tradition have become the focus of attention of Cruz Vélez, Guillermo Hoyos, Daniel Herrera Restrepo (b. 1930), and others. Indeed, the phenomenology-existentialism axis seems to have dominated the nonscholastic history of philosophy in Colombia since the 1940's.[8]

Of course, other philosophical currents are present. Marxism, for example, has been known in Colombia since early in the century. The Partido Socialista Revolucionario was founded in 1926. But Marxist philosophy was not seriously studied until after the fall of the military regime in 1957. The publication of the Marxist magazine *Estrategia* in the 1960s helped to spread theoretical Marxism and prepared the way for the alliance between some Marxist and Catholic ideas evident in the work of some recent Catholic philosophers, such as Alfonso López Trujillo (see, for example, his *Liberación marxista y liberación cristiana*, Madrid, 1974, published earlier in Bogotá).

In general, then, the most important philosophical currents in Colombia are continental European – existentialism, phenomenology, Marxism, and neo-scholasticism. There is some evidence of a recent interest in philosophical analysis that is beginning to yield promising fruits, but it is still too early to tell how far Colombian philosophers will go in this direction. Since I have dealt with these developments elsewhere, I shall omit further reference to them here.[9] I shall conclude by saying that, in general, the philosophical literature in Colombia tends to be expository and of reverent absorption, although there are exceptions. The work of Rubén Sierra Mejía and Danilo Cruz Vélez, for example, is well beyond that stage. Although philosophy in Colombia has achieved a state of "normalcy," using Romero's famous term, it has yet to achieve a state of self-confident maturity.

Ecuador[10]

The philosophical situation in Ecuador is not so precarious as that in Bolivia, although it is not by any means close to that of the other, more philosophically developed Andean countries. In 1953 an international congress of philosophy and philosophy of education took place in the country, but since then no major philosophical events have developed. There are indications, however, of renewed activity, particularly in areas that have to do with the history of Ecuadorian ideas. The impetus has come from various sources and individuals, but one of the decisive figures is Andrés Roig (b. 1922), an Argentinian who settled in Ecuador after he was forced to leave his own country for political reasons. Thanks to his efforts and those of Carlos Paladines (b. 1947), Carlos Freile Granizo and others, Ecuador has developed a team of individuals devoted to the study of Ecuadorian ideas. There is a journal, entitled *Bibliografía Básica de la Filosofía Ecuatoriana*, as well as the series "Biblioteca Básica del Pensamiento Ecuatoriano" sponsored by the Central Bank of Ecuador. Other journals, such as *Pucará* and *Puce*, occasionally publish philosophical articles and the country has several universities that have faculties of philosophy and/or humanities. However, the number of faculty teaching solely philosophy in Ecuadorian universities is not more than fifty.

As far as philosophical orientation is concerned, the most important Ecuadorian universities are Catholic. This implies, of course, that, as in Colombia, much of the philosophy of the country tends to be traditional and neo-scholastic. Among the other traditions strongly represented are phenomenology, existentialism, and Marxism. Phenomenology had some impact on the founder of Ecuadorian philosophy, Julio Enrique Moreno (1879-1952), who, like many of his contemporaries in Latin America, followed Ortega, Bergson, and Scheler. Among more recent supporters of phenomenology is Hernán Malo González (b. 1931). There are a very few individuals who work in mathematical logic and related fields, but in general analytic philosophy is ignored. However, as the journal and series mentioned indicate, there is considerable interest in the history of Ecuadorian and Latin American thought. The impact of the philosophy of liberation has been felt through the influence of both Roig and Horacio Cerutti Guldberg. All in all, however, philosophy in Ecuador has not gone beyond the stages of absorption and critical interaction, and certainly has not achieved anything like the maturity displayed in other countries of Latin America. In general Ecuadorian philosophers remain isolated. Unfortunately, both Roig and Cerutti Guldberg have left the country; Roig to return to Argentina, and Cerutti Guldberg for Mexico.

Peru[11]

The philosophical situation of Peru is in many ways different from that of most other Latin American countries, in that it has a well-established tradition in philosophy. The Universidad Mayor de San Marcos was founded in the sixteenth century and scholastic philosophy was taught there throughout the colonial period. Moreover, Peru has had and still has some philosophical figures of the first rank: Alejandro Deústua (1849-1945), one of the "founders" of Latin American philosophy, Francisco Miró Quesada (b. 1918), a versatile and original thinker with an international reputation, Augusto Salazar Bondy (1925-72), a major historian of Latin American philosophy whose systematic thought took on some interesting directions, and José Carlos Mariátegui (1895-1930), an original interpreter of Marx, regarded by many as the foremost Marxist in Latin America. Peru has failed, however, to develop a philosophical group strong enough to support a national philosophy journal. This failure has forced Peruvian philosophers to publish in widely different forums, preventing them from having a strong impact on philosophy outside the country; the international philosophical profile of Peru has always underrepresented its real strengths.

The current philosophical panorama of Peru reflects in many ways the panorama of Western philosophy. The emphases are primarily in continental European philosophy (phenomenology, existentialism, and Marxism) and philosophical analysis, with the usual representation of scholastic philosophy in Catholic institutions.

According to Sobrevilla, it was probably Alberto Wagner de Reyna (b. 1915) who introduced phenomenology and existentialism in Peru. He studied with Hartmann and Heidegger and brought their ideas to Peru when he returned in 1935, tempering his position, however, with traditional scholastic and Christian ideas. Wagner de Reyna's views initiate the discussion of phenomenological and existentialist ideas. Among those who became interested in them were Honorio Delgado (1892–1969), Oscar Miró Quesada (1884–1981), Luis Felipe Alarco (b. 1913) and others. Francisco Miró Quesada also falls into this group and published several works within this tradition in the 1930s and 1940s, before moving in the direction of philosophical analysis. Like Miró Quesada, although younger, Augusto Salazar Bondy also worked initially within the phenomenological-existentialist tradition before changing course in the direction of philosophical analysis in the 1960s. The continental European perspective is still well-represented and is still the dominant philosophical current in Peru. Among its most recent supporters have been or are Luis Felipe Guerra (1930–76), José Ignacio López Soria (b. 1937 in Spain), and most important of all, David Sobrevilla (b. 1938), who has already achieved visibility outside Peru. Sobrevilla's most important book is *Repensando la tradición occidental* (1986).

Largely as a result of Miró Quesada's early interest, philosophical analysis has had an important impact on Peruvian philosophy. Miró Quesada himself has published extensively in the areas of logic, epistemology, and the philosophy of science, and Salazar Bondy had begun, before his untimely death, to produce analytic materials in ethics. Since I have dealt with the development of philosophical analysis in Peru elsewhere, I will omit further discussion of it here.[12] Peru is an important philosophical center in Latin America, but has yet to realize its full potential and to be given the recognition it deserves.

Venezuela[13]

Chile and Colombia have both enjoyed an important philosophical life throughout the twentieth century, even though philosophical activity has not progressed so much as one would have wished in recent years. The situation in Venezuela, however, is different. Forty or fifty years ago, philosophical activity in Venezuela was considerably inferior to that carried out in Chile and Colombia, but recently the situation has changed in such a way that Venezuela in the 1970s and 1980s has enjoyed a more favorable philosophical situation.

This change is the result of several factors, among which I would like to mention four. The first and perhaps most important is the political climate of the country. There is complete freedom of expression in Venezuela; there is no political repression and the government keeps itself away from academic matters. This benign political atmosphere has helped the free exchange of ideas and criticism, which in turn has opened the doors to the free and frank discussion of views that in other countries are considered taboo, and has helped to develop a dialogue among philosophers.

The second factor has also to do with politics, but only indirectly. Owing to the political instability that other countries have experienced in the last two decades, and also owing to the economic opportunities and the security that can be found in Venezuela, the country has attracted an important intellectual immigration. The departments of philosophy of Venezuelan universities have attracted important Argentinian and Uruguayan philosophers, such as Arturo Ardao and Angel Cappelletti, both of whom have contributed to the intellectual ferment of the country.

The third factor also has to do with immigration, although its impact was felt much earlier than the recent Argentinian-Uruguayan wave of immigration. I am referring to the Spaniards that emigrated from Spain as a result of the Spanish Civil War (Juan D. García Bacca, Eugenio Imaz, Domingo Casanova, and Manuel Granell, among others) and to others that followed them (like Juan Nuño, b. 1924). The influence of this group of emigrants has been decisive, not only in terms of developing philosophical activity, but also in establishing Franco-German philosophy as predominant in Venezuela.

Finally, we must not forget the influence of a group of Venezuelan philosophers who, having studied with some of the foreign philosophers who brought new philosophical ideas to Venezuela, have carried forward their ideas and charted new courses of development. The most important of them and a key figure in philosophical and intellectual circles in Venezuela is Ernesto Mayz Vallenilla (b. 1925). Apart from several books on various major philosophical figures, he is the author of five original works: *El problema de América* (1957, 1969), *Esbozo de una crítica de la razón técnica* (1974), *El dominio del poder* (1982), *Ratio technica* (1983), and *El sueño del futuro* (1984). He presided until recently over the Universidad Simón Bolivar, the most important philosophical center of the country, and it was thanks to his efforts that it became so.

The institutionalization of philosophy in Venezuela began in the 1940s, when a group of enterprising philosophers, helped and encouraged by Risieri Frondizi, who had then been invited to join the faculty of the Universidad Central, and Juan D. García Bacca, who had settled in Venezuela, founded the School of Philosophy in the mentioned university. In the following decade, García Bacca founded the Instituto de Filosofía. The institute's function was to coordinate philosophical activities in Venezuela and also to publish the journal *Episteme*. Thanks to these events, philosophical activity continued, but it was not until the following decade, in particular after 1970, that a philosophical flowering was evident. The Sociedad Venezolana de Filosofía, founded in 1962, began publishing the *Revista Venezolana de Filosofía* ten years later. This journal continues to maintain a respectable intellectual level and an open attitude toward all serious philosophical currents.

Apart from the Universidad Simón Bolivar and the Universidad Central, two other important philosophical centers are the Universidad Católica Andrés Bello and the Universidad del Zulia. There is also the Centro de Estudios Latinoamericanos Rómulo Gallegos, where philosophers such as the Uruguayan Mario Sambarino have worked. Overall, there are more than fifty active philosophers in Venezuela and, although this number is smaller than the number of those working in Colombia, for example, the overall level of research in Venezuela seems superior to that of Colombia in various aspects. There is a climate of openness to new philosophical ideas that is not characteristic of Colombian philosophy. This can be seen, for example, in the attitude of Venezuelan philosophical circles with respect to philosophical analysis, the last philosophical current to have arrived at the country.

The first indications of the impact of philosophical analysis in Venezuela are found in Juan Nuño's evolution from a continental European perspective to an analytic one. This change is evident in his *Sentido de la filosofía contemporánea* (1965), where he argues that logical positivism is nothing less than a revolutionary perspective that seeks to move philosophy into a more rigorous and scientific path. Following Nuño's lead in the analytic tradition are Rafael Burgos (1939), Pedro Lluberes (b. 1928) and C. Ulises Moulines (b. 1946, presently teaching in Germany).[14]

In spite of some inroads by philosophical analysis, Venezuelan philosophy today is largely continental European in character and the national philosopher of greater prominence, Mayz Vallenilla, works in the area of phenomenology. Juan Nuño, who now practices philosophical analysis, worked on phenomenology, Heidegger and Sartre throughout the early sixties. Federico Riu (1925–85) and Gloria Comesaña (b. 1946) specialize in Sartre, and Alberto Rosales (b. 1931) studies Heidegger. Among Marxists, Eduardo Vázquez (b. 1927) stands out. He has tried to find bridges between Marxism and existentialism. It should be added that philosophical activity has reached a stage of development well beyond the state of passive absorption characteristic of some other Latin American countries. Venezuelans such as Ernesto Mayz Vallenilla and Pedro Lluberes work in an atmosphere of critical interaction, even though the philosophical climate of the country cannot yet be characterized as "mature." The fact that the 9th Inter American Congress of Philosophy took place in Caracas in 1977 indicates the philosophical importance of Venezuela in the Latin American context. Another point that should not be forgotten is that Venezuelan philosophers have adopted a pan-American attitude – contributing substantially to the international philosophical dialogue among Latin Americans.

Central America[15]

With the exception of Costa Rica, the practice of philosophy in the Central American countries has serious limitations and was started quite late. Guatemala's Universidad de San Carlos was founded in the seventeenth century and from its very beginning taught scholastic philosophy. However, the study of modern philosophy in the country did not begin until 1945, when the Faculty of Humanities was organized. The case with Nicaragua was worse. There the Faculty of Humanities was founded only in 1964, while in El Salvador a Center for the Study of Philosophy was founded in 1961. Since then, philosophical activity has continued, although at a very limited level. The first Ibero-American Symposium of Philosophy, organized by the Sociedad Iberoamericana de Filosofía, took place in Guatemala in 1960 and various colloquia and conferences have taken place throughout the region since then. Moreover, one of the most distinguished philosophers from the hemisphere, Héctor-Neri Castañeda (b. 1924) was born and began his career in Guatemala.

In institutional terms it must be added that, in El Salvador, the Universidad Centroamericana José Simeon Cañas, founded in 1966, has a department of philosophy with a dozen faculty members, and offers a Licentiate degree in philosophy. Moreover, the department publishes a journal, *Tal*, of local circulation.

In Honduras, the center of philosophical activity is the Department of Philosophy of the Universidad Nacional Autónoma de Honduras, where again a dozen philosophers work. Moreover, there is a national philosophical society, the Sociedad Hondureña de Filosofía, founded in 1967, but there are no journals of philosophy in the country.

The situation in Nicaragua and Panama, however, is very precarious. The Universidad Centroamericana de Nicaragua has a philosophy department that reflects the recent ideological changes of the country, and Panama has no pedagogical units devoted exclusively to philosophical study and research.

In all these countries, the unstable political situation in recent years has undermined the limited philosophical advances made earlier. The few philosophical oases in existence are slowly drying up under seriously adverse conditions.

Costa Rica[16]

Costa Rica is, for all intents and purposes, the philosophical center of Central America. In the colonial Universidad de Sto. Tomás scholastic philosophy was regularly taught until the end of the nineteenth century. The present National University was founded in 1941, and its Department of Philosophy was organized in 1956. In 1957 its journal, the *Revista de Filosofía de Costa Rica*, appeared. This is the principal philosophical journal in Central America and is one of the best-established journals of philosophy in the whole of Latin America. In spite of its unparalleled stability, however, it has never achieved the level of quality and visibility characteristic of some journals published in Argentina, Mexico, and Brazil. There is also a national association of philosophers, the Asociación Costarricense de Filosofía, founded in 1958, that organizes conferences and colloquia, such as the 2nd Extraordinary Inter American Congress of Philosophy (1959) and the 1st Central American Congress of Philosophy (1971).

Another university was founded in 1974, the Universidad Nacional de Costa Rica; its philosophy department currently numbers more than thirty faculty members. In all, the number of individuals who teach philosophy at the university level is over sixty. The philosophy department of the Universidad Nacional publishes two journals:

Praxis and *Prometeo* (the latter not to be confused with the journal published in Mexico). The first is a journal with Marxist leanings whose primary end is the investigation and spread of the philosophy of praxis in the context of social problems.

The general orientation of philosophy in Costa Rica is continental: There is a strong emphasis on French and German authors, and in the thought of Ortega, Unamuno and Marx. Of course, other philosophical currents are present: Claudio Gutiérrez, for example, studied at the University of Chicago and upon his return to Costa Rica introduced philosophical analysis in the country.

The Extraordinary Inter American Congress of Philosophy that took place in Costa Rica in 1959 illustrates the importance of the country in Latin American philosophical panorama. An important factor in the development of philosophy in Costa Rica is the emphasis placed on the discipline at both the university and secondary school levels. A look at the *Revista de Filosofía de la Universidad de Costa Rica* reveals a lively interest in curricular planning, and secondary school students are required to take four philosophy courses. Under these conditions it should not be surprising that, in spite of its size, Costa Rica is able to maintain a higher level of philosophical activity than that of some, larger Latin American countries.

The Caribbean

The nations of the Caribbean that are part of Latin America are Cuba, the Dominican Republic, and Puerto Rico. Puerto Rice is not politically independent, but has managed to maintain its Hispanic heritage in spite of the enormous obstacles put in its way by Anglo-American domination.

Cuba[17]

Philosophically, Cuba has always been the most prominent country in the Caribbean and, indeed, its intellectual and philosophical life surpassed that of many of the larger countries of Latin America during various periods of its history. Cuba's philosophical tradition goes back to Félix Varela (1788–1853), an intellectual of note, and reached its high point with Enrique José Varona (1849–1933), one of the most important positivists of Latin America.

The fundamental event in the recent development of philosophical ideas in Cuba is, of course, the Cuban Revolution. Before the revolution, philosophy was primarily academic. Its center of activity was located at the Faculty of Philosophy and Letters of the Universidad Nacional de La Habana, where philosophers from every major Western philosophical tradition practiced their craft. Continental philosophy was dominant, although the background of Enrique José Varona's positivism and the proximity to the United States had made possible the acquaintance with American pragmatism. The strong imprint of phenomenology and existentialism can be clearly seen, for example, in the work of Jorge Mañach (1898–1961) and Humberto Piñera Llera (b. 1911). On the other hand, philosophical analysis was practically and surprisingly unknown or at least ignored, as is clear in the various issues of the *Revista Cubana de Filosofía*.

This situation changed radically after the revolution. Of all the faculty members working at the Universidad de La Habana, only one remained after the revolution – the rest emigrated to the United States and with their departure philosophical pluralism ended in Cuba. From 1960 onwards Marxism became the official Cuban philosophy. The philosophical model followed since then has been that of Soviet philosophy, and Cuban philosophers study in Moscow or other Eastern European countries. The history of philosophy in particular, except for the history of Latin American thought, is neglected; it is considered a luxury of interest only to antiquarians. The emphasis is placed on the practical aspects of philosophy, and the philosopher, the economist and the sociologist are not easily distinguishable in this context. The more theoretical and abstract philosophical disciplines, such as logic, are ruled by Marxist models.

A look at the philosophical journal, *Pensamiento Crítico*, published by the philosophy department of the Universidad Nacional de La Habana supports these points. And the same is revealed by the three seminaries offered for university students in Havana, in which only texts from Marx, Engels, and their followers are studied.

Current Cuban philosophy, then, is Marxist. In a meeting of Cuban and North American philosophers that took place in the early 1980s the papers presented by Cuban philosophers clearly indicate the direction of their thought. The titles of the most important papers were as follows: "Concerning the Transformation of the National Revolution of Liberation into the Cuban Socialist Revolution," by Thalia Fung; "The Principles of Economic Transformation of the Cuban Revolution," by Héctor Ayala; "Concerning the Distortions of the National and International Dialectic of the Cuban Revolution," by Arnaldo Silva; "The Participation of the Cuban People in Social-Political Life," by Antonio Díaz; and "Culture in Revolutionary Cuba," by Carlos Trápaga.

Puerto Rico and the Dominican Republic[18]

Unlike Cuba, neither Puerto Rico nor the Dominican Republic have had a strong philosophical tradition. In both countries the development of philosophy as a professional discipline was fairly late. The University of Puerto Rico was founded in 1903, but it did not have a department of philosophy until the 1940s. Indeed, it was only in 1950, when Risieri Frondizi (1910–83) visited Puerto Rico, that a rigorous philosophical curriculum was developed. An important subsequent development was the foundation of *Diálogos*, an exclusively philosophical journal published by the Department of Philosophy. Its founder, L. Schajowics, was primarily interested in nineteenth-century German philosophy and the journal echoed these interests for many years. The change of direction in both the journal and the Department of Philosophy from a primarily continental to a more pluralistic approach that included a strong analytic component began in the 1970s. The background had been prepared by the work of Jorge Enjuto (b. 1922), born in Spain and a student of Frondizi, who worked on Anglo-American philosophy, particularly that of Whitehead. But it was only with the arrival of Roberto Torretti from Chile that the new orientation was cemented. Torretti's interest in the history and philosophy of science, originating in his work on Kant, led him into a progressively more analytic framework. As editor of *Diálogos*, and the best-known member of the department, he began a change of perspective for the philosophers of Río Piedras.

There are other centers of philosophical study in Puerto Rico, although of lesser importance. Among these are the Departamento de Filosofía of the Universidad Católica of Puerto Rico and the Departamento de Humanidades of the Universidad Interamericana in Hato Rey. Overall, Puerto Rico has about fifty active philosophers, of whom nearly a dozen are located at Río Piedras.

In Pan-American terms, the main problem with philosophy in Puerto Rico is that the philosophers from Río Piedras have not done enough to enter into the international Latin American dialogue. The efforts of Roberto Torretti have been directed toward the Anglo-Saxon world, and the other philosophers have not tried to join the mainstream of Latin American philosophy.

With respect to recent philosophical developments in the Dominican Republic, there is very little that can be said. Unlike many other countries of Latin America, the Dominican Republic published an exclusively philosophical journal as far back as 1965, the *Revista Dominicana de Filosofía*. It was founded by Waldo Ross and, reflecting the orientation of its founder, its articles generally fell within the recent Franco-German philosophical tradition, with an emphasis on phenomenology and existentialism. Unfortunately, Ross emigrated to Canada, leaving a vacuum that has not yet been filled. There are hopes of a turnaround, however, as there are some younger Dominican philosophers, like Andrés Paniagua, who are currently studying in the United States.

Uruguay[19]

The development of philosophy in Uruguay parallels that of Argentina. The geographical proximity of Montevideo, its capital, to Argentina's Buenos Aires, and the similarities between the populations of both countries account for the parallels. Like Argentina, Uruguay experienced a revolt against positivism early in the century. The leader of this revolt was Carlos Vaz Ferreira (1872–1958), who developed a "philosophy of experience" inspired by the thought of European vitalists such as Henri Bergson and José Ortega y Gasset.

In addition to Vaz Ferreira's contributions to philosophy and the history of ideas, he was an important teacher. He helped keep Uruguay up-to-date on philosophical developments in Europe. As a result, and in spite of Uruguay's size and the unavoidable and overwhelming presence of Argentina, the country has produced a series of important native thinkers. Phenomenology, for example, was represented by Juan Llambías de Azevedo (1907–72), who was greatly influenced by Scheler and Hartmann and applied the phenomenological method to axiology and the philosophy of law. As many Latin Americans of his generation, Llambías de Azevedo defended an objective theory of value. The phenomenology-existentialist current is also represented by Aníbal del Campo, who translated Hartmann, and Manuel Arturo Claps, who worked on Martin Buber.

Working within the same continental tradition but more recent is Mario Sambarino. In a book published in 1959, entitled *Investigaciones sobre la estructura aporético-dialéctica de la eticidad*, Sambarino offered a dialectical interpretation of ethics. More recently his attention was directed to the question of the identity of Latin American thought. But this work was done in Venezuela, where he and also Arturo Ardao (b. 1912), one of the most important historians of Latin American philosophy, took refuge from political persecution.

From all of this it should be clear that in the 1960s Uruguay had not only a well-established tradition of doing philosophy, but also important philosophical figures. The development of philosophy in the country, however, came to a standstill owing to the political unrest of the 1970s. Most philosophers who had an international profile emigrated. This wave of emigration helped other Latin American countries, particularly Venezuela, but devastated Uruguay. It is only recently, after the re-establishment of democracy in the country, that we find renewed philosophical vigor. Among recent developments is the progressive presence of philosophical analysis. The journal *Sintaxis*, directed by Carlos Caorsi, is trying to spread analytic ideas and techniques in Uruguay and is having some success. It looks, therefore, as if Uruguay might regain its important philosophical position in Latin America in the not-too-distant future.

Concluding Remarks

Let me finish this brief and schematic survey of recent philosophical developments in various countries of Latin America by pointing out several things. First, for the most part Latin American philosophy seems to follow in the footsteps of continental European philosophy. There are signs that Anglo-American philosophy is making some headway, particularly in the major centers of philosophical development. But in the rest of Latin America it is phenomenology, existentialism, and Marxism that dominate non-scholastic philosophical circles.

The second is that in spite of enormous obstacles most Latin American countries, except for the most backward ones, have groups of individuals devoted to philosophy. These groups constantly aim to keep up-to-date with what is happening outside their countries in Latin America, in Europe, and in the United States.

Finally, it should be evident that the main obstacles for the philosophical development of Latin America are political. True, there are also problems of poverty, communication, and education. But it is primarily government interference and repression, from the Left and the Right, that have repeatedly prevented the normalization and growth of philosophical activity in Latin America. The cases of Central America, Chile, Uruguay, and Cuba should serve as clear examples of the negative effect that government interference has on philosophy. Only when such interference stops can Latin America hope to achieve full philosophical maturity and development.

PART II
LITERATURE

Writers

Introduction

MIREYA CAMURATI

Miguel Angel Asturias, the Guatemalan writer and winner of the 1967 Nobel Prize for Literature, commented that the beliefs of the ancient Maya-Quichés included a good definition of what constitutes poetry when they said that poetry happens when words meet for the first time. What they were suggesting was a sort of magical conception of language, but the image is a valid one that might be applied to the works of all writers who are able to organize words to meet for the first time.

Basically, the ability that differentiates a writer from one who is not is that, while using the same words that are available to everyone else, a writer makes them say more and say it better. If we accept this premise it is possible to conclude that reading writers' works is an excellent way for us to be in communication with others and to be able to interpret their thoughts and actions. Following this line of reasoning, it might be proposed that knowledge of the literature of a country or a region is one of the most useful instruments, not only for appreciating its aesthetic values, but more importantly, for studying that society and its culture. In relation to Latin America, these assumptions can be supported by a number of authors and works that frequently transcend that which is specifically literary to provide information relevant to anthropology, history, sociology, political science, economics, and the arts. For example, during the period of the conquest of Peru we encounter the figure of Garcilaso de la Vega Inca (1539–1616). The son of a Spanish conquistador and an indigenous princess, Garcilaso is the perfect *mestizo*, respectful of the two bloods and the two languages of his heritage. This respect is demonstrated by the dividing of his major work into two parts: the first, the *Comentarios reales de los incas*, in which he describes and pays homage to his mother's tradition, and the second, *Historia general del Perú*, with an account of the battles and heroic deeds of the Spaniards, his father's lineage.

Born and educated in Cuzco, the center of the Inca Empire, Garcilaso went to Spain when he was 21 years old. There, in perfect Renaissance prose, he wrote about the people and things of his native land: not only about the emperors and soldiers, but also about the myths and the cosmologies, the sciences and the plants, the temples and the stones.

In Mexico in the second half of the seventeenth century we find Sor Juana Inés de la Cruz (1651–95), a woman obsessed with a desire for knowledge in the middle of a dogmatic and patriarchal society. In her cell in the convent she accumulated a library of more than 2,000 volumes, together with astronomical, mathematical, and musical instruments. She corresponded with the gifted minds of the time, and the viceroys and intellectuals of Mexico came to the convent to visit her. Nevertheless, the nun was unsuccessful in her fight against the limitations imposed upon her because of her sex. Sor Juana's letters and poems remain as early testimony to the long road toward the recognition of women's rights.

As we move on to the final years of the colonial period and the beginning of the revolutions for independence, the position of the writer becomes even more prominent. This is the case with Andrés Bello (1781–1865), the Venezuelan poet, philologist, jurist, legislator, and model of humanist erudition. In 1810 the revolutionary junta of Caracas sent Bello to England as a member of the diplomatic mission presided over by Simón Bolívar, the future liberator. From 1829 until his death Bello lived in Chile, his adopted country, to which he devoted his abilities and energies by founding the university, writing the Chilean Civil Code, and other civic activities.

Years later in the Caribbean, we come upon the pure and heroic figure of José Martí (1853–95), who always places his patriotic passion before his literary passion. The magnitude of Martí's work is all the more astonishing when we consider his total dedication to the cause of Cuban independence, the cause for which he finally gave his life.

A combination of Bello, in his qualities as civilizer and educator, and Martí, in his furious condemnation of tyrants, is the Argentinean Domingo Faustino Sarmiento (1811–88). Sarmiento was the author of powerful prose and a statesman who in 1868 occupied the office of president of the republic. Sarmiento was not the only writer who reached the highest political office. Others were Rafael Núñez, a man of letters and president of Colombia between 1880 and 1888; and, in the present century, the novelist Rómulo Gallegos, president of Venezuela in 1948.

Active political participation is more the norm than the exception in the case of Latin American writers. This is apparent in recent decades with the poet Ernesto Cardenal serving as a minister in the Sandinista government of Nicaragua and the novelist Mario Vargas Llosa performing similar functions in Peru. On occasion, political commitment has ended tragically, as in the case of several writers who have fallen as victims of unbridled persecution or extermination at the hands of repressive regimes.

But the authors of today respond to more than their political responsibilities. As inhabitants of an immense region with all of its racial diversity, all the possible climates, and all the imaginable landscapes, divided into more than twenty nations similar and distinctly different at the same time, the position of the Latin American writers is multiple. In their eagerness to interpret this conglomeration of lands and peoples some writers, such as Alejo Carpentier, speak of the "real-maravilloso americano." He refers here to a juxtaposition of circumstances – impossible in other places on the planet – that occur in Latin American time and space, or to an acceptance, based on faith, of that which is magical or miraculous for others.

For his part, Pablo Neruda, in that magnificent frieze that is the *Canto general*, chooses to rewrite the history and the geography of the continent. From a different perspective, Jorge Luis Borges plays in the metaphysical dimension:

> I maintain . . . that only new countries have a past; that is to say, an autobiographical memory, a living history. . . . Time – a European sentiment of a people with a long past, and their very justification and glory – moves more boldly in the New World. Young people, in spite of themselves, sense this. Over here we are contemporary with time, we are brothers of time.[1]

All this richness of possibilities that constitutes the reality of Latin America, a multiplicity that overwhelms its inhabitants with the impossibility of expressing it, and that confuses outsiders when they try to measure it using their own yardsticks, was what García Márquez was referring to in his 1982 Nobel Prize acceptance speech:

> Poets and beggars, musicians and prophets, warriors and scoundrels, all creatures of that unbridled reality, we have had to ask but little of imagination, for our crucial problem has been a lack of conventional means to render our lives believable.[2]

More than ever, the writers of today are committed to making believable the life and essence of Latin America. Their basic instrument is a language made flexible in order to express hyperboles and ambiguities, humor and absurdity, pain and passion. These are the voices of the continent that in the past several decades has achieved a position of worldwide prominence.

In the papers included in this section we will find critical comments on contemporary poetry, narrative, and drama followed by the words of writers themselves: the Cuban poet, José Kozer; the Puerto Rican fiction writer, Ana Lydia Vega; and the Mexican playwright, Emilio Carballido. As we noted in the beginning, it is they who know how to place words in order for them to convey their true meaning. To read these words is, in a profound sense, to begin to read the verbal map of Latin America.

CHAPTER 6

An Introductory Outline to Contemporary Spanish-American Poetry

Jaime Giordano

In offering an overview of contemporary Spanish-American poetry we are faced with an unusually vast, rich, and complicated maze of literary texts. The magnitude of this task is evident considering that, according to one critic, in Chile alone more than fifty excellent poets under fifty years of age can be identified from among hundreds, perhaps thousands of writers of poetry who find easy, fast, and cheap consolation in this form of art.[1]

Many anthologies of Spanish-American poetry offer selections representing the scope of contemporary production, such as those compiled by Aldo Pellegrini, José Olivio Jiménez, Jorge Rodríguez Padrón, Pedro Lastra, Julio Ortega, and Juan Gustavo Cobo Borda.[2] We also can list a number of specialized anthologies, for example, works of women poets: Juan Villegas' *Antología de la nueva poesía femenina en Chile*[3] includes seventeen poets of high quality; Ramiro Lagos' *Mujeres poetas de Hispanoamérica*[4] is very complete. There are national anthologies in almost every country, and many regional anthologies that give some account of the poetry written in cities or towns like Temuco, Chillán, Córdoba, Tucumán, San Sebastián, and even New York.[5] There are anthologies of poetry selected according to certain themes, like "the sea," "love," etc. For example, there is one exceptionally good theme-anthology of Spanish-American poetry by María Elena Walsh entitled *A la madre*.[6] The amount of poetic activity manifests itself in the publication of poetry magazines everywhere, but most of them are short-lived.

The reasons for the proliferation of poetry are diverse but two explanations come to mind: (1) the fact that poetry is a vehicle of expression at which most people at some time in their lives feel competent; (2) the persistence of a strong Spanish-American cultural identity (as it has been defined by most essayists since Rodó and Vasconcelos) that assumes a special preference for the aesthetic realm, the magic of words, the forces of illusion and compensation, and a certain vague collective idealism that reveals a soul conditioned by a variety of religious feelings. Could it be true that Latin America has been born under the sign of Ariel?[7] Or is it that this trend is derived from a generalized vanity, and/or a desire for easy respectability?

In order to design a list of recommended readings that could be subsumed under the title "Contemporary Spanish-American Poetry," we could choose among a number of arbitrary criteria. One of these is the distribution of authors along successive time intervals in the form of generations according to the patterns established by Ortega y Gasset and Petersen.

If we identify four generations within the time-span referred to as "Contemporary Spanish-American Poetry," ten to twenty outstanding poets who could be considered representative of each of those generations can be listed. (See the appendix at the end of this chapter.) These generations are spread between Gabriela Mistral, born in 1889, and Raúl Zurita, born in 1951. This determination of periods is based on a reading of thousands of Spanish-American poets.

From Gabriela Mistral to Juan Gelman we have distinguished three generations that correspond to the period designated as "contemporary." This period is more or less a continuation of what in Europe and the United States has been called "Modernism." (Our "Spanish-American Modernism" refers to a period that coincides with the turn of the century, between 1880 and 1916, and which, according to Ivan Schulman and Evelyn Picón-Garfield,[8] should be considered as part of a first stage in the development of modern culture in Latin America.)

This "contemporary" poetry prevails today. Certainly, we cannot say that this poetry is "official," or that it is the "discourse of power"[9] that dominates society. There is no need to explain what kind of forces are the most powerful in Spanish-American society today. The political situation there precludes saying that the officially approved forms of discourse have anything to do with poetry. Perhaps this is the reason why there are no evident gaps between generations as could be expected, at least in Spanish-American poetry.

The fourth and last generation includes poets that I find difficult to call young. They range from Jorge Teillier, born in 1935, to Raúl Zurita, born in 1951. This group corresponds to what has been called in the United States "post-modernism." It would be preferable to name it "post-modernity," or "post-vanguardism," or "neo-vanguardism" because Spanish-American criticism is used to calling "post-modernismo" that literature prevailing from approximately 1916 to 1940.

The recommended list in the appendix could be considered as a draft for a possible corpus, and it could be easily enlarged. Clearly, there is room for disagreement, especially about the poets selected to represent the last two generations.

The four-generational evolution of Spanish-American poetry since 1916 can be illustrated through several examples:

(I) At the end of Huidobro's "Arte poética" is a definition of the poet: "El poeta es un pequeño Dios." ["The poet is a little God"] This is far more than Rubén Darío would have dared to say. This verse does not really refer to what the poet *is*, but to what the poet should be. There is a moralistic point in this, and, of course, a high level of expectancy.

(II) But in "Test," by Nicanor Parra, one encounters the opposite view:

> Qué es un antipoeta?
>
> Un comerciante en urnas y ataúdes?
>
> Un sacerdote que no cree en nada?
>
> Un general que duda de sí mismo?
>
> . . .
>
> Un pequeño burgués?
>
> Un charlatán?
>
>   un dios?
>
>   un inocente?
>
> un aldeano de Santiago de Chile?
>
>   ("La camisa de fuerza")

[What is an antipoet? / A dealer in urns and coffins? / A priest who believes in nothing? / A general who doubts himself? / . . . / A petty bourgeoise? / A charlatan? / a god? / an innocent? / a peasant from Santiago de Chile? ("The Strait Jacket")]

Parra's definition is as bold as Huidobro's, but with such irony and sarcasm, that the effect is not just comic, as it appears at a first reading, but also tragic. First of all, Parra defines himself as an *anti-poeta*. And the *antipoeta* is not stating dogmas or moral laws that everybody has to follow. The chaotic enumeration of questions ranges from the obviously blasphemous ("A priest who believes in nothing") to the explicit, sardonic series: "Un charlatán? / un dios? / un inocente? / un aldeano de Santiago de Chile?" The fact that the reader is invited to choose among those possibilities is a further step into satire.

(III) From skepticism and disbelief, the third generation – represented by Enrique Lihn, Juan Gelman, Alvaro Mutis, Olga Orozco – finds the road toward the hallucinatory resurrection of previous illusions, and keeps shuttling between these opposite views. That is how Ernesto Cardenal prays to a simple and powerful creator independently of any evidence of his/her presence. In "Salmo 5" ("Psalm 5") he talks to a familiar ghost: "Escuchad mis palabras oh Señor / Oye mis gemidos / Escucha mi protesta / Porque no eres tú un Dios amigo de los dictadores / ni partidario de su política / ni te influencia la propaganda / ni estás en sociedad con el gangster." ("Listen to my words, oh Lord / Hear my grieving / Listen to my complaint / Because you are not a God who is a friend of dictators / nor a follower of their politics / nor are you influenced by propaganda / neither are you associated with the gangster.") The same in the "Oración por Marilyn Monroe": "Señor / recibe a esta muchacha conocida en toda la tierra con el nombre de Marilyn Monroe / aunque ese no era su verdadero nombre / (pero Tú conoces su verdadero nombre, el de la huerfanita violada a los 9 años." ["Prayer for Marilyn Monroe": "Lord / accept this girl known in all the earth by the name of Marilyn Monroe / although that was not her real name / (but You know her real name, that of the little orphan raped when she was nine years old.")] It is clear in Ernesto Cardenal's poems that the speaker is not a "pequeño dios," not even his parody, but someone who believes that he can translate and verbalize the inner feelings of God or whatever divine entity may achieve the role of incarnating an illusion. The poets of this generation becomes either sincere or cynical evangelists of a naive and desperate gospel.

In the first three generations there is a clear progression: god (Huidobro); god? – with an ironic question mark – (Parra); and the illusion of god (Cardenal). Of course, this is only a generalization. In Neruda's poetry one can trace all three stages. However, he is not generally admired for his *Estravagario* or his posthumous *2000*; the most admired of Neruda's works are his early *Crepusculario* and later "Alturas de Macchu-Picchu," *Los versos del Capitán*, and perhaps some of his "odas elementales." It would have been more complicated for a general outline to have chosen Lihn instead of Cardenal; however, it would be easy to demonstrate that Lihn is a seeker of illusions by fictitious characters, illusions which he enjoys destroying within the text.

(IV) Among the poets born after 1934 it is more difficult to find a real poetical response to the word "god." What can be seen is a general rejection of this type of vocabulary, and a sort of serene and routine handling of those terms that had been considered of value before. Important words, such as "god," or the name of poets, or the vocabulary associated with beauty — *cisne, ensueño* — are regularly conveyed more from intertextual references than from a perception of intrinsic value.

These poets show a remarkable inclination for simplicity, humility, objectiveness, testimony; they do not refer to themselves as god or anti-god. This can be perceived in *Vida*, by Gonzalo Millán; *Mal de amor*, by Oscar Hahn; *Animal fiero y tierno*, by Angelamaría Dávila; *Bajo este cien*, by José Kozer; *Agua que no has de beber*, by Antonio Cisneros; *Tiempo de bolero*, by José Luis Vega. This could be the result of belonging to a generation destroyed by social repression and terrorism. There is no point in imagining that you are or you are not god if you lie in a prison cell or your friends have died at Tlatelolco, as in *Irás y no volverás*, by José Emilio Pacheco. You may prefer to find happiness in the simple things that remain available to you.

Such deprivation may explain the difference between this generation and the emerging one that constitutes a whole new cultural scene. You can find an aggressive, perhaps suicidal resurrection of the son of god only to be followed by his disappearance in the poetry of Raúl Zurita. But with Zurita a point is reached in which everything is being reborn or redestroyed. There is a sort of renaissance from zero, a new foundation after the defeat of the previous generation. One can feel the strength of this in the last stanza of "Aclaración preliminar," a poem included in *Contradiccionario*, by Eduardo Llanos. Basically, the objectivity, the simplicity, the displacement of value from the realm of myth to the realm of change, are all evident in the verses: "si ser poeta obliga a enterarse de que un Juan violó a su madre y a su propio hijo / y que luego lloró terriblemente sobre el Evangelio de San Juan, su remoto tocayo . . . " ["if to be a poet forces one to learn that some John raped his mother and his own son / and that later he cried profusely over the Gospel according to St. John, his distant namesake . . . "] One can feel the enormous distance from the "Gospel according to St. John." It is the painful realization that something too remote cannot be recalled and, worst of all, has no immediate value. The poet does not want salvation; he just wants to add a certain relief or "breath" to the "mist" of life. The poet stays among everybody else. There is no presumption that he enjoys any kind of superiority; on the contrary, it seems that the poetic point is to be able to write poetry from anonymity or a feeling of sameness.

Summary

Briefly, it is clear that what changes from one generation to another has to do with the expectations that poets have of their readers, like in Huidobro's verse: "y el alma del oyente quede temblando" ("and the soul of the listener is to be left trembling"). This defines the highest expectation of all. Readers are to be shocked, leaving the innermost parts of their soul in awe.

The contrary happens in Parra's antipoetry: the reader becomes an accomplice of the poet's sarcasm. The speaker asks them, in "Test," (a) to underline the correct sentence, and (b) to place a cross indicating the correct definition. Of course, no one is going to perform these tasks. Parra really expects the reader to be clever, and to laugh along with him. It would be very unlikely that naive readers will really do what they are told. So readers are not expected to bow in deep respect, but to laugh and disregard any form of what is considered as empty veneration.

Cardenal, in some ways, returns to the high expectations of the first generation, but with simplicity, and in a manner that is supposed to be convincing. The poet is a prophet: a believer, as it seems in the case of Cardenal, or a cynic who tries to persuade us about the banality of everything, as in the poetry of Enrique Lihn.

Later, Jorge Teillier, in *Muertes y maravillas* expects readers to be able to appreciate poetry as they may appreciate a bottle of wine (Chilean red wine, of course). Poetry will teach the readers to breathe. He wants them to share in his detachment. Readers may not be saved, but they do not care. They are invited to stay at the threshold of illusions but without bothering to trespass.

The same is true of José Kozer. In his book *Bajo este cien*, he adopts several disguises, but there is always a speaker who talks to someone: "You remember, Sylvia, how the women worked at home." The image of his father is not the godlike figure implied in *Los heraldos negros* by César Vallejo; although he smokes and there are some references that remind us of "Sinfonía en gris mayor" by Rubén Darío, there is really nothing of the sort. His "air of mystery" does not reveal a superior condition: the reader can smile or admire the simplicity of this father, "Papá," who "didn't ever seem to do anything." The poetic voice does not make any effort to embellish or transcend the real father. That is why this poetic voice enjoys, as in the works of Cisneros and Roque Dalton, long verses that imitate the hesitations, parentheses, and undulations of verbal prose. There is a sense of not caring about what everybody thinks he should do.

This is especially true about a poet like Néstor Perlongher, in his *Austria-Hungría*. If to be a poet means to perspire, defecate, to contradict oneself, to fall in distress, to listen, to seek knowledge, then perhaps this speaker may accept to be called a poet.

It is obvious that in Teillier and Kozer, the poet does not feel that he must relate to any implied reader because *he is* the reader; the poet is at the same level as the reader.

Most of the lyrical standards of previous poetry have been deconstructed and its values rendered obsolete. Traditional notions about the presence of a subject within lyrical discourse; the prestige of the imaginary; the unescapable beauty/horror duality; the building of overlapping systems through analogies; the fetishism of the text as an isotopic structure, have all been displaced from the center of poetry. It is more common to observe the treatment of speech as palimpsest; the intentional diversity of meanings, and prosaism as a liberation from the musical rhythm as well as from the notion of the intrinsic prestige of certain privileged images. Intertextuality is not a relation between selected discourses but a generalized dialogue among all human (and inhuman) utterances. Poetry has turned from a hierarchized imaginary world to a notion of the world as truly open.

Appendix: Four Generations in Contemporary Spanish-American Poetry

I

Gabriela Mistral (Chile, 1889–1957)
Oliverio Girondo (Argentina, 1891–1967)
Alfonsina Storni (Argentina, 1892–1938)
César Vallejo (Peru, 1892–1938)
Vicente Huidobro (Chile, 1893–1948)
Juana de Ibarbourou (Uruguay, 1895–1979)
Luis Palés Matos (Puerto Rico, 1898–1959)
Jorge Luis Borges (Argentina, 1899–1986)
José Gorostiza (Mexico, 1901–1973)
Jorge Carrera Andrade (Ecuador, 1902–78)
Nicolás Guillén (Cuba, 1902)
César Moro (Peru, 1903–56)
Pablo Neruda (Chile, 1904–73)

II

Humberto Díaz Casanueva (Chile, 1908)
Martín Adán (Peru, 1908)
Enrique Molina (Argentina, 1910)
Oscar Cerruto (Bolivia, 1912–81)
José Lezama Lima (Cuba, 1912–76)
Vicente Gerbasi (Venezuela, 1913)
Nicanor Parra (Chile, 1914)
Octavio Paz (Mexico, 1914)
Juan Liscano (Venezuela, 1915)
Gonzalo Rojas (Chile, 1917)
César Fernández Moreno (Argentina, 1919–85)
Alberto Girri (Argentina, 1919)

III

Eliseo Diego (Cuba, 1920)
Idea Vilariño (Uruguay, 1920)
Jorge Eduardo Eielson (Peru, 1921)
Jaime Sáenz (Bolivia, 1921)
Eunice Odio (Costa Rica, 1922–74)
Juan Sánchez Peláez (Venezuela, 1922)
Olga Orozco (Argentina, 1922)
Alvaro Mutis (Colombia, 1923)
Rosario Castellanos (Mexico, 1925–74)
Roberto Juarroz (Argentina, 1925)
Ernesto Cardenal (Nicaragua, 1925)
Ida Vitale (Uruguay, 1926)
Blanca Varela (Peru, 1926)
Carlos Germán Belli (Peru, 1927)
Enrique Lihn (Chile, 1929–88)
Roberto Fernández Retamar (Cuba, 1930)
Fayad Jamís (Cuba, 1930)
Juan Gelman (Argentina, 1930)

IV

Jorge Teillier (Chile, 1935)
Roque Dalton (El Salvador, 1935–75)
Oscar Hahn (Chile, 1938)
Alejandra Pizarnik (Argentina, 1939–72)
José Emilio Pacheco (Mexico, 1939)

José Kozer (Cuba, 1940)
Antonio Cisneros (Peru, 1942)
Angelamaría Dávila (Puerto Rico, 1944)
Hanni Ossott (Venezuela, 1946)
Tamara Kamenszain (Argentina, 1947)
Gonzalo Millán (Chile, 1947)
José Luis Vega (Puerto Rico, 1948)
Alexis Gómez Rosa (Dominican Republic, 1950)
Raúl Zurita (Chile, 1951)
Néstor Perlongher (Argentina)
Eduardo Llanos (Chile)

CHAPTER 7

The Poetic Experience: The Logic of Chance*

JOSÉ KOZER

Only for an instant can man bear the wholeness of the divine.
— Friedrich Hölderlin

I have but twenty minutes in which to read and comment on four of my poems. I have chosen these at random from a total of nearly 2300 poems written since 1970. Three of these poems I have read in public on other occasions.

A fourth, "Buchenwald," I have never read in public. I perceive it as a problematic poem, as a poem I would not like to read out loud and which, perhaps perversely, I will force myself to read, having chosen it.

I must comment on these four poems and, without giving a great deal of attention to the matter, I have decided to comment on them by using notes, quotes, the words of others that I have been collecting throughout the years on cards — words that I have read here and there, going from one book to the next, in my disorderly readings.

I have chosen four entries from the file where I keep hundreds of ideas and images and words that have impressed me. I do not know exactly why I have chosen these four and I have no idea of what order they will impart to my reading.

The night before the reading I reflected on these four entries. Suddenly I realized that of the four two were thoughts and two are images embodied in anecdotes. And just as suddenly, in a sort of *satori* ('illumination,' 'revelation') I understood that behind all this there was a logic, a perfectly ordered sequence (how so?) that, as in a jigsaw puzzle about to be completed, has found its own shape.

---

*Kozer's remarks preceeding the poems were translated by Jorge Guitart.

And so it is that each of the two thoughts chosen at random can precede — and direct — a particular poem. And similarly each of the two images fits a particular poem.

You Remember, Sylvia

Paul Celan, the poet of Bukovina, who suffered in the concentration camps, the suicidal poet, the poet of the image and of the rupture of the image, the poet of language and of the rupture of language: to him is attributed the phrase — the dictum — "Poetry does not impose; it exposes."

This phrase heads the first poem that I will read; in this poem where the central character is (supposedly) my father, he (I am telling the audience) is not imposed but simply exposed.

And I expose the long geographic, psychological, affective, and spiritual trek of this character: an immigrant, the traveler that comes to be at anchor, the unknown land, the language unknown and unknowable. From the poem there emanates the character, revealing himself; embedded in the poem he does and says things, opening up, staying before the others, the others who have the option of receiving him or discarding him. I will now read:

"You Remember, Sylvia"

You remember, Sylvia, how the women worked at home.

Papa didn't seem to do anything.

He held his hands behind him leaning like a rabbi smoking a stubby
    birchwood pipe, the curls of smoke giving him an air
    of mystery,

I'm beginning to suspect that Papa must have had a touch of Asian in him.

Maybe he'd been a nobleman from Besarabia who'd freed his serfs in
    the days of the Tsar,

or perhaps he'd been in the habit of taking his ease in fields of oats
    and dreamy at winnowing time had sat hunched over
    gently in a damp spot among the ferns in his ancient
    longcoat a bit threadbare.

It's likely that he became thoughtful when he came across an apple on
    the steppe.

He knew nothing of the sea.

Confidently eager for the image of the foam he confused anemone and sky.

I think the weepy crowd of eucalyptus leaves unnerved him.

Imagine what he felt when Rosa Luxemburg appeared with a tract in her hand before the Tsar's judges.

He would have to emigrate, poor Papa, from Odessa to Vienna, Rome, Istanbul, Quebec, Ottawa, New York.

He would reach Havana as a document and five passports, I can see him rather wearied by the trip.

You remember, Sylvia, when Papa would come home from the stores on the Calle Muralla and all you women in the house would start to bustle.

I swear he came through the parlor door, two-toned shoes, blue pinstripe suit, elegant oval-spotted tie

and Papa didn't ever seem to do anything.

(Translated by Gregory Rabassa)

"Te acuerdas, Sylvia"

Te acuerdas, Sylvia, cómo trabajaban las mujeres en casa.

Parecía que papá no hacía nada.

Llevaba las manos a la espalda inclinándose como un rabino fumando una cachimba corta de abedul, las volutas de humo le daban un aire misterioso,

comienzo a sospechar que papá tendría algo de asiático.

Quizás fuera un señor de Besarabia que redimió a sus siervos en épocas del Zar,

o quizás acostumbrara a reposar en los campos de avena y somnoliento a la hora de la criba se sentara encorvado bondadosamente en un sitio húmedo entre los helechos con su antigua casaca algo deshilachada.

Es probable que quedara absorto al descubrir en la estepa una manzana.

Nada sabía del mar.

Seguro se afanaba con la imagen de la espuma y confundía las anémonas y el cielo.

Creo que la llorosa muchedumbre de las hojas de los eucaliptos lo asustaba.

Figúrate qué sintió cuando Rosa Luxemburgo se presentó con un
   opúsculo entre las manos ante los jueces del Zar.

Tendría que emigrar pobre papá de Odesa a Viena, Roma, Estambul,
   Quebec, Ottawa, Nueva York.

Llegaría a La Habana como un documento y cinco pasaportes, me lo
   imagino algo maltrecho del viaje.

Recuerdas, Sylvia, cuando papá llegaba de los almacenes de la calle
   Muralla y todas las mujeres de la casa Uds. se alborotaban.

Juro que entraba por la puerta de la sala, zapatos de dos tonos, el
   traje azul a rayas, la corbata de óvalos finita

y parecía que papá no hacía nunca nada.

Franz Kafka's Sprout

For the second poem I propose an image. It comes from the *Diaries*
of the Russian writer, Maxim Gorki, from a very amusing chapter in
which he recalls how he would spy on famous writers in an attempt
to catch them unawares doing something unusual.

In our case it has do with an appointment in Yalta that Gorki
had with his countryman, the playwright and short-story writer,
Anton Chekhov. It is 1904, the year that Chekhov was to die of tuber-
culosis. We must picture him in an autumn day, touched by impend-
ing death, in a Russian city of Mediterranean character and luminous
temperament.

Unobserved, Gorki is watching Chekhov, who is waiting for him
sitting on a stone bench in the garden of his house in Yalta. Gorki is
hiding behind a hedge and sees Chekhov dressed in tails and wearing
a top hat.

It is sunny, but not very, and quiet. A sun ray coming through the
trees creates a round, tiny puddle of light by Chekhov's feet. And
Chekhov looks at it absorbed in thought, seemingly absorbed in
thought. Suddenly, he takes off his top hat and describing an arc with
his right arm he moves it as if to catch the puddle of light with his hat
and then puts his hat back on, as if he wanted to retain that light over
his head under the hat. This action, Gorki tells us, will be repeated
time and again by the master Chekhov.

The poem is an attempt to gather a light related to Kafka, the idea
of the house, the lost paradise of childhood, the loneliness, and opacity of all death.

In the poem the house has two levels, just as does the anecdotal reality described. Kafka has plural levels, unfathomable; the poem, working dialectically the two levels, attempts in some obscure way to penetrate the Kafka mystery, the mystery of plurality, of the agglomeration seeking its essence, its simplicity, its single voice. Here is the poem:

"Franz Kafka's Sprout"

It's a small two-story house not far from the river on a Prague

back street. In the early hours

between the eleventh and twelfth of November he had a start, he went
    down to the small kitchen with the round table
    and the basswood chair, the portable stove and
    the blue methylene flame. He lighted

the gas ring

and at the same time (three) the fire greened flames on the three
    windowpanes: it smelled of brimstone. He wanted

to go

into the small dining room and drink some boldo-leaf and honey tea,
    he pulled out the chair and settled down in
    front of a sienna mug that he had placed who
    knows how long ago on the six-colored wicker
    glass rack a gift

from Felicia: and once more

Felicia appeared with a stripe in the middle, the two braids and a
    glow of candles in the white oval of that avid
    face of flour and consecrated bread, a face

three times

a flame on the windowpane: she appeared. And once more three times
    she was the little girl of her dead,

to the sound

of a triangle some chamber players came and to the sound of the
    bell (it's three) in the tall belfry not far
    from the river: they spread out, ten

cups, ten

chairs in the huge mansion with garrets, the house where the bay
    windows and the sideboards (stables and
    sheds) were open day and night, the water

and the sponges

gleamed. Well, yes: it was a different time and a chorus of girls
      watched over the tea kettles (bubbling)
      the eucalyptuses (bubbling) the marjoram
      and some digestive water (mint) waters

for breathing: everything

tranquil (finally) everything tranquil, he went up the steps and
      saw that he was leaning on the windowpane
      (at last) without a crowd of birds

at the window.

(Translated by Gregory Rabassa)

"Rebrote de Franz Kafka"

Es una casa pequeña a dos niveles no muy lejos del río en un

callejón de Praga. En la madrugada

del once al doce noviembre tuvo un sobresalto, bajó a la cocinilla con
      la mesa redonda y la silla de tilo, el anafe y la
      llama azul de metileno. Prendió

la hornilla

y el fuego verdeció a la vez (tres) llamas en los tres cristales de la
      ventana: olía a azufre. Quiso

pasar

a la salita comedor a beber una tisana de boldo y miel, corrió la
      silla y se acomodó delante de una taza de barro siena
      que había colocado no se sabe hace cuánto sobre el
      portavasos de mimbre a seis colores, obsequio

de Felicia: y una vez más

apareció Felicia con la raya al medio, las dos trenzas y un resplandor
      de velas en el óvalo blanco de aquel rostro ávido de
      harinas y panes de la consagración, rostro

tres veces

una llamarada en el cristal de la ventana: apareció. Y era una vez
      más la niña tres veces de sus muertos, acudían

al golpe

del triángulo unos músicos de cámara y al golpe de la esquila (las
      tres) en el alto campanario no muy lejos
      del río: se arrellanaron, diez

tazas, diez

sillas en la inmensa casona de las mansardas, la casa en que los
    miradores y las cristaleras (establos y galpones)
    se abrían día y noche, el agua

y las esponjas

relucían. Pues, sí: era otra época y un coro de muchachas vigilaba
    las teteras (bullir) los eucaliptos (bullir) la mejorana
    y un agua digestiva (mentas) aguas

de la respiración: todo

tranquilo (por fin) todo tranquilo, subió los escalones y vio que se
    tendía en el cristal de la ventana (por fin)
    sin una aglomeración de pájaros

en la ventana.

Buchenwald

Third entry, third poem, third situation. Gerard de Nerval: "Poetry is dream overflowing into life."

I will twist his words: "Poetry is nightmare overflowing into life."

That is an aspect, real, alive, of poetry, of the so-called poetic experience. Every poem is a joy of light or of opacity. Every poem is a dream or a nightmare that has overflown. Sometimes the poet sings with joy; sometimes the commotion comes from horror.

"Buchenwald" is the poem of horror, of organized destruction, horror methodic and rigorous.

In this poem a woman is walking toward the most disproportioned and least natural death that we can conceive: the death imposed by the Nazis in the concentration camps.

She knows and doesn't know that is happening to her. She is being taken to the "showers," to the gas chambers. She moves forward, crosses the threshold (of death). And there, she turns: she remembers her wedding; the image of the wedding emerges: orange blossoms, love, happiness.

Simultaneously she is (another sort of wedding) among the other women, all naked, victims. And among them she finds and does not find support. And she sings her servitude to Elohim, to the God of Israel.

At the same time, the terror that invades her makes tar – shit – come out of her private parts. And she is forced, as if she were at that moment a housewife, to clean the bathrooms, the floors, with a mop, with her tongue.

All that constitutes a simultaneity, the essence of the act or gesture of dying.

And as a part of that death, of that simultaneity, from the place where shit, tar, is emerging, a baby boy is born. He (the poetic self presents him thus) is born with a birthmark: a hairy wart in his face from the pubic hair of (his mother) the woman.

She is left broken, decomposed, in a Cubistic manner, as seen in the final line of the poem ("Her forearm").

And I go on to read "Buchenwald." I had never read it. During the reading I experienced a moment of total surrender. I felt something ripping inside me, something similar to the ripping one feels and hears at the point of getting a hernia.

"Buchenwald"

She smiles.

Her gold tooth is lightly tarnished green.

She raises her right hand has a handkerchief she would wave.

A turtledove pecks at her left earlobe.

She has turned around: and with her, ruffles.

The branch of orange blossom has turned with her: some specks
    of ash fly out through the opening.

She is naked.

Hair grows on her shoulders.

Caterpillars spin from dregs her glowing shawl her alabaster bonnet.

Her buttocks, turn: tar.

Tar, along the cleft: merde, monarch.

Flanked: the forensics gather in flashlight circles, her dung.

A fly circles the invisible thread of tar.

It enters the cleft of her buttocks: buzzes.

It pushes the woman: she stopped a moment, at the threshold.

Perpetuated, she enters.

And all the Jewish women smile, seated: a miniscule fly scratches
    their glands.

Buzzes, the nipples: Elohim.

And the gun-butt blow resounds: echo, the showers.

Echo, in the yellow tilework in the breeze that gently ruffles the white oilcloth curtains.

Dustclouds: the hinges.

Echo: the loud slam of two shutters.

Through the dusty panes of nine clerestories light filters thick as milk: nine puddles.

Lap them up.

Mops dustcloths the unembraceable rags for scrubbing kitchens: lap them up.

Toothless.

And among them, she sat down: I am born this time through the front, covered.

With tar: the opening.

The singed spider of her pubic hair left its birthmark, scratched on my face.

Her forearm.

(Translated by Diane J. Forbes)

"Buchenwald"

Sonríe.

Su diente de oro está tocado de verdín.

Alza la mano derecha tiene un pañuelo que agitaría.

Una tórtola pica en el lóbulo izquierdo de su oreja.

Ha girado: y con ella, sus vuelos.

El ramo de azahar con ella ha girado: unas motas de ceniza se desprenden por el agujero.

Está desnuda.

El vello crece sobre sus hombros.

Las orugas tejen con sedimento su toquilla de lumbre su toca de alabastro.

Giran, sus nalgas: brea.

Brea, por el tajo: mierda, monarca.

Escoltada: los forenses recogen en los círculos de una linterna, sus cagajones.

La mosca recorre el hilillo invisible de la brea.

Penetra, el tajo de sus nalgas: zumba.

Impulsa, a la mujer: se detuvo un momento, en los umbrales.

Se ha perpetuado: entra.

Y todas las hebreas sonríen, sentadas: una mosca minúscula rasca
    sus glándulas.

Zumba, en sus pezones: Elohim.

Y suena el culatazo: eco, las duchas.

Eco, en el crema amarillo del alicatado en el viento que riza
    levísimo las cortinas de hule blanco.

Tolvaneras: los goznes.

Eco, el golpe alto de dos batientes.

Por el cristal de nueve ventanucos filtra la luz un espesor de
    leches: nueve charcos.

A lamer.

Los palos de trapear las bayetas del polvo los inabarcables
    retazos de restregar las cocinas, a lamer.

Encías.

Y entre todas, se ha sentado: yo nazco esta vez por su
    agujero anterior, embreado.

Era, la salida.

La araña chamuscada de su pendejera dejó un lunar de pelos,
    prendió en mi cara.

Su antebrazo.

Attached to What is Us

The home stretch, the fourth and last poem; the circle will be completed, the hole of twenty minutes of public reading.

For this last poem, another image. It comes from a Zen anecdote that I cherish deeply, the probable meaning of which I have been trying to decipher for years.

I found it in Eugen Harrigel's *Zen in the Art of Archery*. A Japanese archer, through practice and meditation, comes to be ranked highest in the country in archery. He has become, he thinks, the best archer in Japan.

He says he is that, he feels he is that: a sign of vanity.

He is told that there is an old man who lives on top of a mountain who is superior to him as an archer. The champion, who is forty, climbs up the mountain to find out. And there he finds an old man who is about eighty.

"I am the best archer in Japan but they have told me that you are better than I. And I would like you to show me."

The old man asks the younger archer to stand on a flagstone that gives onto an abyss and from there shoot and kill a heron. The young archer stands on the flagstone, glances at the abyss, feels dizzy, takes a step backwards, sees the heron flying by, aims, shoots, and kills it.

The old man, without uttering a word, stands up with great effort, places himself on the same flagstone, looks toward the abyss for an instant. And now, seeing another heron flying by, *without* a bow or an arrow, he executes the motions of shooting and kills the heron.

The last poem is a long complex piece that was written in ten, fifteen minutes and was published as is, without any changes.

This poem, given its instantaneous quality, serves to explain the theme that guides and orders my reading. And I say: the poetic experience *is* the poem. There is no bow or arrow. There is no objective; there is no paper or pencil; no goal or target or bull's-eye. The only thing there is is the instant, mysterious, simultaneity which suddenly thrusts forth that strange and new (new?) thing that is the poem.

The arm, in its prolongation of instantaneousness, produces the poem.

That is all. And here it is: "Attached to what is us," a poem with such an illogical (ungrammatical) title, which I love so much:

"Attached To What Is Us"

— For Guadalupe

Tell me, why so many dawns?

What is (was) this year?

I warned you: A juicy pear might appear on the apricot tree, laden
    with fruit, the sap from the rose bush
    might turn crimson; you would smile. And
    now we laugh,

we burst out laughing, a flax sailor blouse, a sepia

belt with a geometrical emblem, I warned you, too: and you see,
    a harp on the pear tree in the backyard,
    a harp? It's been three years since it
    last

rained

and underneath the apricot tree it reeks of dampness, of fierce
      maggots that devour everything that falls;
      they would devour rain itself

if it were to fall. If it were

to fall, we would remember that daily routine that we loved so
      much: dip

the aniseed crackers

in the coffee (I taught you to say, *café retinto y carretero,*
      coffee black as ink, peasant's coffee; you
      would smile) dip. A serene

couple. And

all your wonder gathered in that phrase that captured us: "It is
      that we know how to run our affairs well."

Don't say

I didn't

warn you, there were so many signs: the trellis we found inexplicably
      broken; the rung missing

suddenly

from the ladder for picking the fruit of the pear tree?, the apricot
      tree? How: I just knew. Look,

you were still

asleep and suddenly (so early) I was left at the edge, high by the
      lattice windows, under the bend of an arch turned

upwards; perhaps you are still

dozing: ten, twenty years. Have they gone by? What happened? What
      became

of the second

movement andante sostenuto, remember that at that time we discovered
      the poems of the beloved Sugawara no Michizane?
      Oh my beloved, my beloved,

descend

from the harp

let your countless fingers descend from the stringed instruments,
      let them touch my shoulder, warn me; coffee
      is served. The ceramic dish from Granada

with the aniseed crackers on it and the two mugs of black coffee
        facing each other. Coffee

is served

and we would pretend there was a butler I was your butler and your
        maid ("Coffee is served, madam") Remember? How

afraid

we were of the dish how could it slip from your hand number seven
        moonlight the moon becoming larger entering
        through the lattice, turning iridescent

under

the bell jar apricot flowers, pear flowers, a tulle flower, a wax
        flower this whole room, this table set

for two.

(Translated by Jorge Guitart)

"Apego de lo nosotros"

– Para Guadalupe

Di, di tú: para qué tantos amaneceres.

Qué año es, era.

Te previne: podría aparecer una pera de agua en el albaricoquero
        cargado de frutos, hacerse escarlata la savia del
        rosal; sonreías. Y ahora reímos,

rompemos a reír a carcajadas, blusón de lino, faja

sepia con un emblema geométrico, también te previne: y ves,
        un arpa en el peral del patio,
        ¿arpa? Tres años

que no llueve

y debajo del albaricoquero hiede a humedad: a gusaneras
        fortísimas que devoran cuanto cae, devorarían
        la propia lluvia

si cayera. Si

cayera, recordaríamos aquel tren de vida metódico que
        tanto nos gustaba: mojar

las galletas

de anís en el café retinto (yo te enseñé a decir, café
        retinto y carretero; sonreías): mojar. Qué seres

tranquilos. Y

toda tu admiración volcada en aquella frase que nos resumía:
"es que sabemos administrarnos bien." No digas

que no

te previne, había tantas señales: el varaseto que apareció
roto inexplicablemente el peldaño que faltó

de pronto

a la escalera de coger los frutos ¿del peral, del albaricoquero?
Cómo: yo lo supe, yo lo supe. Mira,

dormías

aún y me quedé de pronto (tan temprano) en la arista en altas
celosías en la revuelta de un arco hacia

arriba, quizás

aún dormitas: dos lustros, o dos décadas, ¿pasaron? Qué hubo. Qué

del segundo

movimiento *andante sostenuto*, ¿recuerdas que por aquella época
descubrimos los poemas del amado Sugawara No
Michizane, amantísima? Amantísima, del arpa

desciendas, de

los instrumentos de cuerda desciendan tus dedos numerosísimos
que me toquen al hombro, que me prevengan: la mesa,
está servida. El plato de cerámica

granadina

con las galletas de anís y frente por frente los dos tazones
de café tinto. Servida

la mesa

e imitábamos como si hubiera un mayordomo yo fui tu mayordomo
y mayordoma ("la mesa está servida, Señora"),
¿te acuerdas? Qué

miedo

le cogimos al plato cómo pudo resbalársete de la mano el plato
el número siete la luz crecer de la luna al entrar
por el enrejado de la ventana, irisar

bajo

la campana de cristal las flores del albaricoquero las flores
del peral, flor de tul flor de cera toda esta
habitación esta mesa

servida.

CHAPTER 8

Women Writers into the Mainstream: Contemporary Latin American Narrative

ROSEMARY GEISDORFER FEAL

There is a well-worn phrase, handed down by generations of critics, that decries: "Latin America: a novel without novelists." And while it is implausible that Latin America can ever be *written* as such, it is readily evident to any observer of world literature that Latin American narrators do write extremely successfully, thereby securing themselves a conspicuous place on the modern fiction scene.[1] The sensational "boom" in Latin American narrative that was sounded in the sixties echoes well into the eighties, but, as I hope to suggest, the register of the authorial chorus has been raised by the feminine voices that have finally made themselves fully heard. After all, the "lowering of the boom" was largely a masculine phenomenon, for not only did it engender the literary coming-out of several major male figures, it also fostered a cultural, social, and commercial alliance from which female authors were markedly absent. But to begin to speak of Latin American narrative with women at the forefront, it would be instructive to go back to the origins of the "boom" and to its major precursor, Jorge Luis Borges, who attained worldwide prestige in the 1940s for his remarkably original short fiction.

There are two facts about Borges that must be taken into account when discussing his role as literary father of a generation of fiction writers: first, Borges did not write novels, even though countless novelists have acknowledged their literary debts to him; second, his idiosyncratic style, characterized by a metaphysical questioning of reality and of writing itself, appears to be less "Latin American" than universal, although it could be argued that he has, in his own way, "written" Argentina. His collection of short stories published under the title *Ficciones* (1944) sets the tone for the new paths that fiction would follow thereafter, paths that often resemble what Borges has called "circular ruins." It took perhaps two decades before the full effect of Jorge Luis Borges was felt by the younger fiction writers in Latin America, but no one can dispute the continuing influence of the Argentine master who shattered once and for all the mimetic mirror of literature.

Borges of course did not stand alone in this endeavor. Before the first shock waves of the "boom" were felt, several other writers were changing the shape of Latin American literature during the forties. Particular mention should be made of Guatemalan Nobel laureate Miguel Angel Asturias, whose novel *El Señor Presidente* (1946) paved the way for future novelistic interpretations of the dictator theme. Asturias further contributed to writing the novel of Latin America in *Men of Maize* (*Hombres de maíz*, 1949), a work that linguistically fuses the past and present, the magical and the real. In his treatment of the indigenous element of his native Guatemala, Miguel Angel Asturias in effect revitalizes the *indigenista* novel through his poetic use of myth, Mayan cosmogony, and ritualistic language. Mexican Rosario Castellanos, like Asturias, created memorable portraits of the indigenous peoples of her native region, Chiapas, in novels such as *Balún Canán* (1957). Cuban Alejo Carpentier accomplished notable achievements in his groundbreaking fiction: Carpentier's exploration of the dictator theme and experiments in what he called "lo real maravilloso" (rendered in English as "magical realism") place him among the most influential authors of this century. A distinguished musicologist, Carpentier was one of the first writers to experiment in the interrelations between music and literature, thus producing some highly innovative texts such as *The Pursuit* (*El acoso*, 1956), with its rigorous structure modeled after Beethoven's Third Symphony. Like Asturias, the Cuban author cultivated historical themes in literature, with particular devotion to the cultural relations between the colonizing Europeans and the colonized Spanish Americans. Both Asturias and Carpentier manifest the impact that surrealism and other avantgarde literary movements have had on Latin American writers of all genres, an influence that cannot be overlooked even in the present.

Of course, the list of those Latin Americans who paved the way for the "boom" of the sixties is a very long one: it includes Mexican Juan Rulfo, whose *Pedro Páramo* (1955) gave us the phantom voices of the ghost town, Comala; Paraguayan Augusto Roa Bastos, with his mythical interpretations of history; Argentine Adolfo Bioy Casares, master of the fantastic: Peruvian José María Arguedas, who combined

Quechuan syntax and Spanish lexicon to produce a thoroughly modern interpretation of the conqueror-native problematics; Chilean María Luisa Bombal, explorer of dream-like worlds overshadowed by death. The technical and thematic innovations of these authors certainly had bearing on the new narrative of the sixties, but no amount of retrospective analysis could possibly explain the phenomenon that took place in Spanish-American letters known as the "boom." In his *Historia personal del 'boom*,[2] Chilean writer José Donoso places the "boom" in relation to the international events surrounding the Cuban revolution: the support that the Spanish-American "new" writers lent to Castro at the beginning of his leadership in the early sixties served to unify them, but the gradual disenchantment of some intellectuals – culminating in the Padilla affair in 1971 – eventually divided them, and to some degree, continues to do so.

Donoso establishes three major moments in the "boom." Carlos Fuentes would represent the first true internationalization of Latin American writing: it was he who promoted his own cause as well as that of other writers when he travelled about, manuscripts in hand, as cultural promoter of the new narrative. Fuentes, prolific author of such masterpieces as *The Death of Artemio Cruz* (*La muerte de Artemio Cruz*, 1962) and *Terra nostra* (1975), has also proven himself an astute commentator of the literary and political scenes.[3] The second major moment of the "boom" occurred in 1962 when Peruvian Mario Vargas Llosa published *La ciudad y los perros* (literally *The City and the Dogs*; published in English as *The Time of the Hero*), often considered the novel that catalyzed the new narrative revolution. In his first novel, the Peruvian experiments with temporal and spacial dislocation, setting in motion the narrative ambiguity that was to become a hallmark of contemporary Latin American writers. He also explores the themes of violence, adolescent sexuality, and political corruption, themes that he cultivates from a variety of perspectives – most notably one fused with irony – in future works of fiction, such as *The Green House* (*La casa verde*, 1966) and *Conversation in The Cathedral* (*Conversación en La Catedral*, 1969). Vargas Llosa continues to be one of the most prolific and respected Latin American writers with a solid international standing, and, like Fuentes, remains involved in both literary criticism and the political sphere.

The arrival on the literary market of *One Hundred Years of Solitude* (*Cien años de soledad*), Colombian Gabriel García Márquez's masterpiece, dates the third moment of the "boom" to 1967, and it is this book more than any other that has placed Latin American writing "into the mainstream."[4] García Márquez has been credited with making "magical realism" one of the most readily recognizable features of modern Latin American fiction. And yet *One Hundred Years* is more than a mythical textual world modeled on some variation of a rural Colombian setting: it is also a highly ironic, metafictional piece that ultimately turns against itself and its own genesis. A best-seller worldwide, *One Hundred Years* must be qualified as a commercial triumph as well as a literary one; it has been followed by a series of popular works, such as *The Autumn of the Patriarch* (*El otoño del patriarca*, 1975), a technically innovative "novel of tyranny," and the stylistically lighter *Chronicle of a Death Foretold* (*Crónica de una muerte anunciada*, 1981). García Márquez' 1982 Nobel Prize is testimony to the enormous popularity the Colombian author has commanded. In fact, many critics of Latin American literature see the Nobel Prize as a generational one: the most conspicuous representative of the new narrative, García Márquez has perhaps been awarded the Nobel not only for his own individual success but also for the wave on which he has ridden to that success.

In addition to Fuentes, García Márquez, and Vargas Llosa, the other major writer of the "boom" is Argentine Julio Cortázar, whose *Hopscotch* (*Rayuela*, 1963) is considered a classic narrative experiment, a prototypical anti-novel, an *opera aperta*, to borrow Umberto Eco's term. Cortázar infused a sense of play into his literature that in part derives from the surrealistic mode, but he was not content to write only as *homo ludens*: like many of his co-generationals, Cortázar took strong political stands and expressed them through literature and essays. In his short stories, Cortázar takes literary ambiguity to its extreme when he makes his narrative viewpoint correspond to inanimate objects, such as the camera in "Blow-up" ("Las babas del diablo"), or to a lizard-like creature, the "Axolotl" of the title. Cortázar issues more than a polite invitation to the reader to participate in his textual world in "Continuity of the Parks" ("Continuidad de los parques"): indeed, he literally forces an inscribed reader to sit in the death chair assigned to a character in the story. The creator of the *cronopios* and *famas* is said to have made language bounce, dance, and fly, but he also made language into a critical discourse that transcends the airy quality of his textual games. The fifth chair in the members' gallery of the "boom" supposedly rotates between José Donoso and Argentine Ernesto Sábato, according to popular legend: interestingly, these authors' most significant novels fall outside the core years of the literary output of the other four "official" members of the new narrative circle. Sábato's deeply influential *The Tunnel* (*El túnel*) dates back to 1948, while Donoso's hallucinatory novel, *The Obscene Bird of Night* (*El obsceno pájaro de la noche*), did not appear until 1970, but was then followed by a series of monumental works that have accorded the

Chilean primary residence in that proverbial last chair. Like other new novelists, Donoso shows a remarkable versatility in his literary repertoire. His range includes the supernatural tinged with psychological overtones; the mock erotic novel, which he cultivates in the memorable *The Mysterious Disappearance of the Marquesita de Loria* (*La misteriosa desaparición de la marquesita de Loria*, 1980); ironic criticism of bourgeois society; and the self-conscious confessional mode, which, in *The Garden Next Door* (*El jardín de al lado*, 1981) entails the traumatic experience of exile, something also common to many modern writers of Latin America.

Donoso apologizes for having constructed a finite list of five or six names and dates that would represent the key moments of the "boom" in Latin American literature, for he realizes that in so doing he necessarily omits some extremely influential writers. Such is the situation of Cuban Guillermo Cabrera Infante, whose *Three Trapped Tigers* (*Tres tristes tigres*, 1967) perhaps incarnates all the features we associate with "new" narrative: linguistic ambiguity, in Cabrera's case coupled with wordplay, puns, and a joyful celebration of language; social critique; mythical reconstruction of historical reality; intertextuality; incorporation of "popular" culture into "high" literature, and so forth. Another writer to subvert the notion of "high" culture is Argentine Manuel Puig, who often draws on Hollywood films to structure his fiction, as is apparent in some of the titles of his most popular novels: *Betrayed by Rita Hayworth* (*La traición de Rita Hayworth*, 1968), and *Kiss of the Spider Woman* (*El beso de la mujer araña*, 1976), which is now itself a motion picture. Also to be counted among the renewing forces of Latin American literature is Cuban José Lezama Lima, whose hermetic *Paradiso* (1966) has been compared with works by Proust, Joyce, and Dante.

But the "boom" should not be construed merely as a list of names, dates, and titles, for it was very much a cultural and personal phenomenon as well, as Donoso so vividly points out in his testimony. A great many of the up-and-coming Latin American writers congregated in Barcelona during the sixties, when publishing houses such as Seix Barral served as their principal commercial sponsors. It is here that these writers solidified friendships, exchanged newly discovered works by others, and launched intellectual activities of a truly international stature. In many instances the exile of these authors was voluntary, even unrelated to the political climates in their countries: in other cases, such as that of Cuban writers, exile indeed had direct political motivations, and in the seventies, large numbers of Latin American writers would leave countries such as Chile, Argentina, and Uruguay in search of intellectual freedom. Upon examination, then, a majority of the works belonging to new narrative must be seen as products of exile: Latin America now has the novelists, but they no longer remain physically attached to the motherland. It is the intellectual and physical separation from the motherland, or the *patria chica*, that has allowed many of these writers to return in their imaginations to the very places they left behind, and gain in the process a distanced perspective that enhances the mythical recreation of a Macondo, of Santiago de Chile, of Buenos Aires, or of the jungle regions of Peru.

Surrounding the superstars of the "boom" were the members of the expected entourage of wives, children, reporters, critics, and especially the literary agent of a great number of major Latin American writers, Carmen Balcells. But nowhere in this impressive debut of Latin American narrative on the world stage were the women writers whose contributions are finally receiving significant critical recognition. In fact, according to the version of events in Barcelona offered by Pilar Serrano, Donoso's wife, García Márquez would openly declare his scorn of "intellectual women," as would Vargas Llosa, who actually reproached Serrano for encouraging his wife, Patricia Llosa, to take Italian classes, a sure way to ruin a marriage.[5] And yet, throughout the "boom" years of the sixties, women writers were producing some extremely good literature, as they had been doing in Latin America long before the international acclaim of García Márquez and colleagues; certainly, the literary activity of women in Latin America has become readily visible in the post-boom years. The phenomenon called the "boom" must be viewed as a privileging of the mainstream, the masculine, the universal, and the commercial: this is not to detract at all from the quality of the writers, but to recognize that all literary history is a hierarchical prioritization. In order for those Latin American writers to gain worldwide prominence, they themselves had to displace the regionalists, the traditionalists, the poets, and often had to fill a prevailing culture void. In my own brief survey, I seem most likely to privilege the public forms of writing over the domestic; the technically innovative works over the traditional; the universal themes over the culturally specific; the *criollo* over the native indian, the black, or the mulatto, especially in light of the categorical classifications to which I (regretfully) must appear to subscribe.

Even in this "official" literary history to which I allude, however, it should now be abundantly clear that the place of women writers can no longer be relegated to the sidelines. The sheer numbers alone of Latin American women writers who have been creating outstanding fiction in the sixties, seventies, and eighties would seem to command attention, but neither the quantity nor the quality factor has ever been sufficient to view women's writing in its due critical context. It is the advent of feminist literary criticism that has taught us another way of looking, and it is no exaggeration to say that literary history is being rewritten in light of the critical methodologies imparted by feminism. In fact, the emergence of women's literature in Latin America has led one critic to claim that women may well form the next "boom": "Representing a collective voice not as yet adequately heard from, the women writers of Latin America have given a tremendous injection of energy and vitality to the system of what is already one of the most active, daring, and imaginative bodies of literature in the Western tradition."[6] And if anything characterizes "feminine" narrative, it is the *lack* of homogeneity; in its place is the radical assertion of individuality, the refusal to belong to a category. Jean Franco believes that the negation of feminine writing as such on the part of many Latin American authors is a rejection of the pigeonholing that the history of literature performs on women writers, isolating them in a parenthetical aside.[7] Be that as it may, there is no doubt that Latin American women may make claim to a "literature of their own," one that is often forged in isolation and in rebellion.

It is remarkable that during the "boom" years, one of Latin America's best fiction writers was going virtually unnoticed on the international level: Brazil's Clarice Lispector, whose writing reflects the French *nouveau roman* and existentialist philosophy. Lispector focuses attention on the key role language plays in our sense of reality and identity, a concern shared by most of the new novelists of Latin America. An equally vital narrative voice that made itself heard in the sixties belongs to Mexican Elena Garro, creator of hallucinatory, linguistically ambiguous textual worlds akin to Donoso's and Lispector's; Garro's explorations of the psychological relations between men and women give rise to haunting narratives of singular literary force. Also making her mark in the sixties is Carmen Naranjo of Costa Rica, whose recent *Diary of a Multitude* (*Diario de una multitud*) analyzes a society controlled by technological progress. Argentina has given us a number of outstanding women fiction writers, including Silvina Bullrich, Beatriz Guido, Marta Lynch, and Liliana Heker, to single out a few. A separate mention must be made of Luisa Valenzuela, one of the better-known Latin American writers in this country: Valenzuela's fiction manages to subvert the predominant masculine discourse with irony, humor, and with language once particular to the male domain, especially the infamous *palabrotas* ("dirty words").[8] Valenzuela, like other women writers in recent years, has treated political themes in her works, proving definitively that the public and domestic roles of women are not irreconcilable, something forcefully demonstrated in Argentina by the Mothers and Grandmothers of the Plaza de Mayo. In

Strange Things Happen Here (*Aquí pasan cosas raras*, 1975) she calls
attention to the "dirty war" in Argentina through a variety of narrative
strategies, including ambiguity and black humor. Chilean Isabel
Allende has also achieved prominence in recent years with three
novels that fuse magical realism and political engagement: in Allende's
fiction, women characters take an active role in shaping the destiny
of their country through involvement in opposition movements and
through writing itself.

One of the most original women writers of our times is Ana Lydia
Vega, who "writes" Puerto Rico with her exceptionally vital prose in
the tradition of compatriot Luis Rafael Sánchez and Cuban Guillermo
Cabrera Infante. Like these two authors, Vega attempts to create her
own language based on popular speech: the result is a bilingual,
multicultural idiom that can only be called "puertorriqueño."[9] This is
not to say, however, that only those immersed in Puerto Rican culture
will find Vega's works accessible. Her "Story of Rice and Beans"
("Historia de Arroz con Habichuelas"), for example, is a culinary
allegory of the conquests that Puerto Rico has undergone: arroz and
habichuelas, the eternal enemies, finally band together after almost
four centuries of bellicose coexistence when their plate is invaded by
that skinny sausage from the North, Místel Japi Jordó ("Mister Happy
Hot Dog"). In "Words for a Salsa" ("Letra para salsa y tres soneos por
encargo"), Vega creates a hillarious sketch of the boy-picks-up-girl
cliché by distancing the popular street language with an ironic viewpoint and a multichoice ending. Like Valenzuela, Ana Lydia Vega
creates an individualistic literary language for purposes that go well
beyond facile amusement: Vega shows herself to be a perceptive interpreter of the social and political dynamics not only of her native land
but of neighboring cultures as well, which leads one critic to admire
her "Caribbean consciousness."[10] The title story of *Encancaranublado*,
for example, dramatizes the plight of three refugees, a Dominican, a
Haitian, and a Cuban, as they attempt to make their way to Miami in
a leaky boat, only to be rescued by a U.S. Navy ship where they are
thrown below deck with the Puerto Rican sailors. Vega has infused
Puerto Rican literature with a self-conscious dose of humor, irony, and
popular culture, and in so doing has deconstructed traditional narrative models. Her writing certainly contributes to the growing body of
a Puerto Rican "literature of [its] own," and is "new" narrative in every
sense of the word.

Even though her writing has been interpreted as feminist doctrine, Ana Lydia Vega continually implores critics and readers to avoid
approaching works by women writers as a literature that is exclusively gender-specific or overly inscribed with the mark of the

feminine.[11] As we have seen, she does not stand alone in this insistence. Vega's compatriot Rosario Ferré, also a distinguished fiction writer, makes similar observations to the ones formulated by other women writers of Latin America: "Sospecho que no existe una escritura femenina diferente a la de los hombres. Insistir en que sí existe implicaría paralelamente la existencia de una naturaleza femenina, distinta a la masculina, cuando lo más lógico me parece insistir en la existencia de una *experiencia* radicalmente diferente." ("I suspect that a feminine writing that is different from writing by men does not exist. To insist that it does would correspondingly imply the existence of a feminine nature, different from the masculine, when it seems more logical to me to insist on the existence of an *experience* that is radically different.")[12] To reject the category of "women's literature" is on the one hand to refuse the "tokenization" that Vega and others so rightly deplore, but on the other hand it is also to shun the political and literary traditions within feminism that have created and sustained a central place, and not a marginal position, for women writers. To enter into the mainstream, Latin American women writers have undertaken a long crosscurrent journey, one that is far from complete, as most "histories of literature" readily demonstrate. And yet, Vega is perhaps right: when the literary history of modern Puerto Rico is sketched out, works like hers should not be viewed as a "feminine aside," but rather should be considered side by side, and within the same tradition, with those of her contemporaries, both male and female, such as Edgardo Rodríguez Juliá, Manuel Ramos Otero, Mayra Montero, and Juan Antonio Ramos.

There are two other major currents in contemporary Latin American prose that deserve mention in this summary: one is Afro-Hispanic narrative, and the other is the documentary novel or testimonial literature.[13] In fact, these two groupings often share textual and societal bases, since works that give testimony to the realities of Latin America quite often deal with the experience of blacks. Such is the case of Cuban Miguel Barnet's *Autobiography of a Runaway Slave* (translated title of *Biografía de un cimarrón*, 1966), a collaboration between a former slave, Esteban Montejo, who was not able to write, and the ethnographer, Barnet, who shaped Montejo's oral testimony into a novelistic version of the old man's life. Nelson Estupiñán Bass depicts the realities of his native province of Esmeraldas, Ecuador, in his historical novel, *When the Guayacans Were in Bloom* (*Cuando los guayacanes florecían*, 1954). Estupiñán has written a series of novels that treat the question of Afro-Ecuadorian peoples, including the well-known *The Last River* (*El último río*, 1966). Another Ecuadorian to give forceful definition to black characters is Adalberto Ortiz in his novel

Juyungo (1943). In Venezuela, Ramón Díaz Sánchez takes relations between the races as a point of departure in his *Cumboto* (1950), and proposes several theoretical approaches to the issue of racial amalgamation, some of them quite disturbing. There have been numerous other manifestations of the Afro–Latin American theme in modern literature, including investigative works like those by Cuban Lydia Cabrera, who has collected and analyzed tales of African lore.

Latin American documentary literature has been widely cultivated in recent decades, and has achieved international attention in a manner not entirely different from the recognition accorded to the early novels of the "boom": that is, many of these testimonial works first commanded interest outside their respective countries of origin, where they may not even be known. This material aspect of distribution naturally is an outgrowth of the political situations that gave rise to the testimony in the first place. Of particular importance is the testimonial work from Guatemala, *I, Rigoberta Menchú* (*Me llamo Rigoberta Menchú y así me nació la conciencia*, 1983), a stunning fusion of political denunciation and ethnographic documentation written by Elisabeth Burgos, who spent many days interviewing the young Guatemalan woman. Menchú's work therefore not only reveals in chilling detail the horrors of military repression in Guatemala, but also recounts in poignantly lyric fashion the centuries-old story of the descendants of the Mayans in the highland region of that country. I have mentioned Luisa Valenzuela's literary treatment of the "dirty war" in Argentina: there are also nonfictional testimonies of great value, such as Jacobo Timerman's *Prisoner without a Name, Cell without a Number* (*Preso sin nombre, celda sin número*, 1980), and Alicia Partnoy's *The Little School: Tales of Disappearance and Survival in Argentina* (1986). One of the cornerstone testimonial works of contemporary Latin America is the highly acclaimed *Massacre in Mexico* (*Noche de Tlatelolco*, 1971), now past its fortieth edition. Author Elena Poniatowska includes material gathered from witnesses to the 1968 tragic massacre of students in the Plaza de las Tres Culturas in this classic book that has influenced both fiction writing as well as other works in the testimonial genre. Poniatowska cultivates the documentary novel in her *Until I See You My Jesus* (*Hasta no verte Jesús mío*, 1969), based on conversations with an elderly peasant woman who was able to recall the Mexican Revolution. Other vital manifestations of testimonial narrative may be found in postrevolutionary Nicaragua and Cuba; in the "narrative of the coup" in Chile; in the Uruguayan literature of the *proceso*; in rebel fighters' testimony in El Salvador and Guatemala; and in a variety of documentary writings about matters such as working life, like Domitila Barrios de Chungara's *Let Me*

Speak! ("Si me permiten hablar . . . ": Testimonio de Domitila, una mujer de las minas de Bolivia, written with Moema Viezzer, 1976), one woman's story of the deplorable exploitation of workers in Bolivian tin mines, or those about political life, including the writings of Fidel Castro and Eva Perón, to cite two disparate examples.

It certainly would be possible to round out my schematic overview of contemporary Latin American literature with mention of the dozens of other significant authors whom I have omitted here. Rather than name those who belong on that long list, however, I have chosen instead to point to what I see as the signs along the way. One sign of the times during the decade of the 1980s is the death of a trio of key figures in the "new" Latin American narrative: Julio Cortázar, Juan Rulfo, and Jorge Luis Borges, often considered the father of the "boom." As for the public recognition that Latin American women writers have recently enjoyed, a visible signal may be the ubiquitous paperback, *The House of Spirits (La casa de los espíritus),* Isabel Allende's highly regarded first novel, in English translation. The cover of this book depicts a wide-eyed flowing-haired young girl misleadingly emblematic of the gothic romance protagonist: those who buy *The House of Spirits,* then, may be in for a surprise of the type experienced by readers of Umberto Eco's *The Name of the Rose,* who unsuspectingly mistook the erudite tome for a simple mystery story. I find it noteworthy that Allende's novel, influenced as it is by García Márquez's *One Hundred Years of Solitude,* should be following in the wake of the great Colombian author's masterpiece some twenty years later. Perhaps, to borrow from the title of a novel by Elena Garro, this is a "recollection of things to come," and we are indeed hearing the first sounds of another "boom": if this is the case, our ears certainly have been well-tuned by generations of women writers who have established themselves firmly in the mainstream.

CHAPTER 9

To Write or Not to Write?*

ANA LYDIA VEGA

My first true encounter with Puerto Rican literature occurred in the middle of the 1960s. Until that time, national texts were nothing more than obligatory bores, grumblingly choked down in school. But one fine day, as it goes in fairy tales, my aunt from Arroyo, whom we affectionately called "The Witch" because of her frequent communications with the Great Beyond, left a novel behind in the living room of our house: its torn cover bore the exotic name of *Usmaíl*. The author was Pedro Juan Soto, one of our now-classic narrators, who would later play an important role in my life. As an avid reader of suspense and terror novels, I seized *Usmaíl* with the hope of finding in it a good dose of blood and guts. *Usmaíl* did not let me down. Blood and guts certainly were not missing in that Puerto Rican "Derecho de nacer," a kind of politicized soap opera that thrust me head first into the great national well of the so-called "identity crisis." And so I came to suspect that not everything was well on the Island of Enchantment and that the world did not end at those unsoiled walls of the Catholic school, where each day on the patio I had to sing the inevitable "Oh say, can you see?"

I also remember that during that time of the "Pax Muñoz Marín," impassioned groups of students would hand Puerto Rican flags to René Marqués after each performance of his plays in the Tapia Theatre, to the shouts of "Viva Puerto Rico Libre!" ("Freedom for Puerto Rico!"). Writing for the theatre seemed to me then the most fascinating of occupations. With my eyes moist from such a moving spectacle, I observed the tribute that the enthusiastic audience would

---

*Translated by Rosemary Geisdorfer Feal.

give to the author of *La carreta*, and the premature flutterings of a literary vocation tickled me in the solar plexus. But I was still quite far from assuming the weight of the patriotic tradition that constitutes the agony and the ecstasy of all Puerto Rican writers.

In Puerto Rico, as perhaps in many Latin American countries, the writer exercises a strange marginal leadership. Fairly unproductive in economic terms, the literary vocation carries with it, on the other hand, an almost heroic prestige. Heroic it is to follow that calling without any hope of remuneration, living as best one can from a job that only allows subsistence while, like an implacable vampire, it continues to suck away time and energy! The Puerto Rican writer, then, cannot "vivir del cuento,"[1] and it may be that this same economic desperation paradoxically gives strength to that voice that clamors in the desert. Without intending it – and because of their very existence – writers are the spiritual counterfigures of politicians. Their moral leadership, predicated in a purity mandated by the economic marginality of their occupation, stands in contrast to the opportunism of some of the so-called "public servants." Even if their books do not have a wide circulation, even if the editions, destined for a scanty readership, do not exceed three thousand copies, the word of Puerto Rican writers harbors an inherent moral weight that confers on them an epic halo, comparable to that of Eliot Ness in his Holy War against gangster corruption.

Honorable but hardly enviable, the situation of writers in our country! Their symbolic distinction permits them to indulge in a stunning ego-trip that is flimsy compensation for the financial limitations they endure. But, on the other hand, that very prestige of a warrior monk represents the biggest nail in the cross that they involuntarily bear. To be the "Conscience of the Unredeemed Homeland" and the "Messiah of Culture" is an impossible mission for any flesh-and-blood kid from next door. This quixotic task would exact a total absence of contradictions, a perfect synthesis of virtues, something like an exemplary life, as well as monolithic thought and permanent vigilance against the eternal rebellion of words, which is the equivalent of full-time self-censorship.

Fortunately, no one deliberately sets out to adopt such a difficult role: the magnitude of that project could easily lead to a permanent case of writer's block. Even so, the messianic vocation weighs at all times on the head and shoulders of the Puerto Rican writer. This tradition of writers as national therapists has been giving us "good examples" for more than a century now! From Manuel Alonso on, going by way of the "generación del '30" and the "generación del '50" and ending with the "generación del '70," our literature – and I say this without the least intention of detracting from its quality — constitutes an endless variation on the same musical theme: the symphony of national identity. For this reason, the trappings of social realism stalk us at each step. Our subconscious tyrannically dictates to us the poetic art of our "historical commitment." An imaginary *Manual for the Aspiring Puerto Rican Writer* could propose the following rules: (1) Show, at the least provocation, the most favorable profile possible of our "People-in-their-struggle; (2) Avoid mocking our (always threatened) National Values, whatever these may be; (3) Ensure that you write optimistic endings which will allow the dazzling splendor of the Grand Dawn of the People to be glimpsed — in short order, please; (4) Maintain at all costs a dignified and solemn tone that leaves no room for doubt as to the absolute seriousness of our noble intentions.

The law of Chemical Purity is in force! And, like the governors from the time of the Spanish rule, its powers are all-embracing.

This most complicated situation becomes even more entangled when the writer happens to be a woman.[2] It is not for nothing that Roland Barthes has called the woman writer "a notable zoological species." And if in addition she is Puerto Rican, then she defies all possible scientific classification. Yes, because in addition to Saving the Country, Affirming the Culture and Accelerating the Coming of the Revolution, done within the greatest possible limits of originality and orthodoxy, she is also required at every moment of her literary existence to denounce Vile Male Oppression, a somewhat risqué variant of the beloved Class Struggle. Because why, after all, are we women writers and not male writers? In this league there are equally inexorable canons of governance. Beware of the unequal distribution of textual roles! Do not dare even to suggest the moral weaknesses of our feminine heroines (and let the pleonasm stand)! Much less permit them vile public orgasms achieved through traditional biological means! Let the word villain always be a *he* so that in our creations the most positive and darings *she's* will abound![3] Even in literature the double duty pursues us.

Slight contradictions appear between one group of evangelical missions and the other. And what if machismo turned out to be one of those proclaimed National Values? And if your male characters are poor-Puerto Ricans-oppressed-by-imperialism but at the same time unrepentant oppressors of their poor-Puerto Rican women-oppressed-by-imperialism? Everything turns into a stew with self-censured ingredients, and the only one who will emerge from the mess is she who can dance to *salsa* in skates on the same tightrope that knocked down the Great Wallenda.

The reception of recent texts written by women has met with

singular good fortune in our country. Stories and novels by Rosario Ferré, Magali García, Carmen Lugo Filippi, and my own, have circulated abundantly in more than one edition, and have achieved a favorable reaction not only in our readers but also among critics. Inevitably, during our participation in innumerable forums and conferences, women readers have unloaded on us the fearsome role of marital counselors – some kind of Ann Landers of sin – demanding from us a liberationist theory and praxis for everyday life. Male readers, confusing life and text through "wishful thinking," ask us if what we narrate – especially the "sexiest" episodes of our stories – corresponds to autobiographic reality. This in turn forces us to reveal that we are married and have children so as to save ourselves from the malicious suspicions that accompany the publication of any text by women.

To make matters worse, critics torture us endlessly with the obsessive query: "Does there exist in your writing a language, a perspective, a discourse, that could be properly called feminine?" Not satisfied with their police interrogation, they go so far as to ask us to analyze the question ourselves with the utmost academic rigor, and to disclose in passing our deepest unconscious creative strategies.

From this latter *viacrucis*, male writers are of course exempt, as it would not occur to anyone to ask men to justify their presence in a panel discussion by learnedly expounding on what supposedly characterizes their writing. Why aren't erudite articles written about the literary repercussions of testosterone in the works of Borges or García Márquez? Why don't they hold international conferences to determine whether or not there is a preputial language in literature written by men? Why aren't men asked what they think about abortion, infidelity, incest, and abortion? Why, in sum, do they bother us so much with this blessed "feminine literature" when not one word is breathed about "masculine literature"?

This is a good moment to express a concern which, although it does not prevent me from sleeping at night, nevertheless raises my blood pressure from time to time. If it is true that there exists a basic inequality, that literature has generally been a man's occupation, thus making it necessary to add an *ess* to "poet" when she is a woman, then wouldn't it also follow true that the more we keep spinning that theoretical wheel of difference, the more we run the risk of reaffirming that inequality despite ourselves? Couldn't it be that the idea of presenting ourselves as women writers is one more trap set by that age-old polymorphous sexism? Won't this classification obsession finally lock us up once and for all in the uncomfortable closet of "tokenization," from which they will take us out each time they need a filler figure for the anthologies of the Feathered Phallocracy, or each time that some university out there holds one of those famous Conferences on Feminine Creativity? At times I ask myself if the obligation to be a feminist in one's writing does not correspond to the obligation to be "feminine" in daily life. Girls, play with your Barbie dolls and keep your knees together. Women Writers, speak out about your own things and write like women, if you still insist on writing.

So it is apparent, therefore, that it is no easy matter to exchange the feather duster for the feather pen. But neither is taking up the pen a bed of roses, even when one has never learned to use the duster. In our colonial society, men and women confront the great task of finding what the critics call one's "own voice," one's "own style." And in our literary tradition, tied as it is to politics, the individual and the collective become hopelessly intertwined, to the point where writing almost becomes a ritual act of reaffirming one's roots, of consolidating the ethnic and cultural bonds that make of us something more than a huddled mass of people on a small overpopulated Caribbean island.

Perhaps this explains the purist strain of hispanophilia that our literature sometimes displays in its adherence to a language that is experienced as the last refuge for our National Being. And it may also explain the search for a legitimate Puerto Rican vernacular that could be artistically transposed to the written page, an essential literary project for the most recent generations. These new writers feel that the battle of language, which so appropriately concerned our literary predecessors, has already been won, and that we no longer have to prove to anyone our right to Spanish. Therefore, we dare to play, to subvert, to desanctify, to mix English and Spanish, cultured slang and popular slang, clean and dirty words, thus multiplying through satire and parody the healthy irreverence that the great majority of writers from past generations denied themselves.

But the celebration of the word continues to be a magic act whose fundamental meaning has not changed from the ancestral times of *El Album Puertorriqueño.*[4] The patriotic obsession with Puerto Rican literature, and its self-imposed didactic nature, has not prevented writers from seeking out and finding techniques of considerable quality. On the contrary, the problem of the historical evolution of the country constitutes a kind of cornerstone on which artistic projects are built. And in this respect, Puerto Rican literature relates to the literature of Martinique, Guadeloupe, Quebec, and so many other countries still awaiting their political definition. How can we find the ultimate metaphor to reformulate the old problem of where we are headed and where we have come from; how, to use the image of the poet José Luis Vega, can we face ourselves in the mirror in such a way that it does not excessively deform the image that it reflects back: this is the dilemma. But now political and social conflicts manifest themselves in our literature as questions of form. The content, much to our relief, is starting to be assumed, thus allowing more liberty for true artistic expression. As we write better, we reaffirm our culture – without intending to do so – and, in some sense, we save "La Patria."

Raymond Chandler, one of the North American writers whom I admire most, has said some things that have impressed me deeply concerning the writer's vocation. He has said: "No writer ever wrote exactly what he wanted to write because there was never anything inside himself, anything purely individual that he did want to write." And he wisely concludes: "It's all reaction of one sort or another."

Making more of Chandler's words, I wish to emphasize that all literature is a reaction to the initial state of things, to an original dissatisfaction. In order to write, to create art, one must start from the premise that life is not complete and that the world is not perfect, that there are still things to be done, agendas to carry out. And returning to Chandler to complete this train of thought I am pursuing: "It doesn't matter a damn what a novel is about: the only fiction of any value in any age is the one which does magic with words . . . and the subject matter is merely the springboard for the writer's imagination."

Puerto Rican literature, like all literature on this planet, has as its point of departure the reality that engenders it. There is no escaping this, even if one attempts to do so. But one must attempt it, because evasion is one of the essential driving forces behind the literary endeavor. Because reality will be there in any case, astutely lurking like a traitor behind all our fantasies. And what I narrate, in the final instance, is what remains on the paper in that constant running back and forth between the pole of reality and the pole of the ideal that characterizes artistic gestation. What matters is the word, prime material of our actions, and the magic that the word unleashes. From our obsessions, from our discontents, from our shortcomings, we attempt to perform magic, to transform the ugly into something beautiful, to transmit through the porous paper the slippery nature of our perceptions, the burning pulsation of our emotions. And this magic, when shared, is reproduced in and by the reader, forging between both energy flows that privileged moment of convergence which we call "The Work."

I have tried to give a general idea of the internal and external forces that shape what it is to be a writer, a woman writer in Puerto Rico. But I do not wish to leave the impression that this is a thankless job, a titanic or Sisyphean one, or an abysmal suffering that turns us into eternally tortured souls. We must try to perform the job with love, and, above all, with humor. It is a matter of survival and of transmitting strength and *joie de vivre* to our readers. There is a good deal of pleasure, of enjoyment, of sensuality in literary creation when it is faced without false illusions, without messianic pretentions, but quite simply as one more human activity, perhaps the most human of all.

CHAPTER 10

An Overview of Contemporary Latin American Theater

TERESA CAJIAO SALAS AND MARGARITA VARGAS

To provide an all-encompassing and complete survey of contemporary Latin American theater is a difficult and ambitious task. Nevertheless, our project, which by no means pretends to be exhaustive, aspires to review the unifying forces in the dramatic production of the continent. The present image of Latin American theater, which began to take shape in the early 1950s, is characterized by its richness and multiplicity. The avenues being explored by our dramatists in this process of growth and development exhibit considerable similarities, showing only temporal variants in accordance with their individual theatrical traditions. The similarities in the work of theatrical groups and among individual playwrights are better understood in light of the elements to be discussed in this chapter: the work and influence of independent and popular theatrical groups, including children's theater; the proliferation of festivals and specialized journals; the emergence of a greater number of organizations dedicated to the stimulating of theater itself as well as theatrical research; prevalent themes; other generating sources of theatrical creation; and theater written in exile.

The first expression of the independent theatrical movement began as early as 1928 with the Teatro Ulises in Mexico and was followed in the 1930s by the Teatro Cueva in Cuba and Teatro del Pueblo in Argentina. During the 1940s the theatrical activity of these groups diminishes greatly, but Latin America experienced an upsurge of independent groups in the 1950s. These groups needed both to experiment and to reach the populace, two goals that did not conform to the demands of commercial theater. The groups wanted to produce a national theater concerned with the socioeconomic conditions of the different Latin American countries. Combined with the original desire to experiment, as was the case with Teatro Ulises, the theater of the last three decades manifests a profound sociopolitical commitment.

The number of independent groups has increased tremendously in the last few years, and even though we shall not attempt to name them all, we would like at least to highlight the most prominent ones. Two groups that have distinguished themselves internationally are the ICTUS of Chile, and the Teatro Experimental de Cali of Colombia. Others worth mentioning are the Aleph of Chile, La Candelaria of Colombia, the Teatro Escambray of Cuba, the Mexican group Mascarones, the Teatro Campesino and the Teatro de la Esperanza of California, the Arena of Brazil, El Galpón of Uruguay, and the Libre Teatro Libre of Argentina. Basically, all the groups share a common ideology; they want their own national identity and a society free of cultural, economic, and political dependence from the United States.[1] In order to achieve these goals, the groups perform either plays written by well-known dramatists or works that are the product of "collective creation." When using the latter, the members not only exchange amongst themselves the various roles required of a dramatic production, but at times they invite the public to participate in the creation of their plays. This contact wth the public and the use of collective collaboration leaves the play open for change and makes it suitable to any sociopolitical situation that may arise wherever they perform.

Because of their commitment to the masses, the members generally stage their plays in the most far-away places and usually out in the open. Members of the ICTUS, for example, have helped laborers and farmers form theatrical groups by giving them technical assistance as well as acting lessons and by teaching them how to produce plays. The ICTUS has also reached the masses through television. In 1969 the Chilean national channel invited them to stage some of their most successful plays and to set up a weekly program.[2] It is curious to note the paradox involved in reaching out for the masses via communicative means owned by the government. It seems to us that accepting money from institutions would imply a loss of autonomy. Some groups have tried to solve their economic problems by holding jobs not related to the theater. They end up working for the establishment, but at least there is no direct link between their vocation and what they do for a living.

However, there are a few groups whose job duties become the subject of their plays; such a group is the Ambulantes de Puebla. It is composed of street vendors who re-enact scenes based on their own experiences. Their costumes are the clothes they wear every day and their props are the stands or carts from which they sell their fruits and vegetables on the streets. The plays they perform consist of their daily confrontations with the police as well as established businessmen who pay rent and taxes and do not want freeloaders taking away their customers.[3] Unlike other groups, whose concerns are more international in scope, the targets of their criticism are not foreign imperialists, but the local forces in power. Their struggle is a more immediate one; they are fighting merely to subsist.

Beside their social contribution, several groups have provided Latin American letters with important literary figures. From ICTUS emerged Jorge Díaz; from Fray Mocho, Osvaldo Dragún; and from Teatro Experimental de Cali, Enrique Buenaventura. However, this achievement in itself has created internal problems, because achieving success in the world of letters implies selling yourself to the establishment. Some groups, for example, have agreed to exclude from their repertoire the plays written by Jorge Díaz. Authors of the stature of Mario Vargas Llosa have also been disowned by the more radical groups.[4]

Even though all the groups situate their plays within a reality true to their own lives, it is impossible to escape foreign literary influences, and these influences are manifested in the theatrical techniques they incorporate in their works. Prevailing influences include Brecht's epic theater, the theater of the absurd, Artaud's postulates, as well as Stanislavsky's methods and Grotowski's techniques.

As part of the independent groups and as a consequence of their didactic goals there has been an intensification of children's theater, especially in Cuba, Peru, Argentina, Brazil, Venezuela, and Mexico. Emilio Carballido has written several children's plays; recently he also edited an anthology entitled *Jardín con animales*.

In addition to the significance of independent theatrical groups, the appearance of organizations devoted to the stimulus of theater, the proliferation of festivals and journals, and the increase in the number of women playwrights have all contributed to the development of Latin American theater.

One of the major organizations involved in the promotion of theater has been Casa de las Américas, an institution created since the Cuban Revolution to stimulate all cultural endeavors. Its theater section has sponsored the publication of the influential journal *Conjunto* and is considered the founding force of the Latin American theater festivals. The CELCIT from Venezuela and the INBA from Mexico have also played leading roles in the expansion of theater, the former at the continental and the latter at the national level.

At the initiative of or in conjunction with these organizations, theater festivals have been held throughout Latin America. The first festival took place in Havana in 1961 and it was "presented by Cuban companies for Cuban audiences."[5] It did not become international in scope until 1964. The Manizales Festival, held in Colombia in 1968 set the pattern for future festivals. The festival started out as gatherings for university theatrical groups, but after 1971 this was changed to include many other independent groups. According to Gerardo Luzuriaga, "these events have become a unifying force among noncommercial theater artists across national boundaries, a sounding board for new ideas and ideals that ultimately may transcend theater and art as such, and therefore become a nuisance to many a government."[6]

While the festivals have served as a forum for common intellectual discussions, constructive criticism, exchange of ideas, and methodologies; inevitably, factions have formed and dominant groups have come to reign. In 1972, at the festival in Quito, Ecuador, Enrique Buenaventura and his group Teatro Experimental de Cali were accused of being too dictatorial. The group Rajatabla from Venezuela withdrew from the festival and, in a newspaper article entitled "Down with the Buenaventura Myth," the members of the group explained that they did not want to be "accomplices to a deceitful situation of Latin American fraternity which attempts to hide the demoralization felt by most of the groups that partake in this type of contests."[7] Even though no prizes were awarded for the best performances, they still considered the festival competitive and unfair because everything was measured by the standards established by the Teatro Experimental de Cali.[8]

The fourth Manizales Festival held in 1971 also faced harsh criticism; a university group from Bogotá staged a parody of the festival and then read a manifesto accusing it of being "colonialist and oligarchic," of promoting "foreign cultures," and of using "leftist rhetoric and Latin American apparel" but still being "a mere spokesman of oppression and dependence."[9] It is unfortunate that in spite of the good intentions with which events are organized, factions form and dissensions occur. Part of the problem is that once a group distinguishes itself from the rest, or receives international recognition, it is no longer considered an underdog fighting for freedom from oppression; instead it is seen as one of the oppressors.

However, according to Spanish critic José Monleón, dramatic changes have taken place in the last four years. He perceived the 1984 Manizales Festival (which had been interrupted for eleven years) as being more festive and relaxed in comparison to the previous one, which he termed "compulsive, dominated by radical confrontations."[10] Perhaps its more relaxed atmosphere was due to the numerous street performances and to the fact that two dominant groups were not present, La Candelaria and the Teatro Experimental de Cali. Another noticeable change is the fact that Colombian theater has separated into two main entities: the groups that are associated with Colcultura and those that belong to the Corporación Colombiana de Teatro.

Eduardo Gómez, a member of the Consejo Nacional de Teatro, considers the Corporación as nationalistic and sees Colcultura as an open group that welcomes pluralism and free experimentation within the theater. From an objective perspective, José Monleón questions Gómez's viewpoint by explaining that the Corporación expresses the same willingness to establish an open dialogue, the same respect toward pluralism and a similar concern for aesthetics.[11] Despite the fact that the groups no longer have distinct political tendencies, personal as well as financial problems continue to separate them.

We do not want to give the impression that there is only one festival in Latin America, but because Colombia popularized the concept of "collective creation" and was one of the first to host international festivals, it is considered a landmark in the theatrical field. Other countries that have also sponsored similar festivals are Mexico, Argentina, and Paraguay. The festival held in Mexico City in 1974 was crucial to the Chicano groups because it forced them to examine their identity. They realized how different they were from the Mexicans and consequently to what extent they were a distinct product of two cultures.[12] Other important Latin American festivals have been held in Venezuela, Spain, New York and Montreal.

Unlike the festivals, which provide a forum specifically for the participants, journals have access to theatrical information from all over the world. Journals function both as research tools and as places where critics and playwrights can contribute to the expansion of drama. Among the most respected journals one finds *Tramoya*, *Latin American Theatre Review*, *Primer Acto*, and *Conjunto* in the lead. Other noted reviews include *Tablas*, *Boletín del Instituto del Teatro*, *Intermedio*, *Boletín del Centro de Investigaciones Rodolfo Usigli*, and *Escena*. The majority of these journals publish new plays, critical essays, information about festivals, international events, and plays currently being performed. Some also offer specialized bibliographies, a record of the activities of the different theatrical groups, and reviews of new plays and critical studies. The existence of these journals has proven invaluable for the dissemination of information crucial to the study of Latin American theater.

The significant increase of women devoted to playwrighting and the excellent quality of their work have also contributed enormously to this thriving period in Latin American theater. In countries like Mexico, Argentina, Venezuela, Puerto Rico, and Chile we could cite the names of several women playwrights whose plays have received national and continental acclaim. In certain instances, as is the case of Griselda Gambaro, Isidora Aguirre, Elena Garro, Luisa Josefina Hernández, and Mariela Romero, women have also achieved international fame.

The theater, which has flourished in all four corners of Latin America, also manifests a great thematic multiplicity. Without wanting to sound simplistic, we shall provide a general overview of the thematic constants of contemporary Latin American theater. Along with the themes that reflect the human conflicts of universal projection, such as alienation, existential anguish, and solitude, one finds themes that stand out as inevitable consequences of the tumultuous political, social, and economic problems. Dictatorships and the abuse of power are unavoidable themes in many theatrical creations;[13] plays like Enrique Buenaventura's *Opera bufa* and Ricardo Monti's *El señor Magnus y sus hijos* about dictatorships in the Caribbean, are classic examples. There are also numerous works structured around the topic of violence, while the themes of torture, oppression, exile, the loss of freedom and identity, rebellion, and social injustice compose myriads of plays that reflect upon the Latin American reality.

Even though the treatment of historical themes has a long tradition, it has become predominant in the theater only during the last few years of this decade. The list of works we could mention to illustrate this thematic constant is too long to enumerate, therefore we shall limit ourselves to a few representative titles. To prove the ever-growing interest in historical themes, it should suffice to mention José Luis Rial's *Bolívar*, the play brought to New York's Festival Latino in 1986 by the Venezuelan group Rajatabla, or one of Sergio Arrau's most recent theatrical productions, *Digo que norte sur corre la tierra*, subtitled *Lautaro y el conquistador*.[14]

The lucid article, "Teatro e historia," written by the Colombian playwright Carlos José Reyes explains the reasons for this predominance:

> Theater and history unite and separate in an endless game. Certain historical times tend to relive past events, because as is with a metaphor in spiral by reevaluating the past one can throw a new light on present developments. . . . If today we renew our interest in the historical themes of a given moment, it is because, beyond the plot, the mythical substance takes us back to the past.[15]

To his voice one would have to add Ana Seoane's who, in her review of the 1984 First Latin American Festival of Córdoba, Argentina, states that

> all of Latin America seems to coincide in this search for a genre that not only entertains the most varied public, but that also informs him and forces him to judge history. In one way or another, theater people have agreed on a silent plan of commitment with the past that will result in a better future.[16]

In addition to historical themes, at present there is a tendency to utilize the textual richness of narrative works as a source of dramatic creativity.[17] Some recent examples include El Local's collective creation of Gabriel García Márquez's "La increíble y triste historia de la cándida Eréndira y su abuela desalmada"; 7 veces Eva by Beatriz Seibel, based on texts by four Argentinian novelists; and the ICTUS's collective creation of *Primavera con una esquina rota*, a novel by Mario Benedetti.[18]

The political avatars in Latin America, marked by violence and its horrible charge of repression and censorship, have resulted in the exile, forced or voluntary, of many theater people. Never before has there been "a greater contingent of Latin American political exiles."[19] This historical episode has given way to a "theater of exile" that branches into two different areas of activity: the creation of plays whose themes reflect on its painful conditions – including the dilemma of the return – and the work of theater groups living abroad. To illustrate briefly the problematics of this theater, one should consider the plays *Por la razón o la fuerza* and *Regreso sin causa*, by the young and promising Chilean playwright, Jaime Miranda, and the already mentioned *Primavera con una esquina rota*.[20] Among the theater groups in exile the Teatro Latinoamericano Sandino – formed in Sweden by Chilean, Uruguayan, and Ecuadorian exiles – is one of the most prominent, having contributed to a greater exposure of Latin American theater in Europe. Another example, among many others, is Teatro Lautaro, organized by Chileans exiled in Berlin, East Germany.[21]

It is also necessary to highlight the impact that the theatrical activities of the diaspora have had on the development of the theatre of other countries in the American continent, such as Venezuela and Costa Rica. Venezuela, a country that has taken a leading role in stimulating theater, received at this period the influence of exiles from the southernmost region of South America, independent groups, playwrights, directors, actors, and critics. Names that stand out are

Juan Carlos Gené and Andrés Lizárraga of Argentina; the Duvauchelle brothers, Lientur Carranza (actors), and Orlando Rodríguez, a renowned critic, all from Chile; and the actor Alberto Robinski of Uruguay. In the case of Costa Rica some important figures include the Argentinians Juan Enrique Acuña,[22] the Catania brothers and the Chilean members of the Teatro del Angel under the direction of Alejandro Sieveking.[23]

These theater people have transformed the negativity of exile into a positive force by making valuable contributions to the development of theater in their adopted countries. In Mexico, however, a country with a long theatrical tradition, the presence of Atahualpa del Cioppo and his group El Galpón de Montevideo, cannot be credited with bringing about dramatic changes. Nevertheless, their stay in Mexico will always serve as a reminder of their valuable contributions to continental theater.

Another aspect of the "theater of exile" is the work of playwrights and theater groups who have remained in their own countries in internal exile. They have explored ways to continue writing and producing in spite of repression and censorship. Clear examples of this variant are the works of the Chilean dramatists Marco Antonio de la Parra, Gustavo Meza, David Benavente, Gregorio Cohen, and Juan Radrigán, and the continued efforts of groups such as ICTUS, El Telón, and Imagen.

Within this complex overview of contemporary Latin American theater, the work of the Mexican playwright Emilio Carballido stands out as one of the most significant to its development. Carballido has addressed his efforts to all aspects of theatrical activity; he has not only contributed as a dramatist, but also as a director, critic, and teacher. Above all, he has been a leading figure in the formation of new generations of playwrights. Undoubtedly, he is the most prolific and important dramatist in Mexican theater today. His work has received wide international acclaim; several of his plays have been translated into other languages and have been staged in such countries as the United States, Cuba, Germany, and Russia.[24]

CHAPTER 11

Theater and Its Functions*

EMILIO CARBALLIDO

We are frequently asked, what is the purpose of art? This question is both practical and impertinent because, on the one hand, by denying the concept of art for art's sake and its lack of immediate usefulness, it throws a shadow of laziness and parasitism on the poor artist. On the other hand, socialist realism makes the problem worse by demanding from art a role of didactic proselytizing and immediate social enlightenment. Applying this assumption to dramatic art becomes somewhat pleonastic. Since early times, when theatrical ceremonies first appeared, we have been able to appreciate that ceremonies and representations have been instrumental in attracting the masses. This simple act fulfills a necessary function. We human beings, lonely and confined within ourselves, have found reasons to unite in a transcendental manner. In psychological terms, there is a fusion of beings the moment we are in a crowd: individual intelligence diminishes, emotions increase, and the individual assimilates. This is well known to organizers of political gatherings and we see it at work in labor meetings. Religious ceremonies and theater are the most transcendental forces of congregation we can find; the moment people come together, the elements of this fusion come to life.

The pursuit of enjoyment is always looked upon with distrust, morally as well as intellectually, while "a funny play" evokes frivolity, "a dense or weighty play" evokes seriousness, and people feel edified and transcended. Nothing could be more false. Weariness is not a quality, it is something that distances and separates. To entertain is to make the spectator multifarious; to assimilate him to that which is

---

*Translated by Teresa Cajiao Salas and Margarita Vargas.

diverse, different; to liberate his confined being so that he can identify with others and live in them. Together, the force of congregation and the act of entertainment lead to the third function of theater: to educate.

A work created in beauty and truth – which will unavoidably be found in an artistic work – will have the power to transform and to enlighten. It is not usual that plays cause immediate changes in the society to whom they are addressed. If any social and consciousness-raising changes are prompted by theatrical works, they will be indirect and take a long time to materialize.

Theater also exerts a collective function similar to that of dreams on the individual. Dreaming purifies us and gives us a source of communication with our inner selves. Theater is the dreaming of the community. Aristotle defined catharsis as the mixture of feelings that should be motivated by tragedy for it to have the social result of purification. But there is also farcical catharsis, in which the secret impulses of the spectator are performed on stage as in nightmares, or as in gratifying dreams. This provides the spectator with a comical disarrangement and through laughter he can cleanse his most inner turmoils. Interestingly, these forces of change that theater encompasses sometimes function with greater effect in theater. This is a rarity that deserves to be discussed.

At the most critical time of the Argentinian military dictatorship a group of theater people decided to practice their art. The official position was that theater was in decline and that consequently there were no Argentinian playwrights. The artists got together to perform during unconventional hours: at the end of the workers' day instead of the normal night schedule. They all assumed the various duties: stagehands, ticket office attendants, ushers, etc. Together, actors, playwrights, and directors presented a repertoire of new plays of medium length to be able to offer triple daily programs.

The public response was tremendous. The authors were not making political statements; nevertheless, it was a very potent and mysterious act of political complicity. The movement was called Teatro Abierto (Open Theater) and the echo of its name resounded all over the continent. In a week, a fire bomb was thrown in the theater and it burned down. Another producer came and gave the playwrights a new locale stating that it didn't matter if it were burned again. It was not destroyed, and the plays became more explicit in their denouncements and attacks. Then Cine Abierto (Open Cinema) appeared and many newspapers supporting the movement emerged. Now we can look back on them as one of the demolishing blows that toppled the military dictatorship. The force of congregation and the finding of a common identity were stronger than an explicit social message.

The prolific Chicano theater movement, created by Luis Valdez in the picket lines of the California fields, is another example of an immediate result of theater. It was with the work of these theatrical groups that the important reivindication of a forgotten racial and cultural minority in the United States was accomplished. Theater is very effective in restoring identity, in consolidating one's own values, and in giving people the necessary channels of communication among themselves. As became evident in the Chicano movement, identity is a powerful political force. Hence, all efforts of colonial domination are accompanied by publicity campaigns in the mass media in which the idea is to alter, erase, or modify people's identity.

In Mexico, theater has had a triple division in strata that dates back to the early days of its history. The priests who came during the colonial period found peoples for whom theater was an integral part of their lives; they had dramatic works which were used as entertainment or for didactic purposes, and their religion had grandiose theatrical ceremonies, too. From this situation emerged the colonial religious theater as well as the ties that unite our tradition with the European one. Nevertheless, the pre-Columbian dramatic ceremonial pattern, either for religious or secular reasons, was preserved independently in the memory of these peoples or in the codices that their elders kept in sacred vaults.

The first stratum is represented by a comic theater of an extremely vulgar and aggressive vein, vital and brazen, capable of absorbing any fad and readapting it to its own taste. This vaudeville-itinerant theater, performed in tents, does not touch either in form or in its staging style the other two strata: the European cultivated theater and the popular village theater performed by dancers in the public square.

At present, in the state of Tabasco, a new and extraordinarily original project has appeared. Its originality is due to the fact that it represents the most coveted link, the one that is capable of uniting the three strata of our tradition into a truly national and popular theater. María Alicia Martínez Medrano, the director of this project, went into a rural town in Tabasco located three hours by land from Villahermosa, the capital. There she trained actors and theater people using the Stanislavsky method. Her first work was taken from the universal repertoire, *Bodas de sangre* (*Blood Wedding*). In accordance with García Lorca's ideas, it was staged as a rural rite of love, machismo, and death, and it was performed with earthshaking strength by the country people. Other plays which have followed include, *La dama boba* (The Foolish Lady) by Elena Garro (homonymous to Lope de Vega's play);

Lilus Kikus, based on short stories by Elena Poniatowska; *El evangelio según San Mateo* (*The Gospel According to Saint Matthew*); and two works written by members of the group: *La tragedia del jaguar* (The Tragedy of the Jaguar) and *La bruja y el pueblo* (The Witch and the People). The spectacular ritual development, the participation of the whole town, of large groups of old and young from all social levels, make this theater a unique phenomenon and a great recovering of the best and unutilized force of our tradition. But above all, the most important achievement of the Laboratorio de Teatro Campesino (Rural Theater Laboratory), is a refined aesthetics that makes it the first national group with an original output that is unequivocally Mexican.

From theater's innate power to untie forces of emotion stems the skepticism with which some of us view the attempts to achieve a sociodidactic theater of immediate effect, which functions through reasoning. The Escambray theater in Cuba has found a curious formula: they concentrate their efforts in clarifying an immediate social problem; at the end of the play the public becomes an assembly and the emotions that the actors had untied are now channeled into discussions that lead to the adoption of new measures. This is another way of applying theater energy to the immediate modification of reality.

The strength of theater is undeniable; at present in Latin America, there exists a splendid flourishing of playwrights unrivaled in any other period of its history. In spite of the constant aggression that we, Latin Americans, suffer, and the attempt to exploit and dominate us, the force of our theater constitutes a sign of hope.

Literary Competitions,
Books, and Journals in the United States

Introduction

MIREYA CAMURATI

It is well known that the relationship between Latin America and the United States constitutes a fundamental theme in Latin American studies. This relationship has not escaped the attention of writers who attempt to interpret its meaning and its consequences. The list of authors who have reflected upon this theme is a long one, and includes some of the most important figures in Latin American literature. Among them the name of José Martí stands out. Martí was in an ideal position to know and understand North Americans. For fourteen years he lived and worked in New York, where he was a language teacher and contributor to several newspapers. At the time when he concentrated his efforts on the formation of the Cuban Revolutionary Party and the organizing of an expedition to liberate his homeland, Martí traveled to other cities of the United States, especially in Florida. His numerous articles about the places he visited and the people he encountered fill several volumes of his works. Among these writings are many exemplary pieces in which Martí displays his monumental prose. His essays on Emerson and Whitman, and his commentaries (in the style of chronicles) "The Charleston Earthquake" and "The Chinese in New York" belong in this category. Based on his observations and experiences, Martí recognizes a generous North America, with a tradition of liberty and respect for other nations, but also a North America ambitious for power and desirous of territorial expansion. This latter characteristic is the one that represents a threat to Hispanic America, or in the Cuban's words, "Our America." In an 1891 article using precisely this title, Martí identifies the basis of the problem and proposes a solution:

> The scorn of our formidable neighbor who does not know us is Our America's greatest danger. And since the day of the visit is near, it is imperative that our neighbor know us, and soon, so that it will not

147

scorn us. Through ignorance it might even come to lay hands on us. Once it does know us, it will remove its hands out of respect. One must have faith in the best in men and distrust the worst. One must allow the best to be shown so that it reveals and prevails over the worst. Nations should have a pillory for whoever stirs up useless hates, and another for whoever fails to tell them the truth in time.[1]

Martí's words, written almost a century ago, continue to be valid today and provide the rationale for this section. Its purpose is to consider some of the activities related to the field of literature that contribute to a better understanding between the Americas.

First, Joaquín Roy presents a study of the literary competition *Letras de Oro*. In spite of its recent inception, this contest for works written in Spanish in the United States has achieved considerable success, both in the quantity and the quality of the participants and in the repercussions in the media here and abroad.

Professor Roy's comments are followed by the presentation of Hiber Conteris, the Uruguayan author and winner of the 1986–87 *Letras de Oro* in the short-story category for his collection, *Información sobre la ruta 1*.

The second area of consideration is Hispanic books in the Library of Congress: 1815–1965. Georgette M. Dorn, head of the Hispanic Reading Room of the Library of Congress and curator of the Hispanic Archive, provides a historical overview of this topic. Vincent Peloso, Howard University, adds his comments to Dr. Dorn's paper.

Finally, the discussion of Inter-American journals is presented by Celso Rodríguez, a historian and editor of the *Inter-American Review of Bibliography*, a publication of the Organization of American States. Ian I. Smart, of Howard University, complements this subject with an account of his experiences as co-founder and editor of the *Afro-Hispanic Review*, a journal unique in this field of literature.

That this section is limited to literary competitions, books, and journals that contribute to better understanding between the Americas does not ignore the value of other equally significant endeavors. Examples of these would be the very popular "literary workshops," or, moving into the field of the arts, the study of films and folk songs. These and other areas can become the subjects for future encounters of scholars who, in the tradition of Martí, work toward clarifying the nature of Inter-American relations.

CHAPTER 12

Writing in Spanish in the United States[1]

JOAQUÍN ROY

Hispanics who write literary works in Spanish in the United States form a female–male ratio of 2 to 3. Twenty-eight percent are between 40 and 50 years of age, but 10 percent are younger than 30, and another 10 percent are older than 70. Half write poetry, 20 percent cultivate the novel, 20 percent the short story, and 10 percent other genres. More than a third are teachers and professors. Florida, California, New York, New Jersey, Texas, Massachusetts, Pennsylvania, and Puerto Rico are the most frequent places of residency. The principal countries of origin are, in this order, Cuba, Colombia, Spain, Argentina, Mexico, Chile, and Puerto Rico.

This study is a profile of the Spanish writer in the United States, according to data provided by the first two years of operation of the literary contest Letras de Oro, established by the University of Miami in 1986.[2] The 371 contestants of 1987–88 confirmed the positive reception of 1986–87 (366 entries). Two surveys[3] (with a response level above one third (252 out of 737 contestants) offer interesting dimensions unknown until now.

Hispanics in the United States

The increase of the Hispanic population since 1970 has been spectacular: 61 percent from 9.1 to 14.6 million, as compared with only 8 percent of the total U.S. population, which increased from 203 to 226 million. Table 12.1 shows that total Hispanic population reached almost 17 million in 1985. It is estimated that in the year 2000 the Hispanic population will reach 23–27 million.[4] The United States is

149

now the fifth-largest "Hispanic country" in the world. Bibliography in this field has expanded considerably.[5]

TABLE 12.1
The Hispanic Population in the United States

Total U.S. population in 1985	234,066,000	100%
Total "Spanish-Origin" Population in the United States in 1985	16,940,000	7.2%

Source: Current Population Survey.

The majority of these 14 million identified in the 1980[6] census are of Mexican origin; in the 1985 census there were 10 million, and 60 percent of the total Hispanic population. Puerto Ricans constitute the second Hispanic subsector (29 percent, if statistics include both the island population and the continental residents); the 1985 census counted 2.5 million. Cubans, living mainly in Miami, New York, and a few other urban centers, are the third-largest Hispanic group; the majority are first- or second-generation political exiles that fled to the United States after the Cuban Revolution in 1959.

Hispanics are younger than the general U.S. population: The Hispanic household has a median age of 38.7, in contrast with 45.8 for the U.S. population. While the 1970 census listed 19.9 percent of the U.S. population as foreign-born Hispanics, in 1980 it was 28.6 percent. However, it is estimated that in the 1990 census only 25 percent of the increase in Hispanic population will be caused by immigration. Birth rate is high; Chicano women will have an average of 3 children, in contrast with black women's 2.4, and non-Hispanic whites 1.7. Hispanic families are also larger than the average U.S. family (3.92 members, as compared to 3.16).

In spite of the fact that many Hispanic immigrants come from rural areas, they tend to cluster in large cities in the United States: while 66 percent of Americans live in large urban populations, 83 percent of Hispanics do, with the resulting overcrowding, housing problems, and lack of education and health services.

The economic picture is rather bleak. Median income for U.S. families in 1980 was $23,430; Hispanic families only received $16,230.[7] While 12 percent of U.S. families were under the poverty level (less than $9,866), 16 percent of Hispanic families were legally poor. The 1985 census confirmed this negative profile: median U.S. income was $27,000, while Hispanics received only $18,880. While 31.8 percent of all individual U.S. workers earn less than $20,000 per year, 50 percent of Hispanics fall in this category; 20 percent of

Americans earn more than $50,000; only 2 percent of Hispanics earn as much.

Discrimination and linguistic obstacles are among the reasons for the discrepancy in income, but education is the main cause for the difference. Sixty-five percent of Hispanics beween 25 and 29 years of age have finished high school; 81 percent of blacks and 87 percent of "anglos" of that age group have diplomas. Hispanics lag 12 percent behind blacks and 30 percent behind "anglos" in high school graduation rate. Twenty percent of "anglos" older than 25 have university degrees, while only 8 percent of Hispanics and 11 percent of blacks do.[8] The 1985 census revealed that only 48 percent of Hispanics have high school diplomas, in contrast with 76 percent of all Americans. Forty-five percent of Mexican-Americans have finished high school, while 62 percent of Cubans have.[9] The percentage attending college is similar in all Hispanic subgroups: 11–12 percent.

The Potential Contestants of Letras de Oro

Writing presumes certain reading habits, in English as well as in Spanish. Not all Hispanics registered by the census read at the same level in Spanish. A research study conducted by the National Association of Hispanic Media offers some details.

• While 90 percent of potential Hispanic readers of newspapers know Spanish, 67 percent speak English, but only 57 percent consider themselves functionally bilingual.

• Hispanics generally keep Spanish reading habits: 69 percent read Spanish-language newspapers, while magazines are read by 50 percent. Hispanic newspapers, printed in English, are read by 41 percent. A very popular format (34 percent) is the Hispanic magazine printed in English. Generally, younger readers prefer light topics.[10]

• Sixty-one percent of potential Hispanic readers are male, 56 percent are married, and the median age is 33.4 years. This sex factor will have an impact on the number and proportion of potential contestants in Letras de Oro, as we shall see later.

• Thirty-three percent of Hispanics interviewed in this survey trace their national origin to Mexico, and only 1 percent to Spain, while 12 percent are Colombians and 12 percent come from El Salvador. Cuba is the origin of 8 percent. Fifty-five percent of all potential Hispanic readers reside in California.

Contest Promotion

Letras de Oro was officially established on January 23, 1986, in Washington, D.C., at a ceremony during a press conference held at the Carlton Hotel, with the participation of University of Miami president Edward T. Foote III; James Robinson, president of American Express; and Professor Manuel Durán, of Yale University, representing the executive committee. A luncheon was later offered for three hundred guests from the academic, business, and political sectors; the meeting ended with a speech given by Carlos Fuentes on the topic of the literature written in Spanish in the United States.[11]

The announcement of the contest was well received by the media, both in Spanish and in English. While it is not easy to know exactly how the contestants knew about the project, the 1986–87 and 1987–88 surveys offer some glimpses, summarized in Table 12.2.

The Generic Category

Table 12.3 shows that in 1987–88, entries in the essay category increased, while novels decreased moderately. Poetry suffered a sharper decrease. Drama entries increased, as well as those for short story (possibly due to the elimination of maximum and minimum number of pages, so long as the collection was booklength).

State of Residency

Entries came from authors in all geographical areas of the United States. Successive censuses have corrected figures. Table 12.4 shows the geographic zones where the Hispanic population lived in 1980.

Letras de Oro has basically four ways to locate the state of origin of its contestants: (1) requests for information made by phone or letters; (2) return address placed in envelopes and packages containing copies of manuscripts; (3) explicit addresses provided by contestants along names; (4) surveys mailed to contestants. When Letras de Oro was born, our office received requests for specific information. A study of data based on telephone calls and letters offers the following details,[12] included in Table 12.5.

Since the day the contest was announced for the first time, until it closed on October 12th, 1986, potential contestants from 33 states and Puerto Rico called or wrote. A majority (31 percent) of entries came from residents of Florida, understandable because of the wide

TABLE 12.2

"I knew about the contest by the following way":					
	1987			1988	
Brochures	26	19%		38	28%
Press	48	34%		42	31%
Radio	4	3%		0	0
Television	27	19%		7	5%
Friends	23	16%		40	30%
Board	3	2%		3	2%
Other	9	7%		4	3%
Total	140	100%		134	100%

TABLE 12.3
Generic Categories of Entries

Genre	1986–87	1987–88	Combined 1986–88	
Essay	12	20	32	4.34%
Novel	75	62	137	18.58%
Poetry	208	157	365	49.52%
Short Story	42	92	134	18.18%
Theatre	29	25	54	7.32%
Translation	–	16	16	2.7
Total	366	371	737	100%

TABLE 12.4
The Nine States with the Largest Hispanic Populations (1980)

Rank	State	Population	Percentage
1	California	4,544,331	31.1%
2	Texas	2,985,824	20.4%
3	New York	1,659,300	11.4%
4	Florida	858,158	5.9%
5	Illinois	635,602	4.4%
6	New Jersey	491,883	3.4%
7	New Mexico	477,222	3.3%
8	Arizona	440,701	3.0%
9	Colorado	339,717	2.3%
Total 9 States		12,432,738	85.1%
Total for the United States		14,608,673	100%

press promotion in this state, especially in Miami. Eighteen percent came from California, 12 percent from New York, 9 percent from Texas and 7 percent from New Jersey.

TABLE 12.5
Distribution of Requests for Information by State

Rank	State	Requests	Percentage
1	Florida	178	31%
2	California	105	18%
3	New York	71	12%
4	Texas	49	9%
5	New Jersey	38	7%
6	Puerto Rico	18	3%
7	Pennsylvania	15	3%
8	Washington, D.C.	12	2%
9	Arizona	11	2%
10	Massachusetts	10	2%
11	Connecticut	9	1%
12	New Mexico	8	1%
13	Ohio	7	1%
14	Maryland	6	1%
15	Virginia	5	– 1%
16	Indiana	4	– 1%
17	Wisconsin	4	– 1%
18	Michigan	3	– 1%
19	Illinois	2	– 1%
20	Kentucky	2	– 1%
21	Louisiana	2	– 1%
22	Alabama	1	– 1%
23	Delaware	1	– 1%
24	Hawaii	1	– 1%
25	Iowa	1	– 1%
26	Mississippi	1	– 1%
27	Nevada	1	– 1%
28	New Hampshire	1	– 1%
29	North Carolina	1	– 1%
30	Oklahoma	1	– 1%
31	Oregon	1	– 1%
32	South Dakota	1	– 1%
33	Utah	1	– 1%
34	West Virginia	1	– 1%

Total 33 States and Puerto Rico   572   100%

TABLE 12.6
Distribution of Entries by State (1986-87, 1987-88)

Position	State	1986-87 Entries	%	1987-88 Entries	%	1986-88 Combined Entries	%
1	Florida	100	27%	79	27%	179	24%
2	New York	49	13%	53	14%	102	14%
3	California	46	13%	35	9%	81	11%
4	New Jersey	25	7%	12	3%	37	5%
5	Puerto Rico	9	3%	28	8%	37	5%
6	Texas	15	4%	12	3%	27	4%
7	Massachusetts	10	3%	11	2%	21	3%
8	Ohio	6	1%	9	2%	15	2%
9	Pennsylvania	9	3%	5	1%	14	2%
10	Virginia	8	2%	3	-1%	11	1%
11	Wisconsin	2	-1%	9	2%	11	1%
12	Arizona	6	1%	4	1%	10	1%
13	Illinois	4	-1%	5	1%	9	1%
14	Maryland	4	-1%	4	1%	8	-1%
15	Missouri	4	-1%	3	-1%	7	-1%
16	Iowa	4	-1%	2	-1%	6	-1%
17	Louisiana	4	-1%	2	-1%	6	-1%
18	Michigan	2	-1%	3	-1%	5	-1%
19	Kansas	1	-1%	4	1%	5	-1%
20	Georgia	4	-1%	0	0%	4	-1%
21	North Carolina	3	-1%	1	-1%	4	-1%
22	Indiana	2	-1%	2	-1%	4	-1%
23	Minnesota	2	-1%	2	-1%	4	-1%
24	New Mexico	2	-1%	2	-1%	4	-1%
25	Washington, D.C.	3	-1%	0	0%	3	-1%
26	Colorado	2	-1%	0	0%	2	-1%
27	Connecticut	2	-1%	0	0%	2	-1%
28	Hawaii	2	-1%	0	0%	2	-1%
29	Utah	1	-1%	1	-1%	2	-1%
30	West Virginia	1	-1%	1	-1%	2	-1%
31	Mississippi	1	-1%	1	-1%	2	-1%
32	Alabama	1	-1%	0	0%	1	-1%
33	Arkansas	1	-1%	0	0%	1	-1%
34	Idaho	1	-1%	0	0%	1	-1%
35	Rhode Island	1	-1%	0	0%	1	-1%
36	Tennessee	1	-1%	0	0%	1	-1%
37	Washington	1	-1%	0	0%	1	-1%
38	Wyoming	1	-1%	0	0%	1	-1%
39	Canada	0	0%	1	-1%	1	-1%
40	U.S. Virgin Islands	0	0%	1	-1%	1	-1%
41	Alaska	0	0%	1	-1%	1	-1%
42	Nebraska	0	0%	1	-1%	1	-1%
43	New Hampshire	0	0%	1	-1%	1	-1%

44	Oregon	0	0%	1	– 1%	1	– 1%
45	South Dakota	0	0%	1	– 1%	1	– 1%
Entries under Pseudonym		23	7%	70	19%	93	13%
Total 45 States[13]		363	100%	370	100%	733	100%

Table 12.6 shows distribution of entries by state in 1986–87, 1987–88, and the combined results. In the first year, Florida produced 100 entries, or 27 percent of the total, a figure that compares with 178 requests for information (31 percent of the total). The net result is 56 percent of requests followed up by one entry.[14] New York generated 71 requests and 49 entries, a follow-up rate of 69 percent. California had 105 requests, with a follow-up of 44 percent. New Jersey had 38 requests and 25 follow-ups (66 percent).

The 1986–87 survey shows that 23 entries, or 7 percent of the total were submitted under a pseudonym in a sealed envelope. In 1987–88 this percentage almost tripled to 70 (19 percent). Perhaps more experienced writers and professors entered the contest, and therefore they took the option of anonymity.[15]

Table 12.7 shows a comparative picture between the initial interest in 1986–87, the number of entries, and the 1980 census.

TABLE 12.7
Combined Results (1986–87) and the 1980 Census

State	Requests		Entries		1980 Census	
	%	Position	%	Position	%	Position
Arizona	2%	9	1%	10	3%	8
California	18%	2	13%	3	31%	1
Colorado	0%	–	– 1%	20	2%	9
Florida	31%	1	27%	1	6%	4
Illinois	– 1%	19	– 1%	13	4%	5
New Jersey	7%	5	7%	4	3%	6
New Mexico	1%	12	– 1%	26	3%	7
New York	12%	3	13%	2	11%	3
Texas	9%	4	4%	5	20%	2

Source: U.S. Bureau of the Census: Strategy Research Corporation

Direct surveys of contestants offer similar, corrected results for 1986–87 and 1987–88 in Table 12.8.

TABLE 12.8
State of Residency (1986–87 and 1987–88 Surveys)

	Question: "Specify state in which you reside"					
		1986–87		**1987–88**		**Combined 1986–88**
State		**No.**	**%**	**No.**	**%**	**No.**	**%**

	State	No.	%	No.	%	No.	%
1	Florida	20	17%	28	21%	48	22%
2	New York	17	14%	27	20%	44	20%
3	California	11	9%	18	13%	29	13%
4	Puerto Rico	4	3%	10	8%	14	6%
5	New Jersey	6	5%	5	4%	11	5%
6	Texas	3	2%	5	4%	8	3%
7	Massachusetts	2	2%	5	4%	7	3%
8	Ohio	3	2%	4	3%	7	3%
9	Pennsylvania	3	2%	3	2%	6	3%
10	Illinois	1	1%	4	3%	5	2%
11	Virginia	1	1%	3	2%	4	2%
12	Wisconsin	2	2%	2	1%	4	2%
13	Arizona	2	2%	2	– 1%	4	2%
14	Louisiana	2	2%	2	1%	4	2%
15	Iowa	1	1%	2	1%	3	1%
16	Indiana	0	0%	2	1%	2	1%
17	Virgin Islands	0	0%	2	1%	2	1%
18	Kansas	1	1%	1	– 1%	2	1%
19	Minnesota	0	0%	2	1%	2	1%
20	North Carolina	1	1%	1	– 1%	2	1%
21	Alaska	0	0%	1	– 1%	1	– 1%
22	Maryland	0	0%	1	– 1%	1	– 1%
23	Michigan	0	0%	1	– 1%	1	– 1%
24	West Virginia	1	1%	1	– 1%	1	– 1%
25	Missouri	1	1%	1	– 1%	1	– 1%
26	Oregon	0	0%	1	– 1%	1	– 1%
27	Georgia	1	1%	0	0%	1	– 1%
28	Washington, D.C.	1	1%	0	0%	1	– 1%
29	Colorado	1	1%	0	0%	1	– 1%
30	New Mexico	1	1%	0	0%	1	– 1%
Total		86	73%	134	100%	220	100%

The comparison between general statistics (Table 12.4) and Letras de Oro results (Tables 12.5, 12.6, 12.7, and 12.8) offers ground for additional comment. Some states (New Jersey, New York, Arizona, California) reflect similarly the ranking in the scale of entries in comparison with the total of Hispanic population. Texas, however, rates very low: 20.4 percent of the U.S. Hispanic population, but only 4 percent of the entries.

The number of entries in the second year increased in Florida, New York, California, New Jersey, and Puerto Rico. The actual percentage shows a decrease in Florida, but this is explained by the increase in the number of sealed envelopes.

Sex and Age of the Contestants

Table 12.9 shows distribution by sex in 1986–87, based on the name used. Out of 366 entries, 202 were submitted apparently by men (a majority of 56 percent).[16] Women offered 104 entries (28 percent). Sixty used a *nom de plume* (16 percent of the total). According to the 1980 census, women accounted for 50.2 percent of the population. However, Table 12.10 gives us a corrected picture, when direct survey netted a male–female rate of 64 percent to 36 percent (a decrease from 56 percent to 28 percent). There is speculation that many women hide their identity under male pseudonyms and faked names. Note that in 1987–88 the rate is 62 percent to 38 percent, and 62.6 percent to 37.3 percent for both years. In any case, the original 28 percent of women (based on the name used) has increased to 37 percent, but it is still lower than their 51 percent of the population.

Careful study, however, of data along surveys on reading habits indicates that Hispanic women are well represented in the contest. As 61 percent of the readers of newspapers are men, the figure matches the 64 percent and 62 percent of the Letras contestants.

The age of the contestants is another factor to study. Table 12.11 shows that 28 percent of the writers are between 40 and 50 years old, but in 1987–88 10 percent are younger than 30, and 10 percent are older than 70. As a whole, Letras de Oro has obtained a balanced generational base.

TABLE 12.9
Distribution of the Manuscripts by Author Gender

Gender of the Author	Manuscripts		1980 Census	
	Number	Percentage	Number	Percentage
Males	202	56%	7,280,000	49.8%
Females	104	28%	7,329,000	50.2%
Authors Using Pseudonyms	60	16%	n.a.	n.a.
Total	366	100%	14,609,000	100%

TABLE 12.10
Sex According to 1986-87 and 1987-88 Surveys

	1986-87		1987-88		Combined 1986-88	
Women	43	36%	51	38%	94	37,30%
Men	75	64%	83	62%	158	62,69%
Total	118	100%	134	100%	252	100%

TABLE 12.11
Age According to 1986-87 and 1987-88 Surveys

	1986-87		1987-88		Combined 1986-88	
29 and less	15	13%	13	10%	28	11.11%
30-39	24	20%	24	18%	48	19.04%
40-49	33	28%	37	28%	70	27.77%
50-59	29	25%	23	17%	52	20.63%
60-69	5	4%	21	16%	26	10.31%
70 and more	12	10%	13	10%	25	9.92%
No answer	0	0%	3	2%	3	1.19%
Total	118	100%	134	100%	252	100%

Occupation

In both surveys of 1986-87 and 1987-88 contestants were asked the question: "Indicate your profession." Table 12.12 indicates the results.

Worthy of note is the increase in the *profesor* (in Spanish) category (which does not distinguish between college professors and school-teachers): a jump from 28 percent to 48 percent. There is, therefore, a significant decrease in "nonprofessionals." This fact can be attributed to the extensive promotion of the contest by mailings to *all* members of the two major professors' and teachers' organizations, the Modern Language Association and the American Association of Teachers of Spanish and Portuguese, in 1987-88. For the same reason, in spite of the explicit elimination of the special categories for "students" in 1987-88, the actual number of "students" increased from 8 percent to 14 percent, a factor that has to be attributed also to the promotion undertaken by teachers and professors among their pupils.

TABLE 12.12

	1986-87		1987-88		Combined 1986-88	
Student	10	8%	19	14%	29	11.50%
Professor	33	28%	64	48%	97	38.49%
Professional	27	24%	29	22%	56	22.22%
Nonprofessional	48	40%	19	14%	67	26.50%
No answer	0	0%	3	2%	3	1.19%
Total	118	100%	134	100%	252	100%

National Origin

Probably the most interesting feature of these surveys is the national origin of the contestants, because it has important repercussions on several literary aspects of the implementation of the contest and the nature of entries (themes, attitude of jury members, jury national balance and composition) and sociological (what means to be a "Hispanic"). Tables 12.13 and 12.14 show the results of surveys on the national origin.

First, let us compare the ranking of certain nationalities of U.S. Hispanics with the Letras de Oro participation in the first year.

The 1987–88 survey expands the data with combined results in Table 12.14.

The modest increase in U.S.-born contestants is mostly attributed to the creation of the new category of translation, and secondarily to the incorporation of a few "natives" to other categories.

The above tables offer some concrete ground for debate, and speculation:

• Although Mexicans are 48.8 percent of the Hispanic population, they submitted only 8 percent of the 1986–87 entries and 5 percent of the 1987–88 entries.

• Colombia is the second-ranked nationality according to entries, 11.7 percent, although they represent just 4.2 percent of the population.

• Spain, with just a small portion[17] of the Hispanic population in the United States, supplied 8.5 percent of the entries.

• Cubans, 11.5 percent of U.S. Hispanics, represented 35 percent of the contestants in 1986–87 and 38 percent in 1987–88.

• Argentina, with 2.1 percent of the Hispanic population, is represented by 7 percent of the contestants.

TABLE 12.13
National Origin of U.S. Hispanics (1980) and Letras de Oro Contestants (1986–87)

	Survey Letras de Oro		1980 Census	
Country	Rank	Percent	Rank	Percent
Argentina	5	7%	7	2%
Chile	6	5%	*	*
Colombia	2	12%	5	4%
Cuba	1	35%	2	11%
El Salvador	9	2%	8	2%
Mexico	4	8%	1	49%
Peru	7	5%	9	1%
Spain	3	10%	4	5%
Venezuela	8	2%	*	*

*Census information does not provide % for Puerto Rico and other Latin American countries, which are grouped together in a general category, as "rest of America" (12%).
Source: U.S. Bureau of the Census; Strategy Research Corporation.

The low representation of writers of Mexican origin can be explained tentatively by the greater linguistic integration of Chicanos than, for example, Cubans. Mexican *braceros* and other immigrants come to the United States with less schooling than other nationalities, especially when compared to the Cubans or the Argentines. This explains the excellent position obtained by the representatives of Argentina, who are presumably professionals before they arrived in the United States fleeing the political and economic crisis of the last decades. Also worthy of consideration is the fact that the abandonment of Spanish as the language of culture is not considered a stigma in some Hispanic communities (in the Southwest), but is slower in the population of Spanish, Argentine, Colombian, or Cuban origin.

However, the aforementioned rankings are based on global data from 1820 to 1985, a century and a half of immigration, according to the last country of residency. The history of immigration shows that numerous groups migrated to the United States after living in a second Latin American country, different from their birthplace, but the total number of these "double" immigrants is not high enough to distort the total picture. Data of 1820–1985 reflect then several generations in which Americans are computed by birth, for example, as "Cuban" because of the place of last residency of their grandparents or great-grandparents in the nineteenth century.

TABLE 12.14
Country of Origin

	Question: "Specify country where you were born"				Combined
		1986–87		1987–88	1986–88
1	Cuba	42	35%	52	39%	37%
2	Colombia	14	12%	14	11%	11.7%
3	Spain	12	10%	9	7%	8.5%
4	Mexico	10	8%	6	5%	6.5%
5	Argentina	8	7%	8	6%	6.5%
6	Puerto Rico	4	3%	12	9%	6%
7	USA	5	4%	9	7%	5.5%
8	Chile	4	5%	7	5%	5%
9	Peru	6	5%	2	– 1%	3.7%
10	Guatemala	1	1%	4	3%	2%
11	Bolivia	1	1%	3	2%	1.5%
12	Panama	0	0%	2	1%	1.5%
13	El Salvador	2	2%	0	0%	1.5%
14	Honduras	0	0%	3	2%	1%
15	Nicaragua	1	1%	1	– 1%	1%
16	Dominicana	2	2%	1	– 1%	1%
17	Uruguay	1	1%	1	– 1%	1%
18	Venezuela	2	2%	0	0%	1%
19	Estonia	1	1%	0	0%	0.5%
20	Ecuador	1	1%	0	0%	0.5%
Total		117	100%	134	100%	100%

For this reason, it is convenient to form another table where data from 150 years can be compared to the data provided by the last two complete decades included in the census (see Table 12.15).

The modified picture of Table 12.15 offers some interesting details:

TABLE 12.15
Spanish-Speaking Immigration to the United States (1820–1985)

Country	Pop. 1985	%	1820–1985	%	1961–70	%	1971–80	%	1960–80	%
Spain	38.7	12.9	274	5.2	44.7	3.8	39.1	2.3	83.8	3.1
Argentina	30.0	10	110	2.1	49.7	4.3	29.9	1.9	79.6	3.2
Colombia	28.1	9.3	219	4.2	72	6.2	77.3	5.1	149.3	5.6
Cuba	9.9	13.3	603	11.5	208.5	18.1	264.9	17.5	473.4	17.8
Dominican Republic	6.1	2	356	6.7	93.3	8.1	148.1	9.8	241.4	9
Ecuador	9.	3	119	2.3	36.8	3.1	50.1	3.3	86.9	3.2
El Salvador	5.3	1.7	98	1.8	15	1.3	34.4	2.2	99.4	3.7
Guatemala	8.1	2.7	66	1.3	15.9	1.3	25.9	1.7	41.8	1.5
Honduras	4.2	1.4	56	1.1	15.7	1.3	17.4	1.1	33.1	1.2
Mexico	77	25	2,568	48.8	453.93	9.4	640.3	42.5	1,094.2	41.1
Panama	2.1	0.7	71	1.3	19.4	1.6	23.5	1.5	42.9	1.6
Peru	19.1	6.3	77	1.5	19.1	1.6	29.2	1.9	48.3	1.8
Puerto Rico	3.4									
Other			641	12.2	106.2	9.2	125	8.3	213.9	8
Total (Spanish speakers)			5,258	10	1,150.2	34.6	1,505.8	33	2,656	33
Total (all countries)			52,520		3,321.7		4,493		7,815	

Note: Total population figures are in millions, and immigration figures are in thousands. Percentage of Spanish-speaking population in all countries is based in the often-used 300 million figure.

• In all statistics, Mexico is the most populous country and the one that provides the highest absolute and relative immigration figures to the United States at all times. However, Mexican immigrants rank very low in Letras de Oro participation.

• Spain is, after Mexico and the Dominican Republic, the country that has provided the second-highest contingent of immigrants over 150 years, but in the last two decades it has been surpassed by Cuba, Colombia, Argentina, the Dominican Republic, Ecuador, and El Salvador. In 1970–80, Spain is only surpassed by Mexico, the Dominican Republic, Colombia, and Cuba.

TABLE 12.16
Country of Birth of the Parents

		1986–87		1987–88		Combined 1986–88	
1	Cuba	39	34%	48	36%	87	35%
2	Spain	15	13%	14	11%	29	12%
3	Colombia	13	11%	11	8%	24	10%
4	Mexico	13	11%	9	7%	22	9%
5	Puerto Rico	3	3%	14	11%	17	7%
6	Chile	6	5%	7	5%	13	5%
7	Argentina	5	4%	6	5%	11	4%
8	Peru	5	4%	2	1%	7	3%
9	Guatemala	1	–1%	4	3%	5	2%
10	Bolivia	0	0%	3	2%	3	1%
11	Honduras	0	0%	3	2%	3	1%
12	USA	0	0%	3	2%	3	1%
13	Dominican Republic	2	2%	1	–1%	3	1%
14	Italy	2	2%	1	–1%	3	1%
15	Panama	0	0%	2	1%	2	–1%
16	Russia	0	0%	2	1%	2	–1%
17	Venezuela	1	–1%	2	1%	2	–1%
18	Nicaragua	1	–1%	1	–1%	2	–1%
19	Uruguay	1	–1%	1	–1%	2	–1%
20	El Salvador	2	2%	0	0%	2	–1%
21	Ecuador	1	–1%	0	0%	1	–1%
22	Austria	1	–1%	0	0%	1	–1%
23	Estonia	1	–1%	0	0%	1	–1%
24	No answer	4	4%	0	0%	4	2%
Total		116	100%	134	100%	250	100%

TABLE 12.17
Citizenship of the Contestants

		1986–87		1987–88		Combined 1986–88	
1	USA	72	61%	90	67%	162	64%
2	Cuba	7	6%	9	6%	16	6%
3	Argentina	4	3%	7	5%	11	4%
4	Colombia	4	3%	7	5%	11	4%
5	Spain	6	5%	5	4%	11	4%
6	Mexico	6	5%	3	2%	9	3%
7	Chile	3	3%	4.	3%	7	3%
8	Peru	4	3%	1	– 1%	5	2%
9	Venezuela	2	2%	2	1%	4	1%
10	Guatemala	1	1%	2	1%	3	1%
11	Uruguay	1	1%	1	– 1%	2	– 1%
12	El Salvador	2	2%	0	0%	2	– 1%
13	Honduras	0	0%	1	– 1%	1	– 1%
14	Nicaragua	0	0%	1	– 1%	1	– 1%
15	Panama	0	0%	1	– 1%	1	– 1%
16	Dominican Republic	1	1%	0	0%	1	– 1%
No answer		5	4%	0	0%	5	2%
Total		118	100%	134	100%	252	100%

• However, if we take into account statistics on the national origin of parents (Table 12.16) of Letras de Oro participants, the result is a match with the global immigration pattern of the last century and a half, while immigration data of the last decade reflect the country of birth of Letras de Oro writers. In literary creation, parental experience may become themes, attitudes, background for fiction, obsessions, identified with a country that is not the author's, but may be idealized in family reunions. Nostalgia produced by emigration can be reduplicated and the country where one was born may disappear in literary works, substituted by the country of parents.

We see from Table 12.16 that the Spanish "nationality" has clinched second place among Letras de Oro contestants. The experience of parental emigration then is added to the trauma caused by political exile. The political loss of a native country is substituted by the romanticized past of the parents' homeland, in this case Spain.

Of further importance is data on the current citizenship (Table 12.17), which reveals naturalization habits and potential political participation.

Acquisition of U.S. citizenship is a matter of concern for Hispanic political leaders. Absolute numbers translate into political power by vote. The Hispanic U.S.-naturalization process has improved in recent years, but it still lags behind that of other nationalities. A study undertaken by NALEO (National Association of Latino Elected Officials)[18] showed disturbing data: in the 1970s, 38.1 percent of all U.S. immigrants applied for citizenship, Hispanics become new U.S. citizens at a rate of 25 percent less: only 13 percent of Mexicans obtained U.S. citizenship, as compared to 71.3 percent of Hungarians and 65 percent of Chinese; Cubans fared better: 58.9 percent. Letras de Oro contestants are well integrated in the United States, at least from the political point of view: 64 percent are U.S. citizens.

The Prize Money and Publication

Letras de Oro contestants seem to be satisfied with the monetary compensation offered by the prizes ($2,000 in 1986–87 and $2,500 in 1987–88, as an advance for royalties). Table 12.18 leaves little doubt of this satisfaction.

Obviously, the organization is aware that this positive answer comes from actual contestants, not from writers who did *not* compete, for many reasons, among them the low prize money.

For the first contest, publication – although always a goal – was not guaranteed. In 1987–88 publishing plans were announced without details. For 1988–89, with the winning works already in print, a contract between the sponsor and a publisher makes publication routine. Table 12.19 shows contestants' opinion of this guarantee.

TABLE 12.18

Question: "Do you consider the monetary compensation sufficient?"				
	1986–87		1987–88	
Yes	77	65%	104	78%
No	30	25%	27	20%
No answer			3	2%
Total	118	100%	134	100%

TABLE 12.19

Question: "Do you consider it necessary that the contest guarantee the publication of winning entries?"

	1986-87		1987-88	
Yes	102	87%	115	86%
No	12	10%	15	11%
No answer	4	3%	4	3%
Total	118	100%	134	100%

Conclusion

Greater publicity of the contest in the Southwest is not expected to increase greatly the number of contestants of Mexican origin, although there certainly will be a smaller disproportion. It is also expected that the more recent waves of political refugees and immigrants will increase the percentages of Cuban, Salvadoran, and Nicaraguan participation. At the same time, many Chileans, Argentinians, and Uruguayans will take up permanent residency in the United States and thus provide more entries. The recent increase in violence in Columbia will likely increase immigration and literary participation in the contest from writers born in that country.

All this advises us to redefine the concept of "Hispanic." This term cannot be confused, for the literary purposes of Letras de Oro, with "Spanish-speakers." A careful examination of these experiences provides a more complete picture, not only of the Hispanic population in the United States, but also a better profile of the entire nation, which Octavio Paz called, in the closing speech of the 1st Letras de Oro award ceremony, "the first plurilingual, multicultural, and pluriracial democracy in history."[19]

Some final comments are due: (1) There exists an interest by different American institutions (both cultural and commercial) in the promotion of the use of Spanish; (2) there is enough generational variety to contemplate the future with hope; and (3) the fifth-largest Spanish-speaking country will continue to contribute works to the only true motherland of the writer: the language.

The Writer and the Language: Reflections on the Linguistic Conditions of Writing

HIBER CONTERIS

Why – or for what reason – and for whom does one write in Spanish in the United States?

During the awards ceremony of the Letras de Oro literary competition (Miami, January 1987), Octavio Paz, the Mexican poet and essayist especially invited for that occasion said:

> The Letras de Oro Awards are a recognition of a reality that is more powerful and complex every day: the existence of twenty million Spanish-speaking people who live in the United States. This considerable geographic reality is also historical and spiritual; these twenty million live, work, love, think, pray, sing, suffer, dance, dream, and die in Spanish. To speak a language is to participate in a culture, to live in it, to be for or against, but always *in* it.[1]

From the writer's standpoint, obstinately to write in Spanish in the midst of a predominantly English linguistic culture is probably – at least in my case – the result of two circumstances: the physical circumstance of living in the United States, and the cultural circumstance (or perhaps "spiritual" as Octavio Paz points out) of not being able to write in any other language but Spanish.

This double circumstance constitutes a situation that I propose to call *linguistic insularity*. The figures collected in the statistic sampling done by the Letras de Oro Administration indicate that, according to

1985 data, the population of Hispanic origin in the United States was 7 percent of the total population, a number close to 17 million. Of this percentage, 48.8 percent are of Mexican origin; 11.5 percent are Cuban; those of Spanish origin, 5 percent; Colombia, 4.2 percent; and those of Argentinian origin are 2.1 percent of the total. Data concerning other nationalities, which constituted 28.4 percent of the total, were not computed because they (the majority supposedly Puerto Ricans) did not participate significantly in the competition.

Considering these figures, one should reformulate in concrete terms the second question in the epigraph: for *whom* do we, Hispanic writers who live temporarily or permanently in the United States, write? Do we write for that group of close to 17 million hypothetical readers living in this country? I believe that none of the writers asked would respond affirmatively to this question. The Hispanic community in the United States is so heterogeneous, diversified, and scattered in population and geographical extension that it could not easily be considered a genuine "community of readers." This internal diversity responds not only to national origin, but also to different nuances of linguistic character derived from implantation in a predominantly Anglo-Saxon environment. Think of Chicano speech, for example, that decidedly attempts a symbiosis of Spanish and English or the characteristic shades of Puerto Rican speech in the United States. The right to write in "Spanglish," that second- and third-generation Cubans proclaimed (I don't know how seriously) as their own during a symposium following the first Letras de Oro awards ceremony, raises a similar problem.

Obviously, even living in their own country, writers should always make a choice concerning the "speech" in which they are going to express themselves. In a strictly national scope, however, the plurality of linguistic styles (not languages) does not invalidate the generic concept of "linguistic community," in which the strictest definition of a "community of readers" must be found. The latter community does not necessarily depend on the number of speakers. My own country, Uruguay, for example, does not quite have three million inhabitants, due to the recent diaspora of the population. However, I do not doubt that Uruguayan authors living in the country have a more precise idea of whom they write for than I do in my voluntary exile. In this sense, from my particular appreciation of the problem, I find it difficult for Spanish-speaking writers living in the United States to think of the rest of the North American Hispanic population as the natural audience of their literary production. One should thus look for other reasons to explain the persistence in the stubborn choice of Spanish as a means of expression in an unfamiliar linguistic environment; those reasons are connected to the question raised at the beginning: *why* does one write in Spanish in the United States?

Putting the question this way is to ask about the essence of literary creation itself and, therefore, about the condition of the writer. According to Heidegger's reflections (Martin Heidegger, *On the Way to Language*, New York: Harper and Row, 1971; "Hölderlin and the Essence of Poetry," in *Existence and Being*, W. Brock, ed., Chicago, 1949), we could relate it to the fundamental ontological question, in that we are asking about the being or ultimate nature of the act of writing. It is a problem whose answer has been attempted innumerable times, from different aesthetic and philosophical perspectives. Without a doubt, it will continue to be raised in the future. I do not pretend here to present a general reply, but rather to answer that question beginning with the real situation described above: the physical circumstance of living in predominately English-speaking surroundings, and the cultural and linguistic circumstance of not being able to express myself literarily in any other language but Spanish. One could say, according to what structuralism has insistently pointed out (in particular, Michel Foucault in *Les Mots et les Choses: Une Archéologie des Sciences Humaines*, Paris: Gallimard, 1966), that men (human beings) do not choose the language they speak, but it is language that chooses its speakers. Language "speaks through us." We have been previously conditioned by the linguistic boundaries in which, consciously or unconsciously, we find ourselves submerged. Accordingly, writers are nothing more than spokespersons for a reality that transcends them. Language structures our thoughts, our ideology, our knowledge, our perceptions, and our reflections of things. It forms and determines the way in which we are going to express and reflect the interior and exterior reality through words. Writers are unconditionally subjected to the language that has molded them. This is probably the truest reason why Hispanic writers in the United States cannot stop writing in Spanish, under penalty of exposure to total alienation, to an act of estrangement that implies the renunciation or alienation of their being.

In this context, one should also understand the question, so often raised, of "literary style." "Style" is no more than the form in which individuals react or transform the transcendental reality that is language. It is their singular way of working with it, their personal way of modifying the generic condition imposed on them by the linguistic boundaries that have determined their thinking and words. Because they are unable to escape this ontologically determinant situation (language), and because they do not abdicate the differential variable of that condition (personal style), writers consubstantiated by Spanish cannot stop writing in that language no matter what linguistic environment they may find themselves in.

Franz Fanon once showed the typical inversion of the situation that the imposition of the dominant foreign language of the colonizer over the colonized presupposes on a linguistic level. Language initially imposes itself on the colonized as a form of domination, one more way – and one of the most important – to mark an oppressive situation. But the moment arrives when this situation inverts itself, because the colonized, who have preserved their national language as the fundamental vehicle of communication with their kind, now "possess" the language of the enemy, the language of the colonizer. In the long run, this double linguistic activity grants them an advantage that will be the decisive condition in their process of liberation.

It is not my intention to carry this simile too far, but it is evident that in pledging to write in Spanish in United States territory, we maintain the ambiguity of the circumstance in which a culture, if not subjected, at least "subordinated to," begins to work retroactively on the dominant culture. The moment when literature in Spanish produced in the United States acquires the status of an autonomous literature, worthy to be classified on the same level as other national literature in the Hispanic language, is still a long way off. But I think that, given current conditions, no one would deny the role it plays as testimony to the cultural transformation that is happening in a great nation, a nation that, because of the nature of its demographic composition and the importance of the means of communcating in Spanish, is turning into a bilingual culture. From this point of view, it is possible to return to the previous reference to Franz Fanon and describe the role of Hispanic literature in Anglo-Saxon America as part of the process of reciprocal influence, interaction and – why not? – liberation to which both cultures – Hispanic and Anglo-Saxon – find themselves open.

To conclude, I want to return to the situation that I described before with the expression *linguistic insularity*, because it appears evident that this situation can be compared, or related, to two other circumstances with similar characteristics. New elements arise from this comparison that can help us understand it better. The first of these circumstances is *exile*: that is to say, that situation in which writers, forced to live outside their countries for some reason or other, keep their native language as a way to preserve their roots and national identity. Concerning the second circumstance, I cannot find a better way of characterizing it than by resorting to an expression, if not first coined in Uruguay, at least widely used there during the military regime that lasted from 1973 to 1985. The term used then was *inxile*: a fortunate word that because of its lexical proximity and the addition of the prefix "in" alludes unmistakably to interior exile, one that occurs inside the borders of one's own country when one finds oneself subjected to censorship and the imposition of a hegemonic ideological discourse by a totalitarian regime. In order to resist, elude, or simply escape that discourse's forms of control and domination, writers who do not renounce their incorruptible stance must find or invent literary strategies that allow them to continue exercising a critical and reflective thinking that ultimately constitutes the justification for the act of writing itself.

On another occasion I explained my interpretation of how the technique of "bricolage" (a term with which Claude Levi-Strauss explains the formation and origin of the myth), can become one of the strategies in which the astuteness of writers filters through or superimposes itself upon their own discourse through cracks in the hegemonic discourse.[2] It would be superfluous to repeat that argument, but I mention it here because the term *inxile* throws some light on the condition of Hispanic writers who continue to write in their own language in the United States. This is the way to exercise their undeniable right (or duty?); it is the critical and reflective function essential to all true intellectual activity.

In this way I believe that the two comparable situations, *exile* and *inxile*, allow us to understand better the circumstance in which we, Hispanic writers, find ourselves in this country, that circumstance being the *linguistic insularity* that I mentioned at the beginning of these reflections. To write in Spanish, here and now, is, for writers, to exercise their social function of critical and independent thinking. At the same time, it reinforces the preservation of their own identity, maintaining roots in the culture and language that formed the way they are. This constitutes, whether they like it or not, their most profound and undeniable heritage.

CHAPTER 14

Hispanic Books in the Library of Congress: 1815–1965

GEORGETTE M. DORN

This paper will trace the first century and a half in the growth and development of the Library of Congress' Hispanic collection. The first books on Latin America and the Iberian Peninsula were acquired by the library in 1815 with the purchase of the Thomas Jefferson private library. The Hispanic collection in 1988 includes approximately two million volumes of books and periodicals on Luso-Hispanic studies.

The Library of Congress was established by an act of Congress and signed into law by President John Adams in 1800, to be housed in a "suitable apartment" in the United States Capitol Building, where it would remain until 1897. A joint congressional committee was to oversee the purchase of books, the preparation of a catalog, and to "devise and establish library regulations." The narrowly based early collection consisted, for the most part, of books on law, geography, and the history and exploration of North America. Unfortunately, the fledgling collection was destroyed when the invading British army burnt the Capitol during the War of 1812.[1]

Thomas Jefferson, in retirement at Monticello, offered to sell his personal library to Congress, provided that it would accept the collection in its entirety. Aware that some members of Congress might object to the purchase of an eclectic and wide-ranging collection on art, architecture, literature, science, politics, and the classics, Jefferson defended his library selection stating in 1814, "I do not know that it contains any branch of science which Congress would wish to exclude from their collection; there is in fact, no subject to which a member of Congress may not have occasion to refer." One congressman worried that Jefferson's books would become instruments in spreading what some viewed as his "suspect philosophy"; others thought that many of his books were written in languages that few could read. Nevertheless, the purchase was narrowly approved by the Congress. The *Boston Gazette* summed up the momentous event commenting, "The grand library of Mr. Jefferson will undoubedly be purchased with all its finery and philosophical nonsense."[2]

Jefferson had been buying books all his life, as can be seen in his correspondence. In fact, the library of 6,700 titles he sold to the Congress was the second major collection he had assembled. This extraordinary collection became the nucleus of what today is the world's largest and most complete library. The catalog George Watterson prepared in 1815 of Jefferson's library became the Library of Congress book classification system used until 1900. Even the system devised in 1900, and still in use today, is partly based on Jefferson's classification scheme.[3]

The library sold by Jefferson, rich in books about the regions of the world and relating to most branches of knowledge, included almost 200 volumes about Spanish and Portuguese America, the Caribbean, and the Iberian Peninsula, in either Spanish, French, Italian, or Latin, all languages which the former president read with ease. Jefferson possessed an insatiable curiosity about the New World, and in his attempt to learn as much as possible about the diversity of human societies, as well as the environment of the Americas, and the conquest of a large portion of it by Spain and Portugal, he had gone to great lengths to amass a representative and learned collection of books. He believed that it was important for North Americans to learn Spanish because "our future connection with Spain and Spanish America will render that language a valuable acquisition," and he also stated that one ought to keep in mind that much of the history of the Americas was written in Spanish.[4]

Jefferson realized the potential importance of Spanish America to the United States and took advantage of his sojourns in Europe to acquire books in Spanish, French, and other languages. For instance, on April 17, 1789, he bought eleven books in Spanish and French about Latin America, among them, José de Acosta's *Historia natural y moral de las Indias* (Seville, 1590); Bartolomé de las Casas' *Tratado comprobatorio del Imperio soberano universal que los Reyes de Castilla tienen sobre las Indias* (Seville, 1553); Diego Fernández, *Primera, y segunda parte, de la historia del Perú* (Seville, 1781); Agustín de Zárate's *Histoire de la découverte et de la conquête de Pérou* (Amsterdam, 1700); Fernando de Pizarro y Orellana, *Varones ilustres del Nuevo Mundo* (Madrid, 1639); José de Veitia Linage, *Norte de contratación de las Indias Occidentales*

(Seville, 1672); Francisco López de Gómara's *Historia de México* (Anvers, 1554); and Bernal Díaz del Castillo's *Historia verdadera de la conquista de la Nueva España* (Madrid, 1632). Díaz del Castillo's eyewitness chronicle of Hernán Cortés' siege of Tenochtitlán and the subsequent conquest of Mexico was one book Jefferson particularly admired. In 1809, he wrote, "Mexico is one of the most interesting countries of our hemisphere, and merits our attention." Some years later, in 1820, he stated, "I should rejoice to see the fleets of Brazil and the United States riding together as brethren of the same family and pursuing the same object."[5]

Other books on Spanish and Portuguese America in Jefferson's collection included *Historia general de los hechos castellanos en las islas de Tierra Firme y del mar*, by Antonio Herrera y Tordesillas (1728 and 1730); Hernán Cortés' *Historia de la Nueva España* (1770) based on his letters; the history of Christopher Columbus by his son; books by Peter Martyr, Antonio Rodríguez de León Pinelo, Antonio de Solís, Juan de Torquemada, and Javier Clavijero. He also read avidly El Inca Garcilaso's *Comentarios reales* and his *La Florida del Inca*; Ercilla's *La Araucana*, the epic of the Chilean Indians; and an account presenting "the dark underside of the American utopia" in *Tyrannies et cruautez des espagnols pérpétrées nez Indes Occidentales*, by Las Casas.[6]

He also had in his collection a copy of the *Diccionario de la Academia de la Lengua*, Giuseppe Baretti's *A Dictionary of Spanish and English* (1778), and Barthelmi Cormon's *Dictionnaire portatif et de prononciation espagnole-français et français-espagnole* (1800), among others. In addition to books about the history of contact between the Old World and the New, and the natural history of the Indies, he also collected works on philosophy and literature. He cherished a bilingual Latin and Spanish edition of the works of Tacitus and also bought a nine-volume set entitled *Parnaso español; colección de poesías escogidas de los más célebres poetas castellanos* by Juan José López Sedano (Madrid, 1766–78), and an edition of *Don Quixote* by the Real Academia of Spain. Experts believe that Jefferson had read Cervantes' classic opus in Spanish, French, and English. Other books by Cervantes that came to the library with the Jefferson purchase include *Los seis libros de Galatea* (1784), *Novelas ejemplares* (1783), and *Los trabajos de Persiles y Segismunda* (1781). These books were in the company of other great classics such as works by Homer, Virgil, Dante, Milton, Tasso, and Shakespeare.[7]

Despite an auspicious start in collecting foreign books, during the early years when it was housed in the Capitol, the library acquired few additional foreign titles. The library was meant to serve but one branch of government, the legislative. Hispanic titles acquired during the 1815–50 period were, for the most part, legal and commercial materials, with some books on geography, exploration, and travel. Members of Congress overseeing the library recommended that the congressional library should be "a vertical library composed of books so organized as to be consulted standing up, rather than read at reclining leisure." It was to exclude 'polite' literature, indeed all literature likely to be found in the personal collections of gentlemen of the Capitol."[8] This policy led George Perkins, a member of Congress, to complain in 1846, that the Library of Congress possessed few titles in Spanish and none in Portuguese. He sensed that the United States would be increasingly interested in trade with Latin America, and maintained that the library should collect books about the area.

Unfortunately, two-thirds of the Thomas Jefferson collection perished in a fire at the Capitol on Christmas Eve in 1851, among them all the books relating to the Hispanic world. Although, over the years all the titles in the original Jefferson collection were replaced with the same editions, of course, the former president's handwritten notations were lost.[9]

In 1865 the Smithsonian Institution transferred to the Library of Congress a wealth of books and periodicals in the humanities and social sciences, greatly expanding the scope of the collections. Numerous Hispanic titles were incorporated into the library's collections with the 44,000 volumes that came from the Smithsonian. One of the books acquired was Domingo F. Sarmiento's *Recuerdos de provincia y Educación común en el estado de Buenos Aires* (Santiago de Chile, 1855), an autographed French translation of Sarmiento's *Civilización y barbarie* (1853), as well as Mary Mann's English translation of the same work (1868), autographed by the translator.[10] At that time the library also initiated a farflung network of exchange programs with foreign institutions and learned societies. At this time, it began seriously to collect codes of law and official gazettes from the Hispanic world. Congress passed a law in 1867 authorizing the library to exchange official United States publications for those produced by foreign governments. By the end of the nineteenth century the Library of Congress held an unsurpassed collection of legal codes and government publications from around the world.

The Library of Congress became the home for copyright deposits in 1870, owing to the efforts of Librarian of Congress Ainsworth Spofford. By the end of the century, the library had accumulated not only substantial North American holdings, but also a respectable collection of foreign publications. To no one's surprise the library's space in the Capitol had become inadequate after the 1860s; books were piling up with no room to shelve them. Unfortunately, repeated entreaties by the library administration for a separate library building were not being heeded in the Reconstruction era until 1886 when the first act was approved, followed by other acts in 1888 and 1889.

The library's diversified holdings made it apparent that it had become the "national library," although Congress has always preferred to keep it as the "congressional library." A building was erected to house the expanding collections and the 1897 inauguration of the ornate neoclassic building, named after Thomas Jefferson, led to the reexamination of the purposes of the library. Librarian of Congress John Russell Young referred to the importance of library holdings about the Americas, stating that "the interblending of Spanish-American history with that of the United States makes it advisable that we should continue to strengthen ourselves in that department to note particularly what pertains not only to the United States but to America in general. Canada, Newfoundland, Nova Scotia, the West Indies, but more especially the countries to the South − Mexico, Central and South America − should have special attention."[11]

Herbert Putnam who served as Librarian of Congress from 1899 to 1939, cited in an address four functions which may be performed by a national library: to serve as a library of special service to the Federal government; as library of record for the United States; as a library of research, reinforcing and supplementing other research libraries; and as a library of national service, which responds to requests from other libraries in the United States, providing cataloging services and printed catalog cards. The library began performing all these services during Mr. Putnam's term.[12]

At the turn of the century several sources contributed to the increasing growth and cosmopolitanization of the collections. The accumulation of materials transferred from the Smithsonian Institution, the titles arriving through international exchange programs, and copyright deposits of United States publications, prompted Herbert Putnam to state that "from these sources the Library has already the largest single collection of American imprints, official documents of all countries and of the publications and societies existing in any single institution."[13]

The Spanish-American War provided the impetus in turning the attention of the library to the Hispanic area. During the following five years bibliographies were prepared and published on Cuba, the Danish West Indies, the Philippines, Puerto Rico, and international canal and railway routes in Mexico and Central America. Materials on Cuba and Puerto Rico became the richest and most diverse core of Hispanic holdings in official publications, books, periodicals, and pamphlets being transferred to the library from other government agencies during the first decades of the twentieth century. For instance, Navy Chaplain Roswell Hoes gave 1,416 Cuban books and periodicals in 1912. Such prompt recognition of an opportunity to strengthen Hispanic holdings brought together what eventually became the most complete collection on Cuba, Puerto Rico, and the Philippines.[14] Periodicals such as *Anuario Borinquén, Bohemia, Revista Bimestre Cubano* all arrived in the early 1900s. The United States government and private companies published detailed surveys of the resources and social conditions in the territories wrested from Spanish control.

Heightened awareness of the library's growing interest in Hispanic materials began to attract important gifts, of books and manuscript collections. The Henry Harisse bequest of 1915 brought the correspondence and the profusely annotated book collection of one of the foremost Hispanic bibliographers, an expert on Columbus, and author of *Bibliotheca americana vetustissima* (1866). In the wake of the First World War, the library appointed its first Hispanic bibliographer, Cecil K. Jones, who made systematic efforts to strengthen and expand the Hispanic collection in all fields through purchase and exchange, not only of general works, but also those of occasional use, essential to the special investigator. Mr. Jones justified the inclusion of literature in the collection because such materials were indispensable for "becoming acquainted with the character and cultural *ambiente* – of our neighbors. History is more than a record of events; it is the interpretation of a social complex. . . . an understanding of the literature and art of a people will afford an intimate acquaintance not to be derived from political history, sociology, ethnology, or political economy."[15]

In 1901 the library held 3,891 titles relating to the history and culture of the Hispanic world; by 1918 the holdings had increased to 15,113 titles. The collection included vocabularies, catechisms, and grammars in Amerindian languages, most of these published in Mexico and Lima in the sixteenth century, in languages such as Náhuatl, Mixtec, Zapotec, or Aymara. Colonial, nineteenth-century and early modern literature were well represented with works by Sor Juana Inés de la Cruz, Carlos Sigüenza y Góngora, Andrés Bello, Alberto Blest Gana, Gertrudis Gómez de Avellaneda, Amado Nervo, Rubén Dario, José María Vargas Vila, José Santos Chocano, Rufino Blanco Fombona, Luis Orrego Luco, Leopoldo Lugones, Manuel Ugarte, José Enrique Rodó, Julio Herrera y Reissig, and many others.[16]

The next impetus in the development of the Hispanic collection came in the 1920s when Archer M. Huntington, Hispanist, poet, and founder of the Hispanic Society of America, established the Huntington Endowment Fund of $100,000, as the first of several important donations. In 1928, Mr. Huntington endowed the first Consultantship in Hispanic Letters at the Library of Congress, which at his suggestion, appointed Juan Riaño y Gayangos to the post. The part-time ambassador was not very active. The first full-time consultant and later Specialist in Hispanic Culture was Father David Rubio, a Spanish Augustinian friar, a graduate of the Universities of San Marcos and Madrid, a member of the Spanish Academy of Letters, and a professor at The Catholic University of America. His energetic efforts in acquiring Hispanic materials increased the collection from 15,000 to 200,000 titles during the 1931–43 period. Efforts were also made to collect in the field of popular culture. An example of these acquisitions was the work of John Lomax, who enriched the Archive of American Folk Song by collecting Hispanic folk music from the Caribbean, and other areas, including the San Antonio, Texas, version of "Las Posadas" and the miracle play "Los Pastores."[17]

A subsequent gift from Mr. Huntington endowed the establishment of the Hispanic Foundation which opened its doors on Columbus Day in 1939, as a center for research and learning in the Luso-Hispanic studies and to further strengthen the library's collections. Librarian of Congress Archibald MacLeish, in his address at the inauguration of the Hispanic Foundation, extolled the Spanish-American experience, saying in part: "No man living in the United States can truly say he knows the Americas unless he has knowledge of these things – a knowledge of this other American past, this older American past which shares with ours the unforgettable experience of the journey toward the West and the westward hope."[18]

The Hispanic Foundation, renamed the Hispanic Division in 1978, became the primary focus for Latin American and Iberian acquisitions and bibliography. Lewis Hanke, the first director, brought with him *The Handbook of Latin American Studies*, the annual, annotated, selected bibliography he had started at Harvard in 1936. *The Handbook* is still prepared in the Hispanic Division by an editorial staff, headed by Dolores Moyano Martin, with the assistance of approximately one hundred scholarly contributing editors. These scholars alert the library about new Hispanic publications and it is partly owing to the existence of *The Handbook* that the library is able to collect such a wide array of Latin American publications.

The Hispanic Division also houses the Archive of Hispanic Literature on Tape, started in 1942 with the strong encouragement of Archibald MacLeish, by Francisco Aguilera, who succeeded Father Rubio as Specialist in Hispanic Culture. The first poet recorded on magnetic tape was the Uruguayan Emilio Oribe. In 1965 the archive contained recordings by 250 Luso-Hispanic and Caribbean writers and intellectuals (today it includes audio- and videorecordings of more than 600 writers). A guide to recordings by the first 272 writers was published by the Library of Congress in 1971.[19] The Specialist in Hispanic Culture began videotaping selected Hispanic writers with an interview of Jorge Luis Borges in 1976.

The Latin American Studies Association was founded at the Library of Congress in 1966 by a group of scholars, among them, Howard F. Cline, the second director of the Hispanic Division, Cole Blasier, who in early 1988 was named chief of the Hispanic Division, Richard Morse, Kalman Silvert, and John J. Johnson. Cline also revived the Conference on Latin American History in 1964 under the aegis of the Hispanic Division. The division has undertaken a number of bibliographic projects such as the multivolume *Handbook of Middle American Indians* (1964–72), three editions of *The National Directory of Latin Americanists* (1967, 1971, 1985), the *Cuban Acquisitions Bibliography* (1970), guides to newspapers and manuscript collections, *Latin America, Spain, and Portugal: An Annotated Bibliography of Paperback Books* (1964, 1967, 1971, 1976), and occasional unannotated bibliographies in the "Hispanic Focus" series (one issue in this series listed books on the Falkland/Malvinas, and another listed publications on the *Sendero Luminoso*).[20]

The decades since 1965–66 witnessed tremendous growth in the Hispanic collection, owing to an increase in the number of books published in Spain and Latin America, and a heightened interest in the subject areas in North American academic communities. The number of scholarly books and articles on Latin America grew to such an extent, that in 1964 the editor of the *Handbook*, which until then included humanities and social sciences in an annual volume of 300 to 400 pages, saw the need to separate the two groups, into alternating years. Each volume on the humanities or social sciences quickly grew to around 500 pages. In recent years the editor had to become increasingly more selective in her choice of materials to include in the bibliography. The establishment of the Library of Congress Office in Brazil, elicited greatly increased contributions from that country.

The handful of Hispanic books that arrived in the Library of Congress with Mr. Jefferson's library, developed during the ensuing century and a half into a large, varied, and in most areas, quite complete, research library. The special strengths of the Library of Congress' Hispanic collection are the legal materials from the Middle Ages to the present, government documents, periodicals, and above all, the extensive holdings in political history, literature, culture, and ethnology of the Luso-Hispanic Area.

CHAPTER 15

Hispanic Books in the Library of Congress, 1815–1965: A Comment

VINCENT PELOSO

The Hispanic Division of the Library of Congress is linked directly to Thomas Jefferson's original intentions for a national library. The Hispanic Division is in fact central to the Library of Congress, an element of the Library's history wholly in keeping with the trend in U.S. scholarship today. I refer, of course, to the growing importance that academia in the United States accords to Latin American studies. After many years of stepchild status, Latin American studies are respected for their contribution to scholarship in general, and the Hispanic Division has played a significant role in that turn of events.

Of the many points worth mentioning in reviewing the place of the Division within the Library's functions, none seems more worthy than the activities of the reference section and the *Handbook of Latin American Studies*. The reference section of the Division, headed since 1970 by Georgette Dorn, consists of the best reference collection on Iberia and Latin America in the country, and perhaps in the world. Here at hand in one room are housed every basic starter bibliography and guide a graduate student might need and many others that experienced scholars seek. The collection houses approximately four thousand titles of ready reference, and it is continuously being updated.

The collection includes a general history in English, and many in Spanish or Portuguese, of every Latin American country. It houses encyclopedias of Latin American history, dictionaries, including Spanish-Guaraní, Latin-Guaraní, Dutch-Spanish, Russian-Spanish, Portuguese-Spanish, and various other specific combinations of that genre, and a complete run of the *Latin American Research Review*. Also among its important reference materials are historical dictionaries of all the Latin American countries, the foremost being Helen Delpar's *Dictionary of Latin American History*. They are supplemented by Who's Whos, literary anthologies, reference volumes on Chicanos, the *Statistical Abstract of Latin America*, and other less well known reference volumes useful to the scholar.

The reference section contains guides to special collections, including the Thomas Mathews guide to the Puerto Rico collection in the Manuscript Division, and a two-volume guide to *The Harkness Collection in the Library of Congress, 1531–1651*. The Harkness Collection, one of the more important such collections in this country, was given to the Library of Congress by Edward S. Harkness in 1929. It is composed of 1405 folios that fall into four classes: notarial documents, royal *cédulas*, viceregal decrees and two *libros de cabildo* of frontier towns established in sixteenth-century Peru. Another important volume is the guide to the official materials in the National Archives of the United States, and there are guides to various other archives in Spain, Mexico, Argentina, and Chile.

Of equal importance to the guides are the catalogues of the reference section. These are the reference materials on the contents of other libraries around the United States where there are extensive collections on Latin America and catalogues on the contents of Latin American repositories. One that stands out in my mind is a multi-volume reproduction of the catalogue of the books in the Sala de Investigaciones of the Biblioteca Nacional del Perú, the country's most important collection of books and manuscripts. This catalogue is vital in understanding the organization of the Sala; without it the investigator faces many hours of worthless searching. Another valuable item is the *Schlagwortskatalog* of the Ibero-Americanisches Institut in Berlin, which houses one of the finest Latin American collections in Europe.

Less well known, the Hispanic reference collection has since 1939 maintained vertical files with up-to-date information on Latin American affairs in the humanities and the social sciences. Alongside these ephemera can be found a handy clipping service entitled *Information Service Latin America* (ISLA), a part of the reference section since 1971. Also of interest is the *Hispanic Pamphlet Collection*. Begun by Father David Rubio in 1961, the pamphlet collection consists of political tracts from each country in Latin America, bulletins issued by the country's private organizations, broadsides, newspaper and magazine clippings, occasional government pronouncements, biographical studies, essays, and a variety of other kinds of occasional publication not ordinarily found in one place. Indeed, the collection of pamphlets on Nicaragua in the Somoza years is a real treasure trove for Central Americanists.

No assessment of the reference section of the Hispanic Division would be complete without making mention of its archive of tapes. While not in themselves books, tapes nevertheless have become an essential source for the creation of books in our era. Oral sources have become a critical element in the reconstruction of biography, family and popular history. Hence, the Hispanic Archive of Tapes is critically linked to the production of books in the Latin American field. It is a basic reference source for the field of literary history, for contemporary folklore, and for literary criticism, among other lines of research.

The Hispanic Archive of Tapes is notable because it has been in existence since 1942 but more because Georgette Dorn has been associated with this ambitious undertaking since 1965, when she began helping the then–reference section chief, Francisco Aguilera, add to the collection. Since 1970, when she became the resident reference librarian of the Division, Georgette Dorn has continued a labor set down by Aguilera and his predecessors.

This invaluable resource contains the thoughts, essays, short stories, poetry, and critical views of every well-known – and many not so well known but highly talented – Latin Americans in the field of writing: among them, Gabriela Mistral, Pablo Neruda, Julio Cortázar, Juan Ramón Jiménez, Rómulo Gallegos, Pablo Antonio Cuadra, Octavio Paz, Jorge Icaza, Ernesto Cardenal, Carlos Fuentes, Mario Vargas Llosa, and Homero Aridjis. Not surprisingly, there are 72 Brazilians in the group, including Carlos Drummond de Andrade, Mario Souza, João Cabral de Melo Neto, and the anthropologist Gilberto Freyre. Clearly this is a source for future historians, literary critics, and students of any of the noteworthy careers of the individuals taped. The size of the archive and the quality of the materials, some of them parts of novels yet to be written, others ruminations, thoughts on themes not yet fully developed, is a credit to the foresight and skill of Georgette Dorn and her predecessors.

Finally, we should note the publications of the Hispanic Division of the Library of Congress. From its very beginning, the Division has published in the Latin American field. Its sponsorship of the three editions of a *National Directory of Latin Americanists* grew from a listing of 1884 specialists in the social sciences and humanities in the first edition, to 2695 in the second, and to 4915 in the third edition of 1985.

The reference section has also been a leader in publishing educational matter. Beginning in 1967 and expanded twice thereafter in new editions until 1976, Georgette Dorn provided a wonderful aid to teachers of Latin American Studies with the publication of *Latin America, Spain and Portugal. An Annotated Bibliography of Paperback Books*. This marvelous little guide helped many of us to find the appropriate reading materials for our classrooms. The last edition before the market swelled to overwhelming proportions listed and annotated over 2,200 titles.

Another continuing publication of the Hispanic Division — indeed, the second-strongest area of the Division — is the *Handbook of Latin American Studies*. An annual publication of annotated bibliographic citations in the field of Latin American Studies since 1936, the *Handbook* is vital to the dissemination of information on Latin American scholarship in the United States. The early volumes, slim but ambitious compilations, were rather general in their approach to Latin American studies, but they reflected the promise as well as the youth of the project. Since then the *Handbook*'s growth has been dramatic.

Under the general editorship of Dolores Moyano Martin since 1977, the *Handbook* is now the basic bibliographic tool in the field for graduate students and for many specialists beginning a new project, strengthening their comparative grasp of a field, or merely "keeping up." The *Handbook* has been organized by fields and by countries within fields where that is practical, but above all by fields, thus reflecting the trends in scholarship and the direction that disciplines have taken in the area of Latin American studies. It publishes in alternate years social sciences (odd years) and the humanities (even years), a development of the mid-seventies when the volume of materials about each country in all scholarly disciplines simply became too large, even with careful selection, to gather into one volume.

A part of that problem is owing to the increasing sophistication of Latin American studies in the United States. Now one can find in the *Handbook* annotations of published books and articles on Latin American subjects in every field from bibliography to philosophy, and from archaeology to sociology. In between, the subdisciplines are well represented, indicating how complex, yet how much more precise and exacting, the field of Latin American studies has become. I need only mention the large sections on linguistics, on folklore, on ethnohistory and on translations. The annotations reflect the universality of interest in the field: There are contributions from editors in Italy, Poland, and Sweden and contributions taken from Japan, India and Hungary.

In conclusion, Thomas Jefferson would hardly recognize what he started. By developing an interest of his own in Latin America, he laid the groundwork for the institutionalization of an intimate link between scholarship in Latin America and that undertaken in the United States. As it sits in a critical position between the two regions, the Hispanic Division of the Library of Congress has taken on a measure of importance, at least as a crossroads of scholarly exchange, that Jefferson could not have dreamed for it, but which he would have welcomed as much as do all his scholarly descendants in both hemispheres.

CHAPTER 16

The Growing Professionalism of Latin American Journals

CELSO RODRÍGUEZ

In spite of the financial constraints afflicting publications in Latin America, the quality of the journals published in that region devoted to the social sciences and the humanities have significantly improved throughout the years. Many of the journals now serve a larger audience of readers and researchers and, more importantly, their scholarly nature is widely recognized. The validity of this broad generalization is not impaired by the problems still plaguing other publications serving those fields. Although today there are more Latin American journals of higher quality available to scholars than ever, there still remains an important gap between them and other professional publications.

Latin American journals can be categorized most simply as "traditional," and "modern." The former applies to journals whose *modus operandi*, throughout the years, remains unchanged, both in content and style. In this category we find journals from some institutions which, for example, reserve their pages for the exclusive use of their members, or that still disregard formalities of style, or − somewhat amusing these days − still include the table of content at the end of the publication.

The "modern" group includes most of the "veteran" journals that have kept pace with changing professional demands, and a growing number of scholarly journals published in the last two decades. Almost all of them are institutional and can be favorably compared with the best academic journals in the United States and other developed countries. They are sponsored by universities, private

187

research institutions, corporations, foundations, and even private and public banks. From a growing list of nonacademic institutions we can cite, for example, FLACSO (Facultad Latinoamericana de Ciencias Sociales); CLACSO (Consejo Latinoamericano de Ciencias Sociales); Konrad Adenauer Foundation; Centro de Investigaciones Sociales sobre el Estado y la Administración, in Buenos Aires; Getulio Vargas Foundation, and the Instituto Universitário de Pesquisas do Rio de Janeiro; Corporación de Investigaciones Económicas para América Latina, and the Centro de Estudios de la Realidad Contemporánea, in Santiago; Banco de la República, in Bogotá; Banco Central del Ecuador, in Quito; Centro de Investigaciones Regionales de Mesoamérica, in Antigua, Guatemala; Sociedad Interamericana de Planificación, in Mexico; Centro de Estudios para el Desarrollo y la Participación, in Lima; Centro de Estudios Rurales Andinos "Bartolomé de Las Casas," in Cuzco, and the Centro Paraguayo de Estudios Sociológicos, in Asunción. Thanks to these institutions, as well as others, a good number of scholarly publications are flourishing.

However, the severity of the financial crisis prevalent throughout the region, and the rearrangement of priorities it entails, has placed many journals, both traditional and modern, in a struggle for survival. Insufficient budgets for publications plus a general market also weakened by serious cutbacks, continue to be one of the major reasons affecting the periodicity of Latin American publications and, in too many instances, force them to disappear.

This misfortune has been happening to journals that were published for many years, as well as to others of which only a few issues were published. Government publications are also victims of the low priority assigned to them in very austere budgets. Other technical factors, unquestionably, also affect the possibilities of journals to survive or expand: For example, Bolivia and Ecuador are totally dependent on the importation of printing material such as paper and ink, as well as technical equipment.[1] Moreover, the lack of economic competitiveness of the region is also obstructing the flow of publications among Latin American countries, and with other markets. In 1985 the freight for transporting one kilo of books from Bogota to Madrid was between 2 and 9 dollars, while from Madrid to Bogota the cost was $1.03.[2]

Other factors also play a negative role in the growth and development of periodical Latin American publications. With very few exceptions, the academic community of the region does not enjoy the vital support of well-established, service-oriented professional associations. In most Latin American universities we still find isolated professors who ignore or disregard the strength which they can obtain from an organization open to all persons devoted to a specific discipline or disciplines; that is, an association functioning to serve the needs and aspirations of the profession nationwide, including the publication of a journal financed through membership fees.

This is a great advantage enjoyed by Latin Americanists in Canada and the United States, as exemplified by *Hispania*, published by the American Association of Teachers of Spanish and Portuguese; The *Journal of American History*, published by the Organization of American Historians; *Revista Iberoamericana*, published by the Instituto International de Literatura Iberoamericana; *American Political Science Review*, published by the American Political Science Association; *Latin American Research Review*, published by the Latin American Studies Association; and the *American Historical Review*, published by the American Historical Association. In Canada there is *North/South*, a publication of the Canadian Association of Latin American and Caribbean Studies.

The purpose of these institutions is to serve all professionals in the nation, without exclusions. But Latin America offers a different picture: In every country there exist a good number of *academias*, and their publications have rendered a valuable service. Regardless of the recognition they receive, however, these institutions are vestiges of an elitist professional life of yesteryear, somewhat out of place in our time. Without considering how well they can satisfy today's professional needs, the fact remains that their membership is highly restrictive. Lacking a wide representation, and without a mechanism to admit those who voluntarily want to become members, the academies appear to be only partially able to fulfill the modern demands of a discipline for an entire nation. Their closed environment prevents the formation of a solid base from which to propel professional growth by means of a truly representative collective action. To some extent, this dilemma reflects the traditional individualistic attitude of Latin American scholars. But in today's circumstances, an individual or a small group has neither the capability nor the clout to generate enough political support for major undertakings of interest to the profession at large.

We may contrast this situation with some examples offered by American professional institutions and their journals. For many years the *Journal of American History*, published by the Organization of American Historians, in Bloomington, Indiana, included bibliographical sections on "Recent Articles" and "Recent Doctoral Dissertations." In June 1987 the *Journal* modified the presentation of these two sections, changing their titles to "Recent Scholarship," and introducing some innovations in the subject classification of the material. These changes disposed of headings so useless as "Miscellaneous" and "General," and incorporated new categories such as "Social History" and "Popular Culture." What is significant to consider in this case is that these changes were made in response to a number of letters written to the editors of the *Journal* by members of the OAH, suggesting modifications considered useful to both teachers and researchers.

In another case, not long ago another academic journal, the prestigious *The Americas*, published in Bethesda, Maryland, by the Academy of American Franciscan History, faced a financial crisis. One of the remedies applied was to request a monetary contribution from those who had published articles in the journal. *The Americas* justified this request based on the consideration that publication of those articles benefited the authors in their professional standing, which is true. As a third example we refer to the action taken sometime ago by the editors of the *Hispanic American Historical Review*, who were considering a new format for the cover of this highly respected journal. They consulted a good number of colleagues, mostly those who had been associated with the *HAHR* in the past, in order to know their opinion on the changes the editors wanted to implement.

These illustrations attempt to emphasize that one of the causes that obstructs the advancement of academic publications in Latin America has its origins, to a large extent, in the lack of strong professional associations. Working in semi-isolation, a scholar's individual initiatives can seldom materialize. On the other hand, national collective efforts channeled through professional associations can make possible the existence of solid journals to serve better their respective disciplines.

A professional association may also contribute in another way to improve the quality of the professional literature. We are familiar with the great diversity, or anarchy, found in the stylistic presentation of footnotes and bibliographical citations made in many books and articles printed in Latin America. Specific norms for material published in Spanish and Portuguese are badly needed. Scholars and students, writers and readers, all will profit by the establishment of uniform guidelines. This could be achieved through the cooperative action of working groups interested in seeking a consensus on specific, reasonable norms that can be uniformly applied within a country. It should not be necessary to duplicate the University of Chicago's *Manual of Style*, but with a basic, standardized manual, a significant degree of uniformity can be achieved.[3] Moreover, this is the lesson that the use of computers and library networks is teaching us every day: no successful computer program or software application can work effectively without first establishing standardized norms for all participants. There are Latin American journals dedicated to the social sciences and the humanities that follow an appropriate style, but they constitute a minority. What we still find, for the most part, is the result of professional negligence, which in our times should not be acceptable. Latin Americanists in the United States can provide a helping hand in this matter. As we frequently attend meetings in our own disciplines with Latin American colleagues, we should take advantage of any favorable occasion to emphasize the need for Latin American publications to establish standardized norms for citing books and articles.

The level of professionalism – a very complex subject – also affects the quality of the journals. We should ask ourselves what level of professionalism can be developed in Latin America when facing an adverse economic or political environment. Even within a good economic or political climate, if favoritism rivals merit, how can the latter prevail? A journal whose first issue was published in Buenos Aires in 1986 established a precise procedure to cope successfully with this predicament. It stated that articles submitted to the editors must not identify the authors. In this way, it was assumed that in evaluating the material received the editors would be free from undue pressure. But is it necessary to apply such an aseptic test to presume, or guarantee, the independent judgment of the editors?

Another burden on the effective circulation of academic journals in Latin America is not related to the editors, its contributors, or its readers; it is a problem that has been nagging us for a long time, and which appears far from being resolved. I am referring to the postal service. We are familiar with mysterious losses or delays that occur not too infrequently. In all fairness, the situation appears to be different from country to country, and even varies within the same country. A recent official report from Argentina, for example, revealed that in Brazil and the United States 95 percent of the mail is delivered within 48 hours of being received, whereas in Argentina only 28 percent is delivered within that time. Of a more complex nature are the barriers raised to the circulation of publications among the countries of the region, especially books. In this regard national professional associations should play a very important role in trying to eliminate the artificial trade walls that today parcel the region.

Turning to the brighter side of this general analysis, it is evident that successful efforts by many Latin American publications are replacing the outmoded, individual enterprises of the past that used to provide the basic support for keeping some publications alive. One example of such individual effort that comes to mind is that of the Uruguayan historian Juan Ernesto Pivel Devoto.

Growing scholarly concerns have led to the emergence of a modern corpus of academic publications. The ascendancy in the number and quality of many Latin American journals is also paving the way for a profitable interaction among journals devoted to the same discipline. A good example is provided by Brazilian publications serving the educational field. In 1986 their editors held their second meeting in Rio de Janeiro, with the participation of twenty-five journals. This significant number reveals an interest in discussing common problems, experiences, and ideas, and in promoting an open dialogue within a homogenous context. The third meeting took place in 1987 in Belo Horizonte, an indication that both the objectives and the format of the meetings are appropriate to discuss how to improve the standing of these publications.[4]

This gathering of editors of Brazilian educational and scientific journals could be a very useful model to imitate, both for journals of the same discipline and for interdisciplinary publications within a country or a region. The Brazilian experience proves that journals and readers alike would be the beneficiaries. The rich variety of publications and styles, even within the same discipline, and their diversity of approaches and viewpoints, provide a very adequate forum in which to discuss how to advance their common interests. Among the important practical matters that can be considered at a meeting of editors are exchange of advertising, exchange of distribution lists, establishment of guidelines to handle multiple submissions, standardization of some essential editorial norms, collective diffusion of journals at professional meetings, prizes to honor the best contributions, and how to improve the distribution of scholarly publications in neighboring countries and elsewhere.[5]

Despite old and new problems, in recent years an important number of journals in the social sciences and the humanities have been published in Latin America. To cite just a few: *Contribuciones*, *Megafón*, and *Letras de Buenos Aires*, from Argentina; *Dados*, and *Letras de Hoje*, from Brazil; *Káñina*, from Costa Rica; *Opciones*, *Estudios Cieplan*, and *Estudios Públicos*, from Chile; *Estudios Sociales*, from the Dominican Republic; *Mesoamérica*, from Guatemala; *Revista Paraguaya de Sociología*, from Paraguay; *Socialismo y Participación*, *Boletín de Lima*, and *Revista Andina*, from Perú; and *Nueva Sociedad*, from Venezuela.

The field of international relations provides an excellent example of the emergence of new journals. Among them can be mentioned:

Política e Estratégia, from Brazil; *Ciencia Política*, from Colombia; *Relaciones Internacionales*, from Costa Rica; *Cono Sur* and *Estudios Internacionales*, from Chile; and *Política Internacional*, from Venezuela. Their content reveals a firm commitment to the elaboration of serious studies in this discipline. The transformation created in the area of inter-American studies by the presence of these and other journals, becomes more relevant when we consider that only two decades ago the important articles published in Latin America in this field derived mostly from foreign works translated into Spanish or Portuguese.

Obviously, Latin American scholars are principally responsible for the growing quality of their publications. But in an indirect way, Latin Americanists from other areas of the world also make a very valuable contribution to that end. English-language academic journals devoted to Latin American studies exert a great influence on our knowledge and research. Opening their pages to Latin American authors is proving another effective way to elevate their professional standing. A recent example is that of the Argentine historian Mario Rapoport, who received the 1986 James Alexander Robertson Memorial Award from the Conference of Latin American History of the American Historical Association, for an article he published in the *Hispanic American Historical Review*. Although it is common for Latin American authors to publish in English-language journals, it is much less frequent for a Latin American author to receive such high academic recognition. We can expect that higher standards in the authors will result in higher standards in the journals to which they contribute.[6]

Journals, like other scholarly publications, are an essential element in the development of the social sciences and the humanities.[7] The comments and suggestions briefly outlined here aim at improving the quality and promoting the expansion of Latin American journals. To achieve this general objective, the continuing support of American scholars and American journals devoted to Latin American studies would be highly beneficial to all our colleagues, from Mexico to the Southern Cone. To make their efforts more valuable and more endurable, however, the main thrust of their advancement should come from Latin American scholars themselves.

CHAPTER 17

The Afro-Hispanic Review

IAN ISIDORE SMART

Latin America is home to countless millions of peoples of African ancestry. Africa, Europe, and native America are the three pillars on which rest the civilization and culture that is peculiar to all of the Americas. Indeed, then, as Richard L. Jackson argues in his recent book, *Black Literature and Humanism in Latin America*,[1] the region's African population is the key to the development of an authentic Latin American humanism. Any program of Latin American studies that undervalues the African factor would be irreparably truncated and necessarily imperfect. Unfortunately, the mainstream of academia has tended to ignore the African presence in Latin America and this sorry state of affairs has been reflected in the history of periodical literature in the region and about the region. Against this background, in January 1982 the first issue of the *Afro-Hispanic Review* appeared, tersely proclaiming itself "a publication of the Afro-Hispanic Institute." The institute had been founded and incorporated in the District of Columbia as a nonprofit organization established for the purpose of promoting the study of and interest in Afro-Hispanic literature and culture and with the concrete objective of publishing in the field, at first a journal, and eventually books.

Black newspapers and journals began appearing in Latin America as early as the nineteenth century. Jackson cites, for example, *La Raza Africana o sea el Demócrata Negro* (*The African Race or The Black Democrat*) and *El Proletario* (*The Proletarian*) published by freedmen in nineteenth-century Buenos Aires.[2] The best-known of the twentieth-century black journals is perhaps the Uruguayan *Nuestra Raza* (*Our Race*), the last issue of which appeared in 1948.[3]

The publications that most immediately inspired the founders of the *Afro-Hispanic Review* were *Meridiano Negro: una revista cultural de los afro-ecuatorianos (Black Meridian: An Afro-Ecuadorian Cultural Journal)* and *Negritud*. Both publications, as is almost universally the case, came into being through the toil of one individual, or at most a very small group of committed souls. The driving force of the *Meridiano* was the renowned African-ancestored novelist and poet, Nelson Estupiñán Bass. *Negritud* owed its existence largely to the immense energies of Amir Smith Córdoba, an African Colombian fully conscious of the plight of millions of his black fellow citizens.

In the second issue (May 1982) of the *Afro-Hispanic Review* it was deemed necessary to state succinctly, but with greater explicitness, the journal's goals and functions. A brief editorial highlighted, among other things, the interdisciplinary nature of the journal's approach, and its welcoming of reader comments. The one-page statement of the "Functions," which became a feature of all succeeding issues, indicated the basic concern for ensuring the survival and full development of the nascent academic disciplines, "Afro-Hispanic literature" and the related "Afro-Hispanic Studies."

We were aware of the significance of our undertaking, for those of us who constituted the founders and associates of the journal and the institute knew full well that, although at Howard University the field of Afro-Hispanic Literature was duly recognized as a worthy object of scholarly pursuit from the first year of university study through the Ph.D., this situation was unique in the United States and perhaps in the world. Without a journal and a press, the future augured ill for the field. However, we harbored no illusions. The very institution that had done the most to grant legitimacy to the field and that, as the "capstone of Black education," had served as the moral strength and central source of inspiration, was extremely hesitant to throw its full administrative weight behind our efforts. The track record of Latin American journals in general and Afro-Hispanic ones in particular contributed to our concerns and intensified our determination to ensure a solid fiscal and administrative base that would withstand the considerable vicissitudes peculiar to our enterprise.

The Afro-Hispanic Institute was set up to provide such a base. It is an association of scholars from a wide range of North American universities united by a common interest in Afro-Hispanic literature and culture. The Institute also numbered among its original members several Afro-Hispanics from Latin America who were engaged either in creative or critical activity in the field. Naturally, Nelson Estupiñán Bass and Amir Smith Córdoba were among these overseas associates. Manuel Zapata Olivella, the distinguished African Colombian man of letters, and Nelly Vélez de Truque, wife of the deceased African Colombian writer, Carlos Arturo Truque, were also included in this special list of associates. The institute and its activities were meant to be self-sustaining financially. Its administrative, academic, and fiscal functions were indivisible. Stanley A. Cyrus, then of Howard University, was the president of the institute, the editor of the *AHR*, and the chief engine that drove the entire enterprise. I served as secretary-treasurer of the institute as well as the managing editor of the journal. The third member of the directing triumvirate was Henry J. Richards, of the State University of New York at Buffalo, who, although listed simply as one of the five associate editors, in fact, shared the major editorial responsibility equally with the official editor and managing editor. An important member of the team was Donna Allen, whose administrative and technical skills and experience made the journal possible. From the very beginning Cyrus predicted that our stamina would not endure beyond a period of five years.

Those first five years were full of almost hysterical activity. The financial situation was unimaginably precarious: we had initiated the enterprise with seed money of approximately $3,000.00 – a little more than the cost of production of one issue – realized through one-time $100 contributions of the "founders" and yearly $20.00 contributions of the "associates." It was expected that the *AHR* would become self-sustaining through subscriptions and sales. We expected, too, a veritable flood of high-quality manuscripts, and the enthusiastic cooperation of our many "associate" and "consulting and contributing editors." We also held out some hope that Howard University, the home institution of the editor and managing editor would eventually render a modicum of practical assistance. The harsh reality belied our expectations. With each financial crisis we turned to the generous and spiritually "deep" pockets of a small handful of "founders." We overloaded a small group of editors with the intolerable burdens of not just assessing manuscripts but at times almost rewriting them to make them publishable – the flood we envisaged never materialized. However, we survived and even evoked the illusory image of good health, a journal happily backed by an understanding and supportive "home" institution, in this case Howard University.

The circumstances surrounding the founding and development of the *Afro-Hispanic Review* are by all accounts not unusual, neither in the United States, nor, certainly, in Latin America. What is quite clear, however, is the fact that the prevailing socioeconomic state of North American academia makes it possible for a journal such as ours to weather the storm. The *AHR* did in fact survive. The three-in-one number of our 1986 issue completed the anticipated initial five-year period. It contained an "Editors' Note" that speaks for itself:

> the founders of the Institute intended and, indeed, hoped that their stewardship of the *Review* would be temporary, exactly analogous to that of a parent over a child. The moment has now arrived for the *Afro-Hispanic Review* to take the final step in its development and become officially associated with a single and outstanding academic institution. As from the 1987 issues the *Afro-Hispanic Review* will be a publication of the University of Missouri–Columbia. . . . At this historic juncture the Institute is singularly pleased to announce the publication of its first book, Ian Smart's translation of Carlos Guillermo Wilson's short stories: *Short Stories by Cubena.* . . . Our second book, Henry J. Richards' translation of the Nelson Estupiñán Bass novel, *Cuando los guayacanes florecían,* is expected to be on the shelves by the summer of 1987. The Afro-Hispanic Institute plans, then, to focus its major attention on this important aspect of the promotion of the field of Afro-Hispanic literature.

The new editors of the journal are Marvin Lewis, one of the original "associates," and Edward Mullen. It is now an official publication of the Black Studies Program and the Department of Romance Languages, University of Missouri–Columbia. Henry Richards, Stanley Cyrus and this author have remained as associate editors. As the *AHR* has taken firm root in its new home, the Afro-Hispanic Institute with the publication of two books and its projected third, fourth and fifth books, has come of age as a publishing house.

The question is now, what impact does the journal have on the scholarly community nationally and internationally, and what is the best agenda for fruitful interaction in the area of Latin American and Caribbean studies.

The journal's focus is interdisciplinary, however its emphasis has tended to be in the humanities rather than the social sciences. In the first year of its existence, it was included in the *MLA International Bibliography.* Felicitously, the Modern Language Association entered into a much more detailed system of subject listing just around the time that the *AHR* came into existence. A perusal, then, of the *International Bibliography* will provide some indication – obviously this is not in any way a strict statistical examination – of our journal's impact on the field of Afro-Hispanic literature. Looking under the subject heading "Afro-Hispanic," one finds that since 1981 the majority of the critics who have authored articles listed under this rubric are those who have been associated with the *Afro-Hispanic Review*. They include such scholars as Richard Jackson, Shirley Jackson, J. Bekunuru Kubayanda, Stanley Cyrus, Lemuel Johnson, and Alan Persico.

Of course, some of the major contributions to the field that have appeared in the pages of the journal have, for some reason or other, not been listed under the subject heading "Afro-Hispanic." Henry J. Richards, for example, who must be considered one of the most authoritative interpreters of the works of Nelson Estupiñán Bass, has published, in the pages of the journal, two seminal articles: "Narrative Strategies in Nelson Estupiñán Bass's *El último río*" (1.1 [1982]: 11–16) and "Nelson Estupiñán Bass and the Historico-Political Novel: From Theory to Praxis" (2.1 [1983]: 5–12), that have escaped categorization as "Afro-Hispanic." Laurence E. Prescott's work on the contemporary African Colombian writer, "*El tambor*: Symbol and Substance in the Poetry of Jorge Artel" (3.2 [1984]: 11–14), or Marvin A. Lewis' insightful analyses: "From *Hacienda* to *Tugurio*: Blacks in Peruvian Fiction" (1.2 [1982]: 17–25) and "From *Chincha* to *Chimbote*: Blacks in the Contemporary Peruvian Novel" (3.2 [1984]: 5–10), or my own studies on the new Central American writers, for example, "Religious Elements in the Narrative of Quince Duncan" (1.2 [1982]: 27–31), have analogously not been listed under the rubric "Afro-Hispanic." For all the unavoidable glitches, it is quite clear that in the realm of periodical literature in the humanities, the *Afro-Hispanic Review* has firmly established itself as a leader.

One of the fruits and, indeed, the most significant demonstration of the *AHR*'s leadership role has been the impetus it has given to general scholarship on Afro-Hispanic creative writers. Some of these writers were already well known to the mainstream academic community, such figures as Cuba's Nicolás Guillén, or the Venezuelan Ramón Díaz Sánchez, or the Colombian Manuel Zapata Olivella, or the Ecuadorians Nelson Estupiñán Bass and Adalberto Ortiz. However, they have not been the subject of such sustained research as has been published in the pages of the *AHR* since 1982. Indeed, in the case of Richards' work on Estupiñán Bass the pages of the journal have been the most significant scholarly forum in both the national and international arenas. Analogous claims may be made with regard to the scholarship that has been published in the journal on those other major Latin American writers of African ancestry that were mentioned earlier.

Clearly, in the case of the "minor" or "lesser known" or "new" Afro-Hispanic writers, the role of the articles published in our journal is more pivotal. The lead article in our initial number was Lemuel A. Johnson's brilliant study on the 1949 novel by the Colombian Arnoldo

Palacios, "The Dilemma of Presence in Black Diaspora Literature: A Comparativist Reading of Palacios' *Las estrellas son negras*" (1.1 [1982]: 3–10). When a scholar of the reputation of Johnson pens a study on a relatively obscure writer, the academic community takes note, and an act of scholarly leadership is committed. That initial issue also contained a brief and poignantly autobiographical piece, "Mi testimonio" ("My Testimony") (pp. 17–22), by the late Carlos Arturo Truque, an African Colombian short-story writer who was born in Chocó in 1927 and died 43 years later without having scaled any particular heights of fame in the literary world. Exposure through the *Afro-Hispanic Review* has most certainly intensified, if not established for the first time, the mainstream academic community's interest in this powerful writer. Laurence Prescott, a most promising North American critic, has done for Jorge Artel what Johnson did for Palacios. My own work on the Central Americans of Anglophone-Caribbean background has similarly helped to bring basically unknown and very promising literary talents before the wider scholarly world.

The editorial process employed by the *AHR* is the usual one for most North American academic journals. We have worked basically with unsolicited manuscripts that we subject to a review by three readers, normally exclusive of the editor and managing editor. These latter make the ultimate decision on whether to publish or not, based largely on the readers' reports but incorporating other factors that are more administrative and technical than academic: for example, the length of the manuscript and the availability of other manuscripts. Some manuscripts coming from outside of the United States, i.e., Latin America and the Caribbean, while substantially publishable, have required significant editorial reworking.

Actually, it is attention to detail that frequently makes the difference between acceptance and nonacceptance of a manuscript, for it is only by way of exception that an editor will be prepared to, so to speak, "clean up" an otherwise good article. The most important of these details is absolute conformity to the required stylistic norms, in our case, those set forth in *The MLA Style Manual* or *The Chicago Manual of Style*. Even such small details as the inclusion of a self-addressed envelope with the appropriate postage, not stamped but in the form of loose stamps perhaps simply clipped to the envelope, the submission of a xerox copy along with the original, and, of course, ensuring that the manuscript can easily receive an anonymous review will help considerably to create a favorable impression on over-extended, underbudgeted editors.

The journal prides itself on its interdisciplinary approach, however, the literary one has predominated, understandably so. This situation offers a particular challenge and invitation to those scholars who are comfortable with innovation. Furthermore, it must be made clear that the term "Afro-Hispanic" has a primarily and exclusively cultural referent. The plain fact of the matter is that culture is generally intimately related to ethnicity. The editors realize, however, that this, like all general rules, brooks exceptions. Thus the race of our contributors is simply not taken into account. All that matters is the level of insight into the relevant subject matter, namely, the literature and culture of Spanish-speaking people of African ancestry.

To maintain its primacy the *AHR* needs a flow of quality manuscripts from a wide variety of scholars seriously committed to exploring the contributions African-ancestored Hispanics have made to literature and culture. In the past there were very few institutions that took seriously the question of Afro-Hispanic literature and culture. To its credit Howard University was one of the first to do so, and is still the only one to translate this commitment into a coherent system of course offering from the first year to the Ph.D. degree. Clearly, this kind of interest is growing throughout the U.S. academic community. Evidence of this is the recent acquisition of the *AHR* by the University of Missouri – Columbia. There is, then, for scholars a rare opportunity to associate themselves with a pioneering journal at that stage of its development that is no longer considered critical and problematic, i.e., the initial five years. The momentum has picked up but the field is still far from crowded.

History, we believe, will look very favorably on the *AHR* and, of course, on those associated with it. The arguments advanced by Jackson and others with respect to the crucial role Africa must play in Latin American humanism have been significantly bolstered by the scholarship of such historian-anthropologists as George G. M. James, Cheikh Anta Diop, Ivan Van Sertima, and Martin Bernal that has very recently begun to have an impact on the mainstream academic community.[4] Now is the period when the benefits of this association far outweigh the risks. There could be no more fitting conclusion to this essay than a general invitation to Latin Americanists and Caribbeanists of every stripe to subscribe to the *AHR*, involving themselves with it to the fullest extent of their academic possibilities. The *Afro-Hispanic Review* and its parent, the Afro-Hispanic Institute – now a full-fledged academic press – constitute the primary academic forum for current research in Afro-Hispanic literature and culture.

Notes and References

Introduction to Part I

1. "Panorama de la filosofía latinoamericana contemporanánea," *Minerva* 1 (1944): 95; reprinted in Jorge J. E. Gracia, ed., *Risieri Frondizi. Ensayos filosóficos* (México: Fondo de Cultura Económica, 1986), 257.

2. See the bibliography of his works prepared by Leopoldo Montoya, in Jorge J. E. Gracia, ed., *Man and His Conduct: Philosophical Essays in Honor of Risieri Frondizi* (San Juan: University of Puerto Rico Press, 1980), 29–39.

3. I have developed this threefold conceptual framework for understanding the development of Latin American philosophy in "Latin American Philosophy Today," *Philosophical Forum* 20 (1988):4–32.

4. See the first issue of a new bibliographic journal entitled *Anuario Bibliográfico de Historia del Pensamiento Ibero e Iberoamericano*, edited by J. L. Gómez Martínez.

Chapter 1.
Contemporary Argentinian Philosophy

1. A brief semantical approach to this point can be seen in my paper, "La expresión filosófica latinoamericana", *Latin American Research Review* 14, no. 2 (1979).

2. Such are the cases of the following centers: Centro de Estudios Filosóficos, Sociedad Argentina de Análisis Filosófico, Fundación para el Estudio del Pensamiento Argentino e Iberoamericano, Asociación Argentina de Investigaciones Eticas, and, also, the case of other entities with more strictly corporate aims. There exist also groups dealing with other trends or activities where, never-

theless, the philosophical "nuance" appears. Such are, for instance: Centro de Estudios sobre Estado y Sociedad and the recently created Centro Argentino de Ciencias del Hombre (Fundación Acta), or not-so-formal nuclei like Club de Cultura Socialista, Club de Pensamiento, and Núcleo Interdisciplinario para la Democracia. The last one holds its meetings at Club del Progreso.

3. For example: *Stromata, Cuadernos de Filosofía, Philosophia, Revista Latinoamericana de Filosofía,* or *Revista de Filosofía Latinoamericana.*

4. For example: *Escritos de Filosofía, Análisis Filosófico, Revista de Estética, Patrística et Medievalia, Anuario de Filosofía Jurídica y Social,* and others.

5. In the current decade, many different international events on various philosophical disciplines were held: three national congresses, annual meetings sponsored by the University of Córdoba; symposia on Argentinian philosophical thought, etc. As regards the last world meeting, see Víctor Bullotts, Congreso Internacional de Filosofía, FISYP, 1987.

6. Juan Adolfo Vázquez, *Antología filosófica argentina* (Buenos Aires: Eudeba, 1965), 160.

7. The period from 1852 onwards is referred to as the period of "Organización Nacional," the time when Argentina set out to become a modern country.

8. In a forthcoming paper, I shall deal with the works mentioned here or those that are not mentioned but could be included.

9. *Fenomenología de la crisis moral* (San Antonio de Padua, Argentina: Castañeda, 1978).

10. (Bogotá: Nueva América, 1983).

11. Part of the argument regarding the philosophy of liberation and the polemic with Dr. Cerutti were collected in the following journals: *Nuestra América* 11 (1984); *Cristianismo y Sociedad* 80 (1984); *Concordia* 6 (1984); and *Prometeo* 2 (1985).

12. The Argentinian "Radical Party" is a political organization of the center. The term 'radical' has nothing to do with what radicalism means in the United States.

13. *Etica y ciencia* (Buenos Aires: Siglo Veinte, 1985), 8–9.

14. The dialogue is taken from an article, "La filosofía, hoy, como la ven los españoles," by Carlos Alemán in the Buenos Aires newspaper *La Nación,* 27 September 1987.

15. See works by Bunge such as *Filosofía de la física* (Barcelona: Ariel, 1982); *Seudociencia e ideología* (Madrid: Alianza, 1985); *Vistas y entrevistas* (Buenos Aires: Siglo Veinte, 1987).

16. As many commentators have pointed out, Frondizi himself has many affinities with that trend. They can be detected, for instance, in his approach to G. E. Moore's axiology. Cf. Héctor-Neri Castañeda, "La base ontológica de la teoría de los valores de Frondizi", in Jorge J. E. Gracia, ed., *El hombre y su conducta* (Río Piedras, Puerto Rico: Editorial Universitaria, 1980).

17. For further information about the Argentinian presence overseas, the reader may refer to my *Panorama filosófico Argentino* (Buenos Aires: Eudeba, 1985), where this fact has been highlighted in many parts of the book. There are various approaches to the period under consideration for instance: J. C. Agulla, *Dependencia y conciencia desgraciada* (Buenos Aires: Editorial de Belgrano, 1985); M. Atienza, *La filosofía del derecho argentino actual* (Buenos Aires: De Palma, 1984); M. G. Casas, "Situação atual da filosofia na Argentina," *Revista Portuguesa de Filosofia* 17, 3–4; A. Caturelli, *La filosofía en la Argentina actual* (Buenos Aires: Sudamericana, 1971); G. Díaz Díaz and C. Santos Escudero, *Bibliografía filosófica hispánica* (Madrid: CSIC, 1982); L. Farré y C. Lértora Mendoza, *La filosofía en la Argentina* (Buenos Aires: Docencia, 1981); A. Klappenbach, "La filosofía en la Argentina actual," *Arbor*, no. 490 (1986); C. Lértora Mendoza, *Bibliografía filosófica argentina* (Buenos Aires: Fecic, 1983); D. Pro, C. Jalif, and G. Prada, *Historia del pensamiento filosófico argentino*, Vols. 1 and 3 (Mendoza: Universidad de Cuyo, 1973 and 1980); O. Terán, *En busca de la ideología argentina* (Buenos Aires: Catálogos, 1986); J. C. Torchia Estrada, *La filosofía en la Argentina* (Washington, D.C.: Unión Panamericana, 1961); M. A. Virasoro, "Filosofía," in *Argentina 1930–1960* (Buenos Aires: Sur, 1961) and the discussion by A. Carpio in *Sur*, no. 275 (1962); H. E. Biagini, "Pensamiento e ideologías en la Argentina (1950–1959)," *Ideas en Ciencias Sociales*, no. 6 (1987); J. Gracia, *et al. El análisis filosófico en América Latina* (México: Fondo de Cultura Económica, 1985). On the general problem of exile, see G. Caro Figueroa, "Exiliados y proscriptos en la historia argentina," *Todo es Historia*, no. 246 (1987).

18. Recently, Professor Evandro Agazzi presented a similar position with respect to the whole Latin American milieu. Cf. "¿Qué espera la comunidad internacional de parte de la filosofía latinoamericana?" *Prometeo* 5 (1986): 58–59, 64–65.

19. *El gaucho Martín Fierro*, by José Hernández, is considered Argentina's national epic. It has been translated into a score of languages. It is a long poem, dealing with the life of nineteenth-century cowboys from the pampas. Martín Fierro, the hero, endures many injustices from the power elite of those times, rich ranch owners, rural police and military men. The *tango* to which the author refers is probably "Cambalache" (approx. the pawn shop). It dates back from the 1930s and, strictly speaking, had nothing to do with the 1976–83 period. Its ironical and scorching lyrics, however, refer to corruption at all levels of society. This, aparently, was an offense that governing military men did not tolerate.

20. Augusto Pérez Lindo, *Universidad, política y sociedad* (Buenos Aires: Eudeba, 1985), 179–180.

References

Keeping in mind the audience of this paper, I have emphasized in this list sources, especially books, either written, published or translated abroad. This does not necessarily imply a judgment on the actual value of the sources referred to. When no city is mentioned, it is to be understood that the publication appeared in Buenos Aires.

AA.VV. *Francisco Romero.* Caracas: Sociedad Interamericana de Filosofía, 1983.

Agoglia, Rodolfo. *Sentido y trayectoria de la filosofía moderna.* Quito: Universidad Católica, 1979.

_____. *Conciencia histórica y tiempo histórico.* Quito: Universidad Católica, 1980.

_____. "Cultura nacional y filosofía de la historia en América Latina," *Cuadernos Salmantinos de Filosofía* 8 (1981).

Aisenson, Aida. *Cuerpo y persona.* México: FCE, 1981.

Albizu, Edgardo. *Estructuras formales de la dialéctica hegeliana.* Lima: Universidad Nacional Federico Villareal, 1984.

Alchourrón, C. and Bulygin, E. *Normative Systems.* Vienna: Springer, 1971.

Alvarez Guerrero, O. *Etica y política social.* Siglo XX, 1986.

Angelelli, Ignacio. *Studies on G. Frege & Traditional Philosophy.* Dordrecht: Reidel, 1967.

Anquin, Nimio de. *Ente y ser.* Madrid: Gredos, 1962.

Arico, José. *Marx y América Latina.* México: Alianza, 1980.

Asti Vera, Armando. *Methodologia da pezquiza científica.* Porto Alegre: Globo, 1983.

Astrada, Carlos. *Nietzsche y la crisis del irracionalismo.* Dédalo, 1960.

_____. *Dialéctica y positivismo lógico.* Devenir, 1964.

_____. *Heidegger.* Juárez, 1970.

Bagu, Sergio. *Tiempo, realidad social y conocimiento.* Siglo XXI, 1970.

_____. *Marx-Engels.* Nueva Visión, 1972.

Battro, Antonio. *Dictionnaire d'épistémologie génétique.* Paris: PUF, 1966. Introduction by Piaget. English translation, 1973.

_____. *O pensamento de J. Piaget.* Rio de Janeiro: Forense, 1976.

Bazán, Bernardo. *Siger de Brabant.* Louvain: Publications Univ., 1972.

Berbeglia, Carlos. *Vida. pensamiento y libertad.* Biblos, 1985.

Biagini, Hugo. "Revaloración del pensamiento y la actividad política," *Revista de Estudios Políticos* [Madrid] 19 (1981).

_____. "En torno a la crisis del liberalismo," *Revista de Estudios Políticos* 30 (1982).

Bonilla, Alcira. *Mundo de la vida* (Husserl). Biblos, 1987.

Botana, Natalio. *La tradición republicana*. Sudamericana, 1984.

Brauer, Daniel. *Dialektik der Zeit* (Hegel). Stuttgart: Fromman, 1982.

Braun, Rafael. *La théorie de la vertu dans la philosophie de Vladimir Jankélevitch*. Louvain: Institut Supérieur de Philosophie, 1966.

Briancesco, Eduardo. *Un triptyque sur la liberté* (San Anselmo). Paris: D. de Brouwer, 1982. Foreword by Paul Vignaux.

Bunge, Mario. *Lingüística y filosofía*. Barcelona: Ariel, 1983.

_____. *Treatise on Basic Philosophy*. Dordrecht: Reidel, 1977–85.

Cabanchik, Samuel. *El absoluto no sustancial* (Sartre). Ed. de Belgrano, 1984

Cappelletti, Angel. *Ensayos sobre los atomistas griegos*. Caracas: Sociedad Venezolana de Ciencias Humanas, 1979.

_____. *Ciencia jónica y pitagórica*. Caracas: Equinoccio, 1980.

_____. *La teoría de la propiedad en Proudhon*. Madrid: La Piqueta, 1980.

_____. *La filosofía de Anaxágoras*. Caracas: Sociedad Venezolana de Filosofía, 1984.

_____. *La idea de la libertad en el Renacimiento*. Caracas: Alfadil, 1986.

_____. *Lucrecio*. Caracas: Monte Avila, 1987.

Carpio, Adolfo. *El sentido de la historia de la filosofía*. Eudeba, 1977.

Casas, Manuel. *Introducción a la filosofía*. Madrid: Gredos, 1970.

Castellán, Angel. *Filosofía de la historia a historiografía*. Dédalo, 1961.

_____. *Tiempo e historiografía*. Biblos, 1984.

Castellanos, Juan. *El pensamiento revolucionario de J. Ingenieros*. S. José, Costa Rica: Educa, 1972.

Castorina, J. and G. Palau. *Introducción a la lógica operatoria de Piaget*. Paidós, 1982.

Ceriotto, Carlos. *Fenomenología y psicoanálisis*. Troquel, 1969.

Cerutti Guldberg, H. *Hacia una metodología de las ideas (filosóficas) en América Latina*. Guadalajara: Universidad de Guadalajara, 1986.

Cirigliano, Gustavo. *Fenomenologia da educação*. Petrópolis: Vozes, 1969.

Clementi, Hebe. *La frontera en América*. Leviatán, 1985–87.

Coffa, Alberto. "Notas para un esquema de la filosofía de la ciencia contemporánea," *Crítica* 16.7 (1972).

Cooper, William. *Francisco Romero's Theory of Value*. Waco, Texas, 1966. Doctoral dissertation.

Cordero, Nestor. *Les deux chemins de Parmenide*. Paris: Vrin, 1984.

Croatto, Severino. *El hombre en el mundo*. La Aurora, 1974

————. *Historia de la salvación*. Paulinas, 1980.

————. *Exodus*. Maryknoll, NY.: Orbis, 1981. A Spanish edition in Peru, 1978, and a Portuguese one in 1981.

————. *Amar y crear en libertad*. La Aurora, 1986.

De Ipola, Emilio. *Ideología y discurso populista*. México: Folios, 1982.

Delacre, Georges. *El tiempo en perspectiva*. San Juan: University of Puerto Rico, 1975.

Derisi, Octavio. *Filosofía de la cultura y de los valores*. Emece, 1963.

Dotti, Jorge. *Dialéctica y derecho* (Hegel). Hachette, 1983.

Dujovne, León. *Martin Buber*. Omeba, 1965.

————. *El pensamiento histórico de Croce*. Rueda, 1968.

Dussel, Enrique. *Histoire et théologie de la liberation*. Paris: Eds. Quvrières, 1974. English version published in the United States.

————. *Ethics and the Theology of Liberation*. Orbis, 1978.

————. *La producción teórica de Marx*. México: Siglo XXI.

Echauri, Raúl. *Heidegger y la filosofía tomista*. Eudeba, 1971. Introduction by Etienne Gilson.

Eggers Lan, Conrado. *El Fedón de Platón*. Córdoba: Univ. Nacional, 1967.

————. *El sol, la línea y la caverna* (Plato). Eudeba, 1975.

Entelman, Ricardo. "Discourse normatif et organization du pouvoir," in *Yearbook of Access to Justice* 6 (1987).

Estiú, Emilio. *Del arte a la historia en la filosofía moderna*. La Plata: Univ. Nacional, 1962.

Estrada, J. M. de. *Ensayo de antropología filosófica*. Club de Lectores, 1958.

Farré, Luis. *Antropología filosófica*. Madrid: Guadarrama, 1968.

_____. *Filosofía de la religión*. Losada, 1969.

Farrel, Martín. *Utilitarismo*. Abeledo, 1983.

Fatone, Vicente. *The Philosophy of Nagarjuna*. Delhi: M. Banarsidass, 1981.

Feinmann, José. *Filosofía y nación*. Legasa, 1983.

Ferrari, Oward. *Historia y ser* (Hegel. Marx). Mendoza: Universidad Nacional de Cuyo, 1971.

_____. *Introducción a Kant*. México: 1974.

Fisher, Sofía. *Linguistique*. Paris: Ecole Hautes Etudes, 1983.

Fornet-Betancourt, R. and C. Lértora Mendoza, *Ethik in Deutschland und Lateinamerika heute*. Frankfurt: P. Lang, 1987.

Frondizi, Risieri. *What is Value?*. LaSalle: Open Court, 1971.

García Astrada, A. *El pensamiento de Ortega y Gasset*. Troquel, 1961.

García Barceló, *Sociedad y derecho*. Estudio, 1979.

García Canclini, N. *Arte popular y sociedad en América Latina*. México: Grijalbo, 1977.

_____. *La producción simbólica*. México: Siglo XXI, 1977.

_____. *Epistemología e historia* (M. Ponty). México: UNAM, 1979.

García, Ward J. *Comparison of Two Liberation Thinkers* (Dussel & M. Novak). Chicago: De Paul University. Doctoral dissertation.

Garmendía, G. and N. Schnaith. *Hobbes y los orígenes del Estado burgués*. México: Siglo XXI, 1973.

Garzón Valdés, E. *Derecho y "naturaleza de la cosa."* Córdoba: Univ. Nacional, 1970.

Gómez, Ricardo. *Las teorías científicas*. El Coloquio, 1977.

González Asenjo, J. *El todo y las partes*. Madrid: Tecnos, 1962.

_____. *Anti-platitudes*. Universidad de Valencia, 1976.

Grau, Néstor. *Notas sobre la antropología platónica*. Tucumán: Univ. Nac., 1968.

Guariglia, Osvaldo. *Quellenkritische und Logische Untersuchungen zur Gegensatzlehre des Aristoteles*. Hildeschein, NY.: Olms, 1978.

_____. *Ideología, verdad y legitimación*. Sudamericana, 1986.

Guillot, Daniel. "Emmanuel Levinas," in E. Dussel and D. Guillot. *Liberación latinoamericana y E. Levinas*. Bonum, 1975.

Harris. Marjorie. *Francisco Romero on Problems of Philosophy.* New York: Philosophical Library, 1960.

Hernández, Enrique. *Positivismo y cientificismo en la Argentina.* Bariloche: Univ. Comahue, 1975.

Iribarne, Julia. *La libertad en Kant.* Lohlé, 1981.

Karsz, Saul. *Théorie et politique* (Althusser). Paris: Fayard, 1974.

Kilgore, William. *A. Korn's Interpretation of Creative Freedom.* Austin: University of Texas, 1958. Doctoral dissertation.

Klimovsky, Gregorio. *El método hipotético deductivo y la lógica.* La Plata: Univ. Nac., 1971.

_____. "Acerca del carácter científico del psicoanálisis," *Revista de Psicoanálisis* 44, no. 4 (1987).

Kogan, Jacobo. *Filosofía de la imaginación.* Paidós: 1986.

_____. *La religión del arte.* Emece, 1987.

Kusch, Rodolfo. *El pensamiento indígena americano.* México: Cajica, 1970.

_____. *Esbozo de una antropología americana.* S. Antonio de Padua: Castañeda, 1978.

Landi, Oscar. *Crisis y lenguaje político.* Cedes, 1985.

_____. *El discurso sobre lo posible.* Cedes, 1985.

Lértora Mendoza, G. *La enseñanza de la filosofía en tiempos de la colonia.* Fecic, 1979.

Lipp, Solomon. *Three Argentine Thinkers* (Korn, F. Romero, Ingenieros). New York: Philosophical Library, 1969.

López Domínguez, F. *La concepción fichteana del amor.* Sudamericana, 1982.

Lorenzano, César. "El materialismo de Marx," *Crítica* 49 (1985).

Lungarzo, Carlos. *Aspectos críticos del método dialéctico.* Ed. Buenos Aires, 1970.

_____. *Introdución a la teoría de la deducción.* Biblos, 1986.

Maci, Guillermo. *La otra escena de lo real.* Nueva Visión, 1979.

Mainetti, José. *Realidad, fenómeno y misterio del cuerpo humano.* La Plata: Quirón, 1972.

Maliandi, Ricardo. *Wertobjektivität und Realiätserfahrung* (N. Hartmann). Bonn: Bouvier, 1966.

_____. *Cultura y conflicto.* Biblos, 1985.

Mari, Enrique. *Neopositivismo e ideología*. Eudeba,1974.

_____. *La problemática del castigo* (Bentham & Foucault). Hachette, 1983.

Martí, Oscar. *The Reaction Against Positivism in Latin America* (Ingenieros). New York: City University of New York, 1978. Doctoral dissertation.

Martín, José. *Filón de Alejandría y la génesis de la cultura occidental*. De Palma, 1986.

Martino, Antonio. *La definizione legislativa*. Torino: Giappichelli, 1975.

Massuh, Víctor. *Nietzsche y el fin de la religión*. Sudamericana, 1969.

_____. *Nihilismo y experiencia extrema*. Sudamericana, 1975.

Mateo, Martha. *Ontología y ética en Sartre*. Tucumán: Univ. Nac., 1975.

_____. *Razón y sensibilidad en la ética de Kant*. Tucumán: Univ. Nac., 1981.

Melano Cough, B. *Hermenéutica metódica* (Ricoeur). Docencia, 1983.

Michelini Dorando, J. *Der Andere in der Dialektik der Freiheit*. Frankfurt, 1981. Doctoral dissertation.

_____. *Scheler y Husserl*. Río Cuarto: Univ. Nac., 1984.

Mondolfo, Rodolfo. *Heráclito*. México: Siglo XXI, 1966.

Noussan-Lettry, Luis. *Spekulatives Denken in Platons Früschriften*. Freiburg: Alber, 1974.

Nudler, Oscar. "Ciencia y metafísica en la teoría de la Gestalt", *Universidad* 94 (1965).

Olaso, Ezequiel de. *Los nombres de Unamuno*. Sudamericana, 1963.

_____. *Escepticismo e ilustración* (Hume & Rousseau). Univ. de Carabobo, 1981.

Orayen, Raúl. *Lógica, significado y ontología*. México: UNAM (in press).

Parker, C. M. *Francisco Romero's "Theory of Man"*. University of Oklahoma, 1973. Doctoral dissertation.

Perez Lindo, A. *La praxis et l'inertie dans l'anthropologie dialectique de Sartre*. Louvain: Univ. Catholique, 1978. Doctoral dissertation.

Pfeiffer, Maria. *Vers l'être brut* (M. Ponty). Paris: La Sorbonne, 1970. Doctoral dissertation.

Picotti, Dina. *Die Überwindung der Metaphysik als Geschichtliche Aufgabe bei M. Heidegger*. München: L. Maximilians Univ., 1969.

Pochtar, Ricardo. "Teoría del languaje, técnica y filosofía", *Cuadernos de Filosofía* 18 (1972).

210 NOTES AND REFERENCES

_____. "El examen de ingenios y la lingüística cartesiana," *Revista Latinoamericana de Filosofía* 2. 2 (1976).

_____. "Regle et cause dans l'analyse du langage," in *Systèmes simboliques, science et philosophie*. Paris: CNRS, 1978.

_____. "Sobre el aspecto creativo del uso del lenguaje," *Escritos de filosofía* (1978).

Ponce, Aníbal. *Storia marxista dell'educazione*. Roma: Partisan, 1970.

_____. *Educazione e lotta di classe*. Roma: Savelli, 1974.

Prado, José. *Voluntad y naturaleza* (Máximo el Confesor). Río Cuarto: Univ. Nacional, 1974.

Presas, Mario. *Situación de la filosofía de K. Jaspers*. Depalma, 1978.

Pro, Diego. *Coriolano Alberini*. Mendoza: Valle de los Huarpes, 1960.

_____. *Rodolfo Mondolfo*. Losada, 1967–68.

Pucciarelli, Eugenio. *El tiempo en la filosofía actual*. Universidad de Buenos Aires, 1970.

_____. "Dos actitudes frente al tiempo," *Cuadernos de Filosofía* 13 (1970).

_____. "El tiempo en la pintura," *Cuadernos del Sur* 11 (1972).

_____. "Tiempo y lenguaje," *Cuadernos del Sur* 1 (1978).

_____. "El instante y el tiempo," *Cuadernos del Sur* 7 (1981).

_____. "El hombre y el tiempo," *Universitas* 23 no. 2 (1985).

Pugliese, Orlando. *Vermittlung und Kehre* (Heidegger). Freiburg: Alber, 1965.

Quiles, Ismael. *Antropología filosófica in-sistencial*, in *Obras Completas* I. Depalma, 1983.

Quintas, Avelino. *Analisi del bene comune*. Roma: Bulsoni, 1979.

Rabossi, Eduardo. *Análisis filosófico, lenguaje y metafísica*. Caracas: M. Avila, 1977.

_____. *Estudios éticos*. Univ. Carabobo, 1979.

Raggio, Andrés. "Alcances y límites de la mecanización en lógica," *Revista de la Universidad Nacional de Córdoba* 11 (1970).

_____. "Estilos perceptivos," *Revista Latinoamericana de Filosofía* 12, no. 1 (1986).

Ravera, Rosa. *En torno a la sociología del arte*. Rosario: Univ. Nac., 1972.

_____. *Cuestiones de estética*. Correo de Arte, 1979.

Rodríguez, Hernán. *Psicología y cibernética*. Siglo XX, 1958.

_____. *La automatización en perspectiva.* Siglo XX, 1959.

Rodríguez Alcalá, H. *Misión y pensamiento de F. Romero.* México: UNAM, 1959.

Roig, Arturo. *Platón.* Mendoza: Universidad de Cuyo, 1972.

_____. *Los krausistas argentinos.* Puebla: Cajica, 1969.

_____. *Teoría y crítica del pensamiento latinoamericano.* México: FCE, 1981.

_____. *Filosofía, universidad y filósofos en América Latina.* México: UNAM, 1981.

_____. *Esquemas para una historia de la filosofía ecuatoriana.* Quito: Educación, 1982.

Rojo, Roberto. *Antinomias del lenguaje.* Tucumán: Univ. Nacional, 1972.

Romero, Francisco. *Historia de la filosofía moderna.* México: FCE, 1959.

_____. *Theory of Man.* Berkeley: University of California, 1964. Introduction by William Kilgore.

Romero, José. *A History of Argentine Political Thought.* Stanford: Stanford University, 1963. Introduction by T. F. Gann.

Rovaletti, María. *Esencia y realidad* (Zubiri). López Librero, 1978.

Rozitchner, León. *Persona y comunidad.* Scheler: Eudeba, 1962.

_____. *Freud y los límites del individualismo burgués.* Siglo XXI, 1972.

Ruda, Osvaldo. *Dialectique de la personnalité* (Sciacca). Ottawa: University of Ottawa, 1973.

_____. *Lexique philosophique-scientifique.* Ottawa: University of Ottawa, 1977.

Saltor, Jorge. *La crisis de la noción de verdad.* Tucumán: Univ. Nac., 1972.

Santa Cruz, María. *La genèse du monde sensible* (Plotinus). Paris: PUF, 1979.

Sazbón, José. *Mito e historia en la antropología estructural.* Nueva Visión, 1975.

Scannone, Juan. *Sein und Inkarnation* (Blondel). Freiburg: Alber, 1968.

_____. *Teología de la liberación y praxis popular.* Salamanca: Sígueme, 1976.

_____. *El rostro del pobre* (Levinas). Patria Grande, 1981.

Scheines, Graciela. *Juguetes y jugadores.* Ed. de Belgrano, 1981.

Schuster, Félix. *Explicación y predicción.* Clacso, 1982.

Seibold, Jorge. *Pueblo y saber en la "Fenomenología del Espíritu" de Hegel.* Universidad del Salvador, 1983.

Sepich, Juan. *La metafísica entre el mito y la razón.* Mendoza: Universidad de Cuyo, 1970.

_____. *Latinoamérica*. Mendoza: Universidad de Cuyo, 1987.

Simpson, Thomas. *Linguagem, realidade e significado*. São Paulo: Universidade de São Paulo, 1976.

Soler, Ricaurte. *El positivismo argentino*. Panamá: Impr. Nacional, 1959.

Stoetzer, O. C. *The Scholastic Roots of the Spanish American Revolution*. New York: Fordham University, 1979.

Tarán, Leonardo. *Academica*. Philadelphia: American Philosophical Society, 1975.

_____. *Speussipus of Athens*. Leiden: Brill, 1981.

Terán, Oscar. *José Ingenieros*. México: Siglo XXI, 1979.

Tola, F. and C. Dragonetti. *Budismo Mahayana*. Kier, 1980.

_____. *Filosofía y literatura de la India*. Kier, 1983.

_____. *The Yogasutras of Patanjali*. Delhi: M. Banarsidass, 1987.

Torchia Estrada, J. C. *Alejandro Korn*. México: UNAM, 1986.

Van Der Karr, J. *José Ingenieros*. New York: Vantage, 1977.

Vassallo, Angel. *Retablo de la filosofía moderna*. Univ. of Buenos Aires, 1968.

Veron, Eliseo. *Conducta, estructura y comunicación*. Tiempo Contemporáneo, 1972.

_____. *Imperialismo, lucha de clases y conocimiento*. Tiempo Contemporáneo, 1974.

_____. *La production du sens*. Université de Paris, 1985. Doctoral dissertation.

Vilanova, José. *Filosofía del derecho*. Cooperadora de Derecho, 1973.

Virasoro, Miguel. *Para una nueva idea del hombre*. Tucumán: Univ. Nacional. 1963.

_____. *La intuición metafísica*. Desclée, 1965.

Warat, Luis. *Semiótica y derecho*. Eikon, 1972.

Yañez Cortés, R. *Contribución a una epistemología del psicoanálisis*. Amorrortu, 1983.

_____. *El efecto de fascinación*. Catálogos, 1986.

Zalazar, Daniel. *Freedom and Creation in the Essays of A. Korn*. Pittsburgh: University of Pittsburgh, 1969. Doctoral dissertation.

Zan, Julio de. "El problema de la identidad nacional del hombre argentino," *Megafón* 8 (1978).

Chapter 2.
On the Diversity of Brazilian Philosophical Expression

1. Most of the first two pages of this paper draw, in a slightly modified version, on my article on "Brazilian Philosophy and National Thought" for the *Dictionary of Brazilian Literature*, Irwin Stern, ed. (Westport, Conn.: Greenwood, 1988), 240–42/

2. I have presented a paper on the subject ("Latin-American Philosophy? – Revisitation of a Recurrent Theme") at a meeting of the Society for Iberian and Latin-American Thought (American Philosophical Association Convention, Eastern Division, December 1984) and I have experienced it myself, even though my position was simply one of attempting to lay out the issue and show the problems involved. For a recently published collection of Spanish-American texts on this issue, see Jorge J. E. Gracia and Iván Jaksić, eds., *Filosofía e identidad cultural en América Latin* (Caracas: Monte Avila Editores, 1988).

3. We should probably follow the suggestion of a recent book by Dean Peabody, *National Characteristics* (Cambridge and Paris: Cambridge University Press and Éditions de la Maison das Sciences de l'Homme, 1985), and talk about "national characteristics."

4. The resurrection of the concern with national character has been acknowledged as legitimate. See Ana Maria Bianchi, *Evolução temática da sociologia brasileira* (São Paulo: Fundação Instituto de Pesquisas Económicas, 1985), pp. 64–73. The author accepts uncritically, however, the view of D. M. Leite, according to whom, along with Caio Prado Jr., "it was possible to move to a non-ideological interpretation of Brazil" (p. 70).

5. See, for instance, Miguel Reale, *Filosofia em S. Paulo*, 2nd ed., revised and restructured (São Paulo: Editora da Universidade de S. Paulo/Editorial Grijalbo, Ltd., 1976); Lídia Acerboni, *A filosofia contemporânea no Brasil* (São Paulo: Editorial Grijalbo Ltda, 1969); João Cruz Costa, *Panorama of the History of Philosophy in Brazil*. Trans. Fred G. Sturm (Washington, D.C.: Pan American Union, 1962); Adolpho Crippa, *As ideias filosóficas no Brasil* (São Paulo: Convívio 1978); Stanislav Ladusans, S.I. ed., *Rumos da filosofia actual no Brasil em auto-retratos*, vol. 1 (São Paulo: Edições Loyola, 1976); Hélio Jaguaribe, *A filosofia no Brasil* (Rio de Janeiro: ISEB, 1959); Geraldo Pinheiro Machado, "A filosofia no Brasil. Appendix", in J. Hirschberger, *História da filosofia contemporânea* (São Paulo: Herder, 1963), 225–312; Luis Washington Vita, *Panorama de filosofia no Brasil* (Porto Alegre, 1968). Marcelo Dascal, "Philosophical Analysis in Brazil," in J. E. Gracia, E. Rabossi, E. Villanueva, and M. Dascal, eds., *Philosophical Analysis in Latin America* (Dordrecht/Boston/Lancaster: D. Reidel, 1984), 277–84; Ernildo Stein, "A filosofia no Brasil," in *La filosofía hoy en Alemania y América Latina*," ed. H. Ortiz (Cordoba, Argentina: Círculo de Amigos del Instituto Goethe, 1984), 238–47.

6. 2nd ed. (São Paulo: Universidade de S. Paulo/Editora Grijalbo, 1974).

7. (Rio de Janeiro: Tempo Brasileiro, 1979), 140.

8. *Ibid.*, 140–41. My translation.

9. Paim refers to de Souza's essay, "O problema do conhecimento em Miguel Reale e o diálogo com Husserl," *Ciências Humanas* nos. 18–19 (1981).

10. António Paim, "Questões teóricas relacionadas à fiilosofia brasileira," *Revista Brasileira de Filosofia* 34 (1985): 357–69.

11. Roberto Gomes, *Crítica da razão tupiniquim*, 6th ed. (São Paulo: Cortez Editora, 1983).

12. *Ibid.*, 87.

13. "Filosofia brasileira *versus* filosofia no Brasil – Notas de leitura á *Crítica da razão tupiniquim*," *Revista Brasileira de Filosofia* 34 (1985): 400–13.

14. *Ibid.*, 107.

15. See in *Leia* (May 1987), the essays by Juarez Guimarães, Renato Janine Ribeiro, Leandro Konder, José Arthur Giannotti, Fausto Castilho, among others (pp. 12–23).

16. These views can be confirmed with a quick glance at the "self-portraits" of contemporary Brazilian philosophers collected by Stanislav Ladusāns, S.I. in his aforementioned *Rumos da filosofia actual no Brasil*.

17. João Paulo Monteiro, "A filosofia do Brasil: por um debate planetário," *Expresso*, 25 February 1984. For the work done in analytical philosophy, see, for instance, Marcelo Dascal "Philosophical Analysis in Brazil," cited above. Interest in analytical philosophy is not new. Williard V. Quine taught at the University of São Paulo in 1942. He actually published there, and in Portuguese, a book that he never translated into English and that still appears with the Portuguese title in his bibliography – *O sentido da nova lógica* (São Paulo: Livaria Martins, 1944). For an account of the conditions of doing philosophy in Brazil in those years, see W. V. Quine's autobiography, *The Time of My Life* (Cambridge: M.I.T. Press, 1985), 158–76.

18. (London: Routledge & Kegan Paul, 1979).

19. (London: Routledge & Kegan Paul, 1980).

20. (Rio de Janeiro: Editora Nova Fronteira, 1985). Actually the Brazilian edition appears as a translation by Donaldson M. Garschagen. The original version was published by the Presses Universitaires de France, Paris, under the title *Michel Foucault ou the nihilisme de la chaire*.

21. (New York: Free Press, 1975).

22. (New York: Free Press, 1977).

23. (New York: Macmillan, 1984).

24. (Cambridge: Cambridge University Press, 1987).

25. (New York: Herder and Herder, 1972).

26. Richard Rorty, in a brief conversation with me before one of his talks at the Congreso Inter-Americano de Filosofía in Guadalajara, Mexico (November 1985), and also during his subsequent talk, mentioned Unger as proof that there is a Brazilian philosophy, and hence a Latin American Philosophy. I suppose he meant to say that it was possible also for Brazilians to do philosophy. But this goes without saying. The Argentinian Mario Bunge and the Guatemalan Héctor-Neri Castañeda are only two of the known Latin American philosophers who reached the high ranks of the Anglo-American philosophical establishment.

27. The theoretical issues concerning philosophical identity, national identity, and national thought are intricately interwined and too complex to even be outlined here. A few important bibliographical sources, however, can be suggested: Berdyaev, *The Russian Idea* (New York: Macmillan, 1948); Alexandre Koyré, *La Philosophie et le Problème Nationale en Russie au Debut du XIX Siècle* (Paris: Librairie Ancienne Honoré Champion, 1929); Andrzej Walicki, *Philosophy and Romantic Nationalism: The Case of Poland* (Oxford: Clarendon Press, 1982); Eduardo Nicol, *El problema de la filosofía hispánica* (Madrid: Editorial Tecnos, S.A., 1961); Alvaro Ribeiro, *O problema da filosofia portuguesa* (Lisboa: Editorial Inquérito, 1943); Martin S. Stabb, *In Quest of Identity: Patterns in the Spanish American Essay of Ideas, 1890–1960* (Chapel Hill: University of North Carolina Press, 1967); Leopoldo Zea, *En torno a una filosofía americana* (México: El Colegio de México, 1945); José Gaos, *En torno a la filosofía mexicana* (México: Porrúa y Obregón, S.A., 1952); Francisco Miró Quesada, *Proyecto e realización del filosofar latinoamericano* (México: Fondo de Cultura Económica, 1981); Paulin J. Hountondji, *African Philosophy: Myth and Reality* (Bloomington: Indiana University Press, 1983).

Chapter 3.
Philosophy in Brazil Today

Notes

1. Many of the statistics in this section are taken from "As Opçores da Filosofia na Universidade," by Antonio Paim in *Revista Brasileira de Filosofia*, no. 125 (1982): 99–107, an article based on a lecture given during the Semana Comemorativa do 40° Ano da Constituição da Faculdade de Filosofia na Bahia (10 June 1981).

2. São Paulo: Editôra Convivio, 1982:91.

3. "E Como Vai A Lógica No Brasil?" In *Convivium* 24, no. 4 (1986): 335.

4. Ibid.: 340.

5. "Manifesto Editorial" in *Marx Hoje*, vol. 1 (São Paulo: Editora Ensaio, 1988), p. 9.

6. A brief summary of recent phenomenological work in Brasil is provided by Aguiles Côtes Guimarães in his article "A 'Segunda Via' de Inspiração do Pensamento Brasileiro" in *Convivium* 30, n° 3 (May–June 1987): 240–243.

Chapter 4.
Mexican Philosophy in the 1980s: Possibilities and Limits

Notes

1. I want to thank Leopoldo Zea, Fernando Salmerón, Carlos Stoetzer, Horacio Cerutti, and Rubén García Clark, for their advice. Responsibility for those mistakes that unavoidably crept in are mine alone. I also want to thank the Centro Coordinador y Difusor de Estudios Latinoamericanos and the Universidad Nacional Autónoma de México for their warm reception; and last but not least, to Harry Iceland and the Fulbright program for their generous support during my tenure as a Fulbright Fellow in Mexico.

2. In literature, José Luis Martínez, *The Modern Mexican Essay* (Toronto: University of Toronto Press, 1968); Martin Stabb, *In Quest of Identity* (Chapel Hill: University of North Carolina Press, 1967); in political science, Michael Weinstein, *The Polarity of Mexican Thought* (University Park: The Pennsylvania State University Press, 1976); in history, James Cockcroft, *Intellectual Precursors of the Mexican Revolution* (Austin: University of Texas Press, 1968), among the many excellent studies available.

3. The adjective *Mexican* is meant only to limit the noun *philosophy*. For a discussion of some problems in the conception of a Latin American philosophy, see my "Is there a Latin American Philosophy?" *Metaphilosophy* 14 (1983): 39–49.

4. It is difficult to think of jobs for philosophers outside academia not because they can only teach, rather because the university has been so intimately linked to the philosophical project.

5. For an excellent evaluation of the profession and the discipline in the 1970s, see Gabriel Vargas Lozano, "Notas sobre la función actual de la filosofía en México (la década de los setenta)," *Dialéctica* 9 (1980), and his excellent "Corrientes actuales de la filosofía en México," *Prometeo* 3 (1987): 45–54. For a 1970 prediction of Mexican philosophy in the 1980s, see Luis Villoro, "La filosofía en México en los 80," in *Perfil de México en 1980* (Mexico: Siglo XXI, 1970).

6. At present there is one history of Mexican philosophy in English: Patrick Romanell, *The Making of the Mexican Mind*, with a foreword by E. S. Brightman (Notre Dame: University of Notre Dame Press, 1967). For a very readable history of Mexico, see Daniel Cosio Villegas *et al.*, *A Compact History of Mexico*, foreword by R. A. Potash, translated by M. Mattingly Urquidi (México: El Colegio de México, 1985).

7. For books cited in the text, refer to the Selected Bibliography of Books Published During the Decade of the 1980s at the end of the chapter.

8. Sor Juana Inés de la Cruz, *Obras* (Mexico: Porrúa, 1978). Octavio Paz, *Sor Juana o las trampas de la fe*, 3rd ed. (México: Fondo de Cultura Económica, 1983).

9. See, for instance, "Bicentenario de la Gazeta de Valdés: 1784–1809. La Revolución Francesa," *Boletín del Archivo General de la Nación*, III Serie, vol. 8, no. 26 (1984), and "Bicentenario de la Gazeta de Valdés: 1784–1809. Miscelánea de Noticias," *Boletín del Archivo General de la Nación*, III Serie, vol. 8, no. 27 (1984).

10. "After three decades of independence, Mexico – dismembered without peace or national unity – could pride itself only on its intellectuals." Luis González y González, "The Period of Formation," in *A Compact History*, 108–09.

11. For instance, Leopoldo Zea, *Positivism in Mexico*, translated by J. Schulte (Austin: University of Texas Press, 1974).

12. José Vasconcelos, *The Cosmic Race*, translated by Didier T. Jaen (Los Angeles: California State University, Los Angeles, Chicano Studies Center, 1979).

13. Witness Roces translation of Karl Marx, *El Capital* (México: Fondo de Cultura Económica, 1946).

14. Samuel Ramos, *Profile of Man and Culture in Mexico* (Austin: University of Texas Press, 1975); Octavio Paz, *The Labyrinth of Solitude: Life and Thought in Mexico*, translated by L. Kemp (New York: Grove, 1961); Abelardo Villegas, *La filosofía de lo mexicano* (México: Fondo de Cultura Económica, 1960). For a general discussion, see Henry C. Schmidt, *The Roots of "Lo Mexicano": Self and Society in Mexican Thought, 1900–1934* (College Station, Texas: Texas A&M Press, 1978).

15. Vicente Lombardo Toledano, *Escritos filosóficos* (México: Editorial Nuevo México, 1937).

16. José Sánchez Villaseñor, *El sistema filosófico de Vasconcelos* (México: Editorial Polis, 1939).

17. Oswaldo Robles, *The Main Problems of Philosophy*, trans. K. Reinhardt (Milwakee: Bruce, 1946).

18. Adolfo Sánchez Vázquez, *Art and Society: Essays in Marxist Aesthetics* (New York: Monthly Review Press, 1973).

19. For an interesting application of the phenomenological method to historical inquiry see Edmundo O'Gorman, *La invención de América*, Colección Tierra Firme (México: Fondo de Cultura Económica, 1977).

20. For instance, Francisco Lizcano, *Leopoldo Zea. Una filosofía de la historia*, Instituto de Cooperación Iberoamericana (Madrid: Editiones Cultura Hispánica, 1981).

21. Leopoldo Zea, *El positivismo en México. Apogeo y decadencia del positivismo en México* (México: El Colegio de México, 1944).

22. Leopoldo Zea, *Filosofía de la historia americana* (México: Fondo de Cultura Económica, 1978); *América como autodescubrimiento*, Pensamiento Latinoamericano, Instituto Colombiano de Estudios Latinoamericanos y del Caribe (Bogotá: Publicaciones de la Universidad Central, 1986); *Discurso de la marginación y la barbarie* (Barcelona: Antropos, 1988).

23. Enrique Dussel, *The Philosophy of Liberation*, trans. Christine Murkovsky and Aquilina Martínez (Maryknoll, New York: Orbis, 1985).

24. For a brief history of higher education in Mexico, see G. F. Kneller, *The Education of the Mexican Nation* (New York: Octagon, 1973), pp. 164–203. A general description of the educational system can be found in Luis Garibay Gutiérrez, "Mexico," *International Encyclopedia of Higher Education*, A. Knowles, ed. (San Francisco: Jossey-Bass, 1977), 6:2848–2856. Also of interest is Fernando Salmerón, *Cuestiones educativas y páginas sobre México* with a prologue by José Gaos, 2nd ed. (Xalapa: Universidad Veracruzana, 1980). For criticisms of the Mexican higher education system, see Josefina Alcázar, *Universidad y financiamiento* (Puebla: Universidad Autónoma de Puebla, 1984); Gastón García Cantú, *Años críticos: La UNAM, 1968–1987*, Textos de Ciencias Sociales (México: Universidad Nacional Autónoma de México, 1987); and Fernando Jiménez Mier y Terán, *El autoritarianismo en el gobierno de la UNAM*, 2nd. ed. (México: Ediciones de Cultura Popular, 1987).

25. *Carreras en el sistema de educación superior en México* (México: Asociación Nacional de Universidades e Institutos de Enseñanza Superior, 1984), 434. The same description can be found in ANUIES, *Catálogo de carreras: Licenciatura en universidades e institutos tecnológicos*, 4 vols. (México: Secretaría de Educación Pública, 1986), 1:63.

26. Figures are for 1986 unless otherwise specified. One should not rely too heavily on statistics. Furthermore, data on the profession and the discipline in Mexico are difficult to obtain. The composites presented here come from several sources. The extraofficial ones are the *Almanaque Mundial, 1987* (Panamá: Editorial América, 1987); UNESCO *Statistical Yearbook, 1984* (United Nations Educational and Social Committee: 1984); James Wilkie and Adam Perkal, *Statistical Abstracts of Latin America.* vol. 23, (Los Angeles: University of California, Los Angeles, 1982); Asociación Filosófica de México; UNAM Personnel Department, and the very valuable essay by Fernando Salmerón, "Tradición filosófica y enseñanza. Notas sobre el caso de México," unpublished, 1987. The official sources are the *Estadísticas básicas del sistema educacional nacional* (México: Secretaría de Educación Pública, 1986); ANUIES *Carreras*; ANUIES *Catálogo de carreras; Anuario Estadístico 1986: Licenciaturas* (México: Asociación Nacional de Universidades e Institutos de Enseñanza Superior, 1987); *Anuario Estadístico 1987: Licenciatura* (México: Asociación Nacional de Universidades e Institutos de Enseñanza Superior, 1988); the *Anuario Estadístico 1986: Postgrados* (México: Asociación Nacional de Universidades e Institutos de Enseñanza Superior, 1987);

Anuario Estadístico, 1987: Postgrado (México: Asociación Nacional de Universidades e Institutos de Enseñanza Superior, 1988).

27. Sixty public and private universities, according to the UNESCO *World Guide to Higher Education* (New York: Bowkers, 1980), p. 188.

28. *Carreras*, 148–50. The *Anuario Estadístico 1986: Postgrado*, and the *1987: Postgrado* list the following institutions as offering a master's in philosophy: the Universidad Nacional Autónoma de México (Mexico City), the Universidad Iberoamericana (Mexico City), the Universidad Autónoma del Estado de México (Toluca), the Universidad Autónoma de Nuevo León (Monterrey), and the Universidad Autónoma de México, Iztapalapa, (Mexico City); the last one offers a master's in the philosophy of science. They also list the Universidad Nacional Autónoma de México and the Universidad Iberoamericana, both in Mexico City, as the only ones offering a doctorate in philosophy.

29. Such as the Centro de Investigación en Ciencias Sociales y Humanidades, Universidad Autónoma del Estado de México, Toluca; the Centro Coordinador y Difusor de Estudios Latinoamericanos, and the Instituto de Investigaciones Filosóficas, both at UNAM. For a history of the institute in the 1970s, see Fernando Salmerón, "El Instituto de Investigaciones Filosóficas," *La Palabra y el Hombre* 26 (1978): 3–19.

30. The names and books listed are those that have come across my desk. Much of value has been omitted; matters are complicated by the lack of an index of Mexican books in print. For books in philosophy, one must rely on the various bibliographies published, such as Rubén García Clark, "Información bibliográfica de publicaciones filosóficas de autores radicados en México, aparecidos durante el año de 1985," *Prometeo* 2 (1986): 125. Published since December 1985 is the useful bibliographic bulletin *Libros de México*.

31. The diffusion value of these journals should not be underestimated, for, in addition to being cultural vehicles, they are the main outlet for dissemination of individual research. Yet many journals have often been accused of publishing anything regardless of quality, of being a faculty, an institute, or a group's house organ. American or European journals are usually put forth as models, for they subject submitted essays to careful editorial scrutiny and peer review, and publish only what has been found to meet rigorous intellectual standards. If this criticism is — to a point — on target, circumstantial but serious reasons do not allow the refereeing of essays in Mexican journals. The intellectual community is too small, and rejection of an essay would have too strong an impact on the author's prestige and the possibility of employment in an economy in which the livelihood is so precarious. Denying the *modus vivendi* is a punishment not commensurable with the production of mediocre essays, or of those that do not interest an editorial committee. Furthermore, mediocrity is a function of time and place. One must remember that Hume's *Treatise on Human Nature* fell stillborn from the presses, that the *Critique of Pure Reason* was not an immediate success, or that in Mill's lifetime, *Utilitarianism* did not cause much interest.

32. Available in English as Jorge J. E. Gracia *et al.*, eds., *Philosophical Analysis in Latin America*, Synthese Library 172 (Dordrecht: D. Reidel, 1984); and Jorge J. E. Gracia, ed., *Latin American Philosophy in the Twentieth Century: Man, Values and the Search for Identity* (Buffalo, New York: Prometheus, 1987).

33. Available in English as Mario de la Cueva *et al.*, *Major Trends in Mexican Philosophy*, translated by R. M. Caponigri (Notre Dame: University of Notre Dame Press, 1966).

34. His earlier book is *Despertar y proyecto del filosofar latinoamericano* Colección Tierra Firme (México: Fondo de Cultura Económica, 1974).

35. The problem of capacitation (academic standards) is a tangled one. Many universities have tried to upgrade their faculty qualifications. But since the number of Ph.D.'s in Mexico is small, this could be a detriment to the profession. Still, circumstances and standards are different. Most philosophy instructors have at least a *licenciatura*, which, if not a doctorate, is professionally far above the American bachelor of arts and the nowadays devalued master's.

36. The concept of interchange is better than that of influence, the last associated with copy or imitation. Exchange means a *bilateral* relation among individuals or groups to discuss ideas, carry out mutual projects, etc.

37. Salmerón, "El Instituto," 7–8.

38. Development in the sense of growth, increase, economic, political, social, academic, or intellectual improvement. For an awareness of the impact of the crisis in education, see Alcázar, *Universidad*, 9–10. For a criticism of the Universidad Nacional Autónoma de Mexico reaction to the crisis, see Jiménez Mier, *Autoritarianismo*, 253–59. For an earlier and very insightful analysis, see Carlos Ornelas Navarro, "El estado y las fuerzas democráticas. La lucha por la reforma universitaria," *Foro Universitario*, no. 43 (June 1984): 23–34.

39. Alcázar, *Universidad*, 51. Jiménez Mier, *Autoritarianismo*, 169–77.

40. Good examples of radio programming are A. J. Ayer *et al.*, *The Revolution in Philosophy* (London: Macmillan, 1959), and D. F. Pears *et al.*, *David Hume: A Symposium* (London: Macmillan, 1963).

41. For instance, *Proceedings and Addresses of the American Philosophical Association* 60 (1986): 71–73. *Cuadernos Americanos* 1 (1987): 107–59.

Chapter 5.
Philosophy in Other Countries of Latin America

1. Some of the data used in this article have been extracted from various previous publications of the author. See, in particular, "Panorama general de la filosofía latinoamericana actual," in *La filosofía hoy en Alemania y América Latina*, ed. Héctor V. Ortiz (Córdoba, Argentina: Instituto Goethe de Córdoba, 1984),

169-85; "Philosophical Analysis in Other Latin American Countries," in *Philosophical Analysis in Latin America*, ed. Jorge J. E. Gracia, *et al.* (Dordrecht, Holland: Reidel, 1984), 365-80; *Directory of Latin American Philosophers — Repertorio de Filósofos latinoamericanos*, ed. Jorge J. E. Gracia (Buffalo — Buenos Aires — México: SUNYAB Council for International Studies and Programs in association with the Asociación Argentina de Investigaciones Eticas, and Colegio de Estudios Latinoamericanos — Universidad Nacional Autónoma de México, 1988); *Latin American Philosophy Today*, a special issue of the *Philosophical Forum 20* (1988), ed. Jorge J. E. Gracia, with articles on Marxism (Adolfo Sánchez Vázquez), feminism (Ofelia Schutte), phenomenology and existentialism (David Sobrevilla), the philosophy of liberation (Horacio Cerutti Guldberg), the problem of philosophical identity (Leopoldo Zea), sources for the study of Latin American philosophy (Iván Jaksić), and philosophical analysis (Jorge J. E. Gracia); and *Latin American Philosophy in the Twentieth Century*, ed. Jorge J. E. Gracia (Buffalo, NY: Prometheus Books, 1986). I have also consulted some general sources of information, such as the philosophy section, compiled by Carlos Torchia Estrada, of the *Handbook of Latin American Studies*, the *International Directory of Philosophers*, José Luis Abellán's *Filosofía española en América (1936-1966)* (Madrid: Ediciones Guadarrama, 1967), and J. L. Gómez Martínez, "Pensamiento hispanoamericano: una aproximación bibliográfica," *Cuadernos Salmantinos de Filosofía* 8 (1981): 287-400.

2. For information about the history of ideas in Paraguay, see Efraím Cardozo, *Apuntes de historia cultural del Paraguay* (Asunción: Colegio de San José, 1963) and Justo Pastor Benítez, "Diagrama de las ideas en el Paraguay," *Revista Dominicana de Filosofía* 2 (1956): 58-62.

3. Concerning philosophy in Bolivia, see Guillermo Francovich, *La filosofía en Bolivia* (Buenos Aires: Losada, 1945; 2nd expanded ed., La Paz: Juventud, 1966) and *El pensamiento boliviano del siglo XX* (México: Fondo de Cultura Económica, 1956); Augusto Pescador, "La filosofía en Bolivia en el siglo XX," *Cursos y Conferencias* 25 (1956): 61-80, and *Cuadernos de Filosofía*, Concepción 6 (1977): 93-109; Manfredo Mercado Kempff, "La filosofía actual en Bolivia," *Notas y estudios de Filosofía* 3 (1952): 67-70; Juan Millán Albarracín, *Orígenes del pensamiento social contemporáneo de Bolivia* (La Paz: Universo, 1976), and *Filosofía boliviana del siglo XX* (La Paz: Alcapana, 1981); and José Luis Gómez Martínez, *Bolivia: un pueblo en busca de su identidad* (La Paz — Cochabamba: Los Amigos del Libro, 1988).

4. Concerning philosophy in Chile, see Enrique Molina, *La filosofía en Chile en la primera mitad del siglo XX* (Santiago: Nascimiento, 1951; 2nd expanded ed., 1953) and *Desarrollo de Chile en la primera mitad del siglo XX*, 2 vols. (Santiago: Universidad de Chile, 1952); Santiago Vidal Muñoz, "Filosofía en Chile," *Cuadernos de Filosofía* 6 (1977): 19-44; Roberto Escobar, *La filosofía en Chile* (Santiago: Editorial Universal, 1976) and "El sentido de lo americano en los filósofos chilenos," *Mapocho* 26 (1978): 25-33; Iván Jaksić, "Filosofía y gobierno militar en Chile," *Prometeo* 1, no. 2 (1985): 63-67, "Chilean Philosophy under Military Rule," *Occasional Papers in Latin American Studies*, University of California at Berkeley, 10 (1984), "Philosophia perennis en tiempos pretorianos: La filosofía

chilena desde 1973," *Cuadernos Americanos* 259 (1985): 59–87, "La vocación filosófica en Chile," *Cuadernos Americanos*, nueva época 2 (1988): 21–42, and *Academic Rebels in Chile: The Role of Philosophy in Higher Education and Politics* (Albany, NY: State University of New York Press, 1989); Thomas Bader, "Early Positivist Thought and Ideological Conflict in Chile," *The Americas* 26 (1970), 376–93; Ricardo Donoso, *Las ideas políticas en Chile* (México: Fondo de Cultura Económica, 1946); Solomon Lipp, *Three Chilean Thinkers* (Waterloo: Wilfrid Laurier University Press, 1975); Allen L. Woll, "The Philosophy of History in Nineteenth Century Chile: The Lastarria-Bello Controversy," *History and Theory* 13, no. 3 (1974): 273–290; *Bibliografía chilena de filosofía: desde fines del siglo XVI hasta el presente* (Santiago: La Biblioteca, 1979); and Félix Schwartzmann, "La Philosophie au Chili," in Raymond Klibanski, ed., *La Philosophie Contemporaine* (Firenze: La Nuova Editrice, 1971).

5. "Philosophical Analysis in Other Latin American Countries," 365–69.

6. Concerning philosophy in Colombia, see Jaime Jaramillo Uribe, *El pensamiento colombiano en el siglo XIX* (Bogotá: Temis, 1964), *Entre la historia y la filosofía* (Bogotá: Revista Colombiana, 1968), and *Antología del pensamiento político colombiano*, 2 vols. (Bogotá: Talleres Gráficos del Banco de la República, 1970); Jaime Vélez Correa, "Proceso de la filosofía en Colombia," *Anales de la Universidad de Antioquía* 36 (1960): 869–1012; Rubén Sierra Mejía, "Temas y corrientes de la filosofía colombiana en el siglo XX," in *Ensayos filosóficos* (Bogotá: Instituto Colombiano de Cultura, 1978), 99–126; Daniel Herrera Restrepo, "El proceso filosófico en Colombia y sus condicionamientos socio-políticos," in *Primer foro nacional de filosofía* (Pasto, 1975), and *La filosofía en Colombia: Bibliografía 1627–1973* (Cali: Universidad del Valle, 1973); Juan David García Bacca, *Antología del pensamiento filosófico en Colombia (1647–1761)* (Bogotá: Imprenta Nacional, 1955).

7. Rubén Sierra Mejía, "Temas y corrientes de la filosofía colombiana," 91–92.

8. *Ibid.*, 98–117.

9. "Philosophical Analysis in Other Latin American Countries," 369–71.

10. Concerning philosophy in Ecuador, see Benjamin Carrión, "Historia de las ideas en el Ecuador," *Revista de Historia de las Ideas* 1 (1959): 251–63; Horacio Cerutti Guldberg, "Aproximación a la historiografía del pensamiento ecuatoriano," *Pucará* 1 (1977): 21–48; Arturo Andrés Roig, *Esquemas para una historia de la filosofía ecuatoriana* (Quito: Universidad Católica, 1977; 2nd ed., 1982); Jorge Carrera Andrade, *Galería de místicos y de insurgentes: La vida intelectual del Ecuador durante cuatro siglos, 1555–1955* (Quito: Casa de la Cultura Ecuatoriana, 1959); C. Paladines, *Sentido y trayectoria del pensamiento ecuatoriano* (México: Centro de Coordinación y de Estudios Latinoamericanos – Universidad Nacional Autónoma de México, 1987).

11. For studies of philosophy in Peru, see Luis Felipe Alarco, *Pensadores peruanos* (Lima: Sociedad Peruana de Filosofía, 1952); Manuel Mejía Valera,

Fuentes para la historia de la filosofía en el Perú (Lima: Universidad Nacional Mayor de San Marcos, 1965); Augusto Salazar Bondy, *Philosophy in Peru: A Historical Study* (Washington, D.C.: Unión Panamericana, 1954; 2nd expanded Spanish ed., Lima: Universo, 1967) and *Historia de las ideas en el Perú contemporáneo: el proceso del pensamiento filosófico,* 2 vols. (Lima: Moncloa, 1965); Mario Alzamora Valdéz, *La filosofía del derecho en el Perú* (Lima, 1968).

12. See "Philosophical Analysis in Other Countries," 371–73.

13. For studies of philosophy in Venezuela, see Luis Beltrán Guerrero, *Introducción al positivismo venezolano* (Caracas: Revista Nacional de Cultura, 1955); Horacio Cárdenas, *Resonancias de la filosofía europea en Venezuela* (Caracas: Universidad Central de Venezuela, 1958); Alicia de Nuño, *Ideas sociales del positivismo en Venezuela* (Caracas: Universidad Central de Venezuela, 1969); Marisa Kohn de Beker, *Tendencias positivistas en Venezuela* (Caracas: Universidad Central de Venezuela, 1970); Agustín Martínez, "La filosofía en Venezuela: recopilación bibliográfica," *Semestre de Filosofía* 1 (1977); Alfonso Armas Ayala, *Influencias del pensamiento venezolano en la revolución de independencia de Hispanoamérica* (Caracas: Instituto Panamericano de Geografía e Historia, 1970); José Ramón Luna, *El positivismo en la historia del pensamiento venezolano* (Caracas: Editorial Arte, 1971); and Pompeyo Ramis, *Veinte filósofos venezolanos, 1946–1976* (Mérida: Universidad de los Andes, 1978).

14. For more information on analysis in Venezuela, see "Philosophical Analysis in Other Latin American Countries," 373–76.

15. For studies of philosophy in Central America, see Jesús Julián Amurrio González, *El positivismo en Guatemala* (Guatemala: Universidad de San Carlos, 1970); Lourdes Bendfeldt and Alba Calderón, *Bibliografía filosófica de publicaciones de las Universidades de Costa Rica y San Carlos de Guatemala y de autores guatemaltecos que exhibió la Biblioteca Nacional* (Guatemala, Universidad de San Carlos, 1964); Diego Domínguez Caballero, "Panamá y la historia de las ideas en Latinoamérica," *Revista de Historia de las Ideas* 1 (1959): 217–35 and *Los estudios filosóficos en la Universidad de Panamá* (Panamá: Universidad de Panamá, 1963); Constantino Láscaris, *Historia de las ideas en Centroamérica* (San José: EDUCA, 1970) and "Algunos pensadores centroamericanos." *Revista de Filosofía de la Universidad de Costa Rica* 15 (1977): 281–307; Ricaurte Soler, *Formas ideológicas de la nación panameña* (Panamá: Treas, 1963; 2nd ed. 1964); Rafael Heliodoro Valle, *Historia de las ideas contemporáneas en Centroamérica* (México: Fondo de Cultura Económica, 1960); and José Luis Balcárcel, "Filosofía de la filosofía en Centroamérica," *Revista de Filosofía de la Universidad de Costa Rica* 15 (1977): 197–200.

16. For studies of philosophy in Costa Rica see previous note and Constantino Láscaris, *Desarrollo de las ideas filosóficas en Costa Rica* (San José: ECA, 1965) and "Desarrollo de las ideas filosóficas en Costa Rica," *Revista de Filosofía de la Universidad de Costa Rica* 8 (1970): 267–84; no. 9 of *Revista de Filosofía de la Universidad de Costa Rica* (1971), devoted to Costa Rica and its thought; Alain Guy, "La filosofía en Costa Rica," *Revista de Filosofía de la Universidad de Costa Rica*

9 (1971): 111–19; and the collection *El pensamiento contemporáneo costarricense* (San José: Editorial Costa Rica, 1980).

17. On philosophy in Cuba, see: José M. Mestre Domínguez, *De la filosofía en La Habana* (La Habana: Ministerio de Educación, 1952); Humberto Piñera Llera, *Panorama de la filosofía cubana* (Washington, D.C.: Unión Panamericana, 1960); Waldo Ross, *Crítica a la filosofía cubana de hoy* (La Habana: Cuadernos de Divulgación Cultural, 1954); Medardo Vitier, *Las ideas en Cuba*, 2 vols. (La Habana: Trópico, 1938), *La filosofía en Cuba* (México: Fondo de Cultura Económica, 1948), "Cincuenta años de estudio de la filosofía en Cuba," *Cursos y Conferencias* 25 (1956): 130–32, and *Las ideas y la filosofía en Cuba* (La Habana: Editorial Ciencias Sociales, 1970); Donald Clark Hodges, "Philosophy in the Cuban Revolution," in *Marxism, Revolution and Peace*, ed. H. L. Parsons and J. Sommerville (Amsterdam: Gruner, 1977); Sheldon B. Liss, *Roots of Revolution: Radical Thought in Cuba* (University of Nebraska Press, 1987).

18. For studies of philosophy in Puerto Rico and the Dominican Republic, see Vetilio Alfau Durán, "Documentos para la historia de la filosofía en Santo Domingo," *Anales de la Universidad de Sto. Domingo* 15 (1950): 243–59; Armando Cordero, *Estudios para la historia de la filosofía en Sto. Domingo* (Ciudad Trujillo: Arte y Cine, 1956) and *Panorama de la filosofía en Sto. Domingo*, 2 vols. (Santo Domingo: Arte y Cine, 1962); Franklin J. Franco, *Historia de las Ideas políticas en la República Dominicana: contribución a su estudio* (Santo Domingo: Editorial Nacional, 1981); José A. Fránquiz, "Panorama de la filosofía en Puerto Rico," *Luminar* 7 (1945): 100–17; Domingo Marrero Navarro, "Notas para organizar el estudio de la historia de las ideas en Puerto Rico," *Revista de Historia de las Ideas* 1 (1959): 159–76; Monelisa Pérez Marchand, "Preámbulos para una historia de las ideas en Puerto Rico," *Revista de Historia de las Ideas* 1 (1959): 143–58; and Eugenio Hernández Méndez, *Antología del pensamiento puertorriqueño: 1900–1970*, 2 vols. (Hato Rey: Universidad de Puerto Rico, 1975).

19. For studies of philosophy in Uruguay, see Arturo Ardao, *Espiritualismo y positivismo en el Uruguay* (Buenos Aires: Fondo de Cultura Económica, 1950), "Tendencias filosóficas en el Uruguay en el siglo XX," *Cursos y Conferencias* 48 (1950): 27–38, *La filosofía en el Uruguay del siglo XX* (Buenos Aires: Fondo de Cultura Económica, 1956), and *Racionalismo y liberalismo en el Uruguay* (Montevideo: Universidad de la República, 1962); Manuel Arturo Claps, "Situación actual de la filosofía uruguaya," *Número* 3–4 (1964): 128–37; and Jesús Caño-Guiral, *Las ideologías políticas y la filosofía en el Uruguay* (Montevideo: Nuestra Tierra, 1969).

Introduction to Part II: Literature — Writers

1. Jorge Luis Borges, *Evaristo Carriego*, Trans. Norman Thomas Di Giovanni (New York: Dutton, 1984), 42.

2. Gabriel García Márquez, "The Solitude of Latin America," Trans. Marina Castañeda, *New York Times* 6 February 1983, sec. 4: 17.

Chapter 6.
An Introductory Outline to Contemporary Spanish American Poetry

1. Gonzalo Millán, "Promociones poéticas emergentes: El espíritu del valle," *Posdata* 4 (Concepción, 1985): 2–9.

2. Aldo Pellegrini, *Antología de la poesía viva latinoamericana* (Barcelona: Seix Barral, 1966); José Olivio Jiménez, *Antología de la poesía hispanoamericana contemporánea: 1914–1970* (Madrid: Alianza, 1971; revised edition: 1977); Jorge Rodríguez Padrón, *Antología de poesía hispanoamericana (1915–1980)* (Madrid: Espasa-Calpe, 1984); Pedro Lastra and Luis Eyzaguirre, "Catorce poetas hispanoamericanos de hoy," *INTI. Revista de Literatura Hispánica* 18–19 (Providence Coll., Fall 1983–Spring 1984); Juan Gustavo Cobo Borda, *Antología de la poesía hispanoamericana* (México: Fondo de Cultura Económica, 1985); Julio Ortega, *Antología de la poesía hispanoamericana actual* (México: Siglo Veintiuno, 1987).

3. Juan Villegas, *Antología de la nueva poesía femenina chilena* (Santiago de Chile: La Noria, 1985).

4. Ramiro Lagos, *Mujeres poetas de Hispanoamérica* (Bogotá: Centro de Estudios Poéticos Hispanos, 1986).

5. The New York anthology is especially representative because it includes outstanding Spanish-American poets of a variety of Hispanic national origins: Iván Silén, *Los paraguas amarillos. Los poetas latinos en Nueva York* (New Hampshire–Binghamton, N.Y.: Ediciones del Norte/Bilingual Press, 1983).

6. María Elena Walsh, *A la madre. Poemas elegidos por . . .* (Buenos Aires: Sudamericana, 1981).

7. See José Enrique Rodó, *Ariel*, 1900 (many subsequent editions).

8. Ivan A. Schulman and Evelyn Picón-Garfield, *Las entrañas del vacío. Ensayos sobre la modernidad hispanoamericana* (México: Cuadernos Americanos, 1984).

9. See Neil Larsen, ed., *The Discourse of Power. Culture, Hegemony and the Authoritarian State in Latin America* (Minneapolis: Institute for the Study of Ideologies and Literature, 1983).

Chapter 8.
Women Writers into the Mainstream:
Contemporary Latin American Narrative

1. All titles of literary works mentioned will be given in English (unless the Spanish title is identical or easily comprehensible). For full citations of Latin American literature in English translation, I refer the reader to the following

sources: Juan R. Freudenthal and Patricia M. Freudenthal, eds., *Index to Anthologies of Latin American Literature in English Translation* (Boston: G. K. Hall, 1977); Bradley A. Shaw, *Latin American Literature in English Translation: An Annotated Bibliography* (New York: New York University Press, 1976); Bradley A. Shaw, *Latin American Literature in English 1975–1978*. (New York: Center for Inter-American Relations, 1979); a good guide to contemporary Spanish-American literature, with all information given in English, has been prepared by George R. McMurray, *Spanish American Writing Since 1941: A Critical Survey* (New York: Ungar, 1987).

2. José Donoso, *Historia personal del 'boom'*. Appendix I, "El 'boom' doméstico," by María Pilar Serrano. Appendix II, "Diez años después," by José Donoso (Barcelona: Seix Barral, 1983). English translation, *The Boom in Spanish American Literature: A Personal History*, trans. Gregory Kolovakos (New York: Columbia University Press and the Center for Inter-American Relations, 1977).

3. See especially his *La nueva novela hispanoamericana* (México: Joaquín Mortiz, 1969) for one of the earliest assessments of the innovations ascribed to the "boom."

4. This is the title of a seminal collection of interviews with major figures of the "boom": Luis Harss and Barbara Dohmann, *Into the Mainstream* (New York: Harper and Row, 1967).

5. See Serrano's "El 'boom' doméstico" (114–15), included in the latest edition of Donoso's *Historia personal del 'boom'*.

6. These are the comments of Earl E. Fitz in his book, *Clarice Lispector* (Boston: Twayne, 1985), 29.

7. Jean Franco, "Apuntes sobre la crítica feminista y la literatura hispanoamericana," *Hispamérica* 45 (1986): 41. In the interviews that Evelyn Picon Garfield conducted with six contemporary Latin American women writers, this negation of feminine writing as a category is particularly evident. Most of the six authors believe that gender difference is less important than class difference as far as access to literary culture is concerned. *Women's Voices from Latin America* (Detroit: Wayne State University Press, 1985).

8. In her article "La mala palabra," Valenzuela concludes: "Hace tanto, ya, que venimos lentamente escribiendo, cada vez con más furia, con más auto-rreconocimiento. Mujeres en la dura tarea de construir con un material signado por el otro. Construir *no* partiendo de la nada, que sería más fácil, sino transgrediendo las barreras de censura, rompiendo los cánones en busca de esa voz propia . . . " ("We have been slowly writing for a long time now, with more and more fury, with more self-knowledge. Women in the difficult struggle to construct with a material signed by another. To construct *not* starting from nothing, which would be easier, but rather by transgressing barriers of censure, by breaking

the canons in search of that voice of one's own . . . "). In *Revista Iberoamericana* 51 (1985): 491. [Trans. mine.]

9. Vega's publications of short stories and novelettes include a collection of stories produced in collaboration with Carmen Lugo Filippi, *Virgins and Martyrs* (*Vírgenes y mártires*, Río Piedras, Puerto Rico: Antillana, 1981); *Encancaranublado* (Río Piedras, Puerto Rico: Antillana, 1983); *Story Passion and other Passion Stories* (*Pasión de historia y otras historias de pasión*, Buenos Aires: Ediciones de la Flor, 1987).

10. This term is employed by Efraín Barradas, "La necesaria innovación de Ana Lydia Vega: preámbulo para lectores vírgenes," *Revista Iberoamericana* 51 (1985): 555. He also remarks: "Ana Lydia Vega ha logrado encarnar en nuestras letras contemporáneas, mejor que cualquier otra escritora boricua, esa corriente innovadora y trastrocante que es el feminismo." ("Ana Lydia Vega has managed to incarnate in our contemporary literature, better than any other Puerto Rican writer, that innovative and transforming current which is feminism" [550]). [Trans. mine.]

11. See Vega's article in this volume for a fuller discussion of the issue of women's writing.

12. Rosario Ferré, "La cocina de la escritura," in *Sitio a Eros* (México: Joaquín Mortiz, 1986), 31.

13. For a general orientation to these fields, see Richard L. Jackson's *Black Writers in Latin America* (Albuquerque: University of New Mexico Press, 1979), and David William Foster's "Latin American Documentary Narrative" in his *Alternate Voices in the Contemporary Latin American Narrative* (Columbia: University of Missouri Press, 1985), 1–44.

Chapter 9.
To Write or Not to Write?

1. "Vivir del cuento" can literally mean "to earn a living through writing stories," but in everyday language signifies "to live by one's wits," that is, without working. [Trans.]

2. Vega uses the term *escritora*, which through grammatical gender denotes 'female writer', as opposed to *escritor*, 'male writer'. Note, however, that the plural *escritores* can include writers of both genders. [Trans.]

3. Vega again plays with the notion of grammatical gender: Let the word *villano* always end in an *o* so that the glory of women, the words ending in *a*, stands out in clear contrast. [Trans.]

4. *El Album Puertorriqueño* is one of the earliest anthologies of Puerto Rican literature; it was first published in Spain in 1844. [ALV]

Chapter 10.
An Overview of Contemporary Latin American Theater

1. Gerardo Luzuriaga, "El IV Festival de Manizales, 1971," in Gerardo Luzuriaga, ed., *Popular Theater for Social Change in Latin America: Essays in Spanish and English* (Los Angeles: UCLA Latin American Center Pubs., 1978), 199.

2. Nizim Charim, "¿Quiénes somos? ICTUS y la creación colectiva," *Tramoya* 12 (July–September 1978): 5.

3. Theodore and Adele Edling Shank, "Chicano and Latin American Alternative Theater," in Gerardo Luzuriaga, ed., *Popular Theater for Social Change in Latin America: Essays in Spanish and English* (Los Angeles: UCLA Latin American Center Pubs., 1978), 227.

4. At the 4th Manizales Festival, held in 1971, the theatrical group from the National University of Bogotá censored Mario Vargas Llosa's presence because of his political position (Luzuriaga, 195–7).

5. Luzuriaga, 189.

6. Luzuriaga, 189.

7. All translations are ours, unless otherwise indicated.

8. Marina Pianca, "El Festival de Quito, 1972," in Gerardo Luzuriaga, ed., *Popular Theater for Social Change in Latin America: Essays in Spanish and English* (Los Angeles: UCLA Latin American Center Pubs., 1978), 210.

9. Luzuriaga, 195.

10. José Monleón, "Polémica y balance con el teatro colombiano al fondo," *Primer Acto* 203–4 (1984): 10.

11. Monleón, 15.

12. In his article, "Report on El Quinto Festival de Teatros Chicanos," *De Colores* 2.2 (1975): 66–72, Juan Bruce-Novoa gives an informative account of the events which took place at the festival held in Mexico City.

13. *Opera bufa* by Enrique Buenaventura is an excellent example of a "dictatorship play" since it was created on the basis of texts by García Márquez's *El otoño del patriarca*, Roa Bastos' *Yo, el supremo*, Carpentier's *El recurso del método*, Shakespeare's *Macbeth*, and poems by Brecht, Neruda, Cardenal, and Darío.

14. For a comprehensive review of the recent interest in historical themes see: Beatriz J. Rizk's "El nuevo teatro en Latinoamérica," *Conjunto* 61–62 (July–December 1984): 11–31.

15. Carlos José Reyes, "Teatro e historia." *Conjunto* 61–62 (July–December 1984): 155.

16. Ana Seoane, "Primer Festival Latinoamericano de Teatro, Córdoba – 1984." *Conjunto* 64 (April–June 1985): 130–41.

17. Even though the interest in narrative as a source for dramatic creation is greater now than ever, this activity has had a long tradition. Roberto Arlt's adaptation – in collaboration with Leónidas Barletta – of his short story "El humillado" from *Los siete locos* supports our opinion. Other examples of plays based on narrative are *El herrero y la muerte*, adapted by Teatro Circular de Montevideo from the same short story by Tomás Carrasquilla that Buenaventura used for *En la diestra de Dios Padre*, was presented in 1986 Manizales Festival. *Doña Ramona*, an adaptation of the novel by José Pedro Bellán presented at the 1986 Cadiz Festival by Teatro Circular de Montevideo; *Doña Flor y sus dos maridos* based on Jorge Amado's novel and presented by an Argentinian collective group in Montevideo; *Diálogo del rebusque* adapted by Santiago García from Teatro de la Candelaria based on *El buscón* by Quevedo; *Corazón al Sur* done in collaboration by Francisco Garzón Céspedes and Sara Larocca on the basis of narrative texts as well as songs and poems; the adaptations done by Rajatabla of Venezuela of Arturo Uslar Pietri's novel, *Las lanzas coloradas* and of Miguel Angel Asturias' *El señor presidente*; and the adaptation of García Márquez's story *El ahogado más hermoso del mundo* done by the Oveja Negra group from Panama, among many others.

18. It is interesting to note that a play based on a typical novel of exile, *Primavera con una esquina rota*, has become by virtue of the ICTUS collective work, a play of "internal exile."

19. Along with the numerous theater people in exile all over the world, one has to include the production of the Cuban playwrights and theater groups working in Miami and other cities of the United States.

20. *Regreso sin causa* by Jaime Miranda and *Retorno al fin* by Héctor Aguilar are two plays thematically structured on the dilemma posed by the return to the native land.

21. Other important theatre groups in exile are Teatro Latinoamericano de Colonia (Germany) and Teatro Popular Chileno (England).

22. Juan Enrique Acuña has distinguished himself in the area of children's theater as a pupeteer.

23. The Teatro del Angel has recently returned to Chile and is actively to the national theater scene.

24. Malcolm Scott MacKenzie, "Emilio Carballido: An Ideational Evolution of His Theatre." Ann Arbor, Michigan: UMI (1981): 8121001.

Introduction to Part II:
Literature — Literary Competitions, Books, and Journals in the United States

1. José Martí, *Our America*, Trans. Elinor Randall, Juan de Onís and Roslyn Held Foner (New York: Monthly Review Press, 1977), 93.

Chapter 12.
Writing in Spanish in the United States

1. This article has been made possible by the support of the Graduate School of International Studies of the University of Miami, which sponsors the Literary Contest Letras de Oro with American Express. This research incorporates data included in a previous article, "Reading and Writing in Spanish in the U.S.," *Hispania* 70 (1987): 830–33, with statistics compiled by Manuel Fernández, Clea Sucoff, María Rivero and Steve Ralph, assistants of the Letras de Oro contest. Editorial comments were very kindly provided by Robert Kirsner.

2. It is funded by American Express, for an initial period of three years. A basic grant of $25,000 was expanded into a $180,000 contract to cover all operations (staff, mailing, telephone, travel, and prizes). In addition, the sponsor independently covers all expenses for the inauguration and award ceremonies, printing and mailing of brochures, attendance at selected conventions, and the cost of publishing the winning entries.

3. 140 (of 366) contestants in 1986–87 and 134 (out of 371) in 1987–88 were kind enough to answer the survey. This high response level (more than a third), added to the consistency of data and allows us to consider results as highly reliable. Although this study combines explicit data on names and return addresses given by contestants, personal data of entries submitted with real names are confidential. Members of the jury receive only titles and an identification number for administrative purposes. The Letras de Oro organization does not supply lists of contestants.

4. These figures are freely tossed around by government officials in the United States and Hispanic countries, and have to be considered with caution as far as predictions.

5. As a sample, see Rodolfo de la Garza, ed., *Ignored Voices: Public Opinion Polls and the Latino Community* (Austin: Center for Mexican American Studies, University of Texas, 1987); Strategy Research Corporation, *U.S. Hispanic Market* (Miami, Fla., 1984): Rufus P. Browning, *Protest is Not Enough: The Struggle of Blacks and Hispanics for Equality in Urban Politics* (Berkeley: University of California Press, 1984); Alberto Moncada, *La americanización de los hispanos* (Barcelona: Plaza y Janés, 1986); Lewis H. Gann, *The Hispanics in the United States: A History* (Boulder: Westview Press, 1986); Pastora San Juan Cafferty and William C.

McCready, eds., *Hispanics in the United States: A New Social Agenda* (New Brunswick, N.J.: Transaction Books, 1985); Diana Balmori, *Hispanic Immigrants in the Construction Industry* (New York: New York University, Center for Latin American Studies, 1983); Development Associates, *The Demographic and Socioeconomic Characteristics of Hispanic Population in the United States: 1950–1980* (Washington, D.C., 1982); David William Foster, ed., *Sourcebook of Hispanic Culture in the United States* (Chicago: American Library Association, 1982); Skelly Yankelovich and White, Inc., *Spanish USA: A Study of the Hispanic Market in the United States: Origins, Characteristics and Life-style, Marketing and Media Behavior* (New York, 1981); Abram Jaffe, Ruth M. Cullen, and Thomas D. Boswell, eds., *The Changing Demography of Spanish Americans* (New York: Academic Press, 1980).

6. For detailed graphs, see Joaquín Roy, "Presencia de España en los Estados Unidos: Economía o cultura. Una propuesta para el 92," *Realidades y posibilidades de las relaciones entre España y América en los ochenta* (Madrid: Instituto de Cooperación Iberoamericana, 1986), 173–97.

7. Data of 1982.

8. Study of the Census Bureau, 1987.

9. See census report, *The Hispanic Population in the United States (March 1986–March 1987)* (1988).

10. *Vista* magazine, distributed as a supplement to twenty major dailies, conducted in 1985 a survey of its readers: 58 percent preferred reading it in English. While 71 percent of the readers claimed to have a good command of English; another 18 percent said that they have a passable knowledge. In summary: most Hispanics prefer to read in English. However, a note of caution is needed: the survey was not on "speakers," but potential "readers." Ninety-two percent said they would prefer receiving the new magazine along with the English newspaper to which they already subscribe. Only 63 percent said that they would buy it separately.

11. See Carlos Fuentes, "How I Elected to Write in Spanish," *Ideas'92* 1.1 (1987): 5–10.

12. When newspapers and magazines announced the contest in Winter–Spring of 1986, potential contestants called or wrote our office for specific rules. Data from individuals who left explicit names and addresses were counted; simple questions about one aspect of the contest were not. This system was discontinued for lack of resources. The 1986–87 mailing contained a poster which was sent to all college Spanish departments in the country. The 1987–88 mailing was sent to all members of the MLA and the AATSP lists, an extensive mailing system that was repeated in 1988–89.

13. Including Puerto Rico, U.S. Virgin Islands and Canada.

14. Literal interpretation is impossible because many originals were entered with no consultation, and many requests for information were not followed by an entry.

15. They will remain that way until the authors explicitly ask for the return of the manuscripts. One year after the call for entries, all remaining copies will be destroyed, along with the sealed envelopes.

16. A word of caution is due here, since it is speculated that some contestants entered their works under common Spanish names that were in fact pseudonyms. Others (especially women) preferred to use opposite sex names. However, it is likely that these exceptions do not have a significant impact upon the global figures and percentages.

17. The 5 percent included in the census is a misleading figure. Very often people who have a very distant Hispanic ancestry, answer with a generic "Spain" about country of origin. Real figures range from 25,000 Spanish citizens registered in the consulate rolls, to 170,000, including U.S. naturalized citizens. See my article "Presencia de España en los Estados Unidos."

18. NALEO later commissioned a study (funded with a $250,000 grant from the Ford Foundation to the Washington firm of David North). Results are still not available.

19. See Octavio Paz, "La literatura escrita en español en los Estados Unidos," Closing speech delivered for the 1st Letras de Oro Award Ceremony delivered in Miami on 22 January 1987. *Ideas'92* 1.1 (1987): 11–14.

Chapter 13.
The Writer and the Language:
Reflections on the Linguistic Conditions of Writing

1. The speech by Octavio Paz was delivered in Spanish. This is my translation of it.

2. "El 'bricolage' como estrategia narrativa del 'inxilio.'" Paper given at the twenty-ninth annual meeting of the Midwest Modern Language Association, 12–14 November 1987, Columbus, Ohio.

Chapter 14.
Hispanic Books in the Library of Congress: 1815–1965

1. John Y. Cole, *For Congress and the Nation: A Chronological History of the Library of Congress* (Washington: Library of Congress, 1979), 3–7.

2. Quoted in Douglas L. Wilson, "Jefferson's Library," *Thomas Jefferson: A Biography*, ed. by Merrill D. Peterson (New York: Scribner's, 1986), 157; about the sale, see also Dumas Malone, "Books in Transit: The Library of Congress," in *The Sage of Monticello* (Boston: Little, Brown, 1981), 169–84.

3. Millicent Sowerby, "La biblioteca de Thomas Jefferson," *Revista Interamericana de Bibliografía* 8 (1958): 116–19; James Gilreath, "Sowerby Revirescent and Revised," *Papers of the Bibliographical Society of America* 78 (Second Quarter, 1984): 219–20.

4. Donald Jackson, *Thomas Jefferson and The Stony Mountains: Exploring the West from Monticello* (Urbana: University of Illinois Press, 1981), 88–89, 96–97; Dolores Moyano Martin, "Hispanic Narrative in the Library of Congress," unpublished paper, presented at a workshop on Alejo Carpentier, Yale University, New Haven, Conn. 30 March 1979, 1–2.

5. Jackson, 88–89; Thomas Jefferson, quoted in William E. Carter, *The Hispanic Room in the Library of Congress* (Washington: Library of Congress, 1984), 1.

6. *Catalogue of the Library of Thomas Jefferson*, compiled and annotated by Millicent Sowerby (Washington: Library of Congress, 1952), vols. 2–5; Frederick R. Goff, "Jefferson The Book collector," *Quarterly Journal of the Library of Congress* 29 (January 1972): 32–47; Georgette M. Dorn, "Las colecciones de literatura hispánica en la Biblioteca del Congreso," *Revista Interamericana de Bibliografía* 29 (1979): 337–38.

7. *Catalogue*, vol. 5, pp. 94–97; Goff, 32–47; Dorn, "Colecciones," 337–38; Martin, 1–2.

8. David C. Mearns, *The Story Up To Now: The Library of Congress, 1800–1946* (Washington, Library of Congress, 1946), 20.

9. Cole, 21–22; Gilreath, 222; Goff, 33.

10. Dorn, 339.

11. John Russell Young, quoted in U.S. Library of Congress, *Hispanic Foundation* (Departmental and Divisional Manuals, no. 12) (Washington: Library of Congress, 1950), 3.

12. Cecil K. Jones, "Hispano-Americana in the Library of Congress," *Hispanic American Historical Review* 2 (February 1919): 96–97.

13. Jones, 96.

14. *Report of the Librarian of Congress and Report of the Superintendent of the Library Buildings and Grounds for the Fiscal Year Ending June 30, 1912* (Washington: Government Printing Office, 1912), 10, 27.

15. Jones, 103; Carter, 14.

16. Jones, 102–4.

17. Georgette M. Dorn, "The Library of Congress and Other Latin American Resources in the Washington Area," *The Americas* 39 (April 1983): 539–40.

18. Archibald MacLeish, "The American Experience," in *The Hispanic Foundation in the Library of Congress,* ed. Robert C. Smith (Washington: Government Printing Office, 1939), 3.

19. Francisco Aguilera and Georgette M. Dorn, *The Archive of Hispanic Literature on Tape: A Descriptive Guide* (Washington: Library of Congress, 1974).

20. *The Handbook of Middle American Indians,* 15 vols. (Austin: University of Texas Press, 1964–72); *The National Directory of Latin Americanists,* compiled by the Hispanic Division (Washington: Government Printing Office, 1985).

Chapter 16.
The Growing Professionalism of Latin American Journals

1. David Block, "Current Trends in Andean Scholarly Publishing: Ecuador, Peru, and Bolivia," *Inter-American Review of Bibliography* 36 (1986): 129–44.

2. Juan Luis Mejía, "Panorama de la industria editorial en Colombia," *Cerlalc. Noticias sobre el Libro* 53 (1987): 17, 19.

3. Rubén Sierra Mejía, however, expressed his disdain for what he considered a citation-mania: "La cita se ha convertido en una norma sagrada de la preceptiva académica. . . . Se cita y se hacen referencias. Y la opinión que no esté amparada en una autoridad, es como una especie de teoría que no describe hechos: simple y llanamente un producto de la fantasía." "Sobre el arte de citar," *Revista Aleph* 63 (October–December 1987): 3–4.

4. "II Encontro brasileiro de revistas de Educação," *Educação em Debate* 9 (2nd semester, 1986): 136–39. With the same purposes, the editors of Brazilian scientific journals are also holding annual meetings, "Documento final do II Encontro de Editores de Revistas Científicas," *Dados. Revista de Ciências Sociais* 29, no. 2 (1986): 271–72.

5. There are two institutions in the United States entirely devoted to these matters: the Conference of Editors of Learned Journals, in Morgantown, West Virginia, and the Society for Scholarly Publishing, in Washington, D.C.

6. The Argentine scholar Gregorio Weinberg, however, considers that under the present economic situation publishing abroad weakens the national journals: "Aminoradas las posibilidades de publicar en el propio país, se procura hacerlo en revistas extranjeras, o se colabora en forma creciente con universidades e institutos donde sus actividades habitualmente encuentran acogida favorable. A su vez esta orientación, que induce a publicar en centros prestigiosos, contribuye como consecuencia a empobrecer aún más las escasas publicaciones nacionales; de aquí a ayudar, por indirecta vía, a su desaparición, sólo hay un paso." "Aspectos del vaciamiento de la universidad argentina durante los recientes regímenes militares," *Cuadernos Americanos,* nueva época, 6 (November–December 1987): 210.

7. The historical evolution of Chilean periodical publications is reviewed in Héctor Gómez Fuentes and Bruna Benzi Bistolfi, "La publicación periódica: un importante vehículo para la transmisión del conocimiento," *Trilogía* (December 1987): 24–28.

Chapter 17.
The Afro-Hispanic Review

1. Richard L. Jackson, *Black Literature and Humanism in Latin America* (Athens: University of Georgia Press, 1988).

2. Richard L. Jackson, *The Black Image in Latin American Literature* (Albuquerque: University of New Mexico Press, 1976), 13.

3. Jackson, *Black Image*, 95.

4. See George G. M. James, *Stolen Legacy*, 1954 (San Francisco: Richardson, 1985); Cheikh Anta Diop, *The African Origin of Civilization: Myth or Reality*, ed. and trans. Mercer Cook (New York: Hill, 1974); Ivan Van Sertima, *They Came before Columbus: the African Presence in Ancient America* (New York: Random House, 1976); Martin Bernal, *Black Athena: The Afroasiatic Roots of Classical Civilization* (New Brunswick: Rutgers University Press, 1987).

Selected Bibliography

With few exceptions, this bibliography includes only books and articles that deal specifically with Latin American philosophy and literature and to which reference has been made in this volume. Generally, Latin American works of literature or of philosophy mentioned in the text are not recorded. Also not recorded are works of literature or philosophy that are not specifically concerned with Latin America.

Abellán, José Luis. *Filosofía española en América (1936–1966)*. Madrid: Ediciones Guadarrama, 1967.

Acerboni, Lídia. *A filosofia contemporânea no Brasil*. São Paulo: Editorial Grijalbo, 1969.

Agazzi, Evandro. "Qué espera la comunidad internacional de parte de la filosofía latinoamericana," *Prometeo* 5 (1986): 58–59, 64–65.

Aguilera, Francisco, and Georgette M. Dorn. *The Archive of Hispanic Literature on Tape: A Descriptive Guide*. Washington: Library of Congress, 1974.

Agulla, J. C. *Dependencia y conciencia desgraciada*. Buenos Aires: Editorial de Belgrano, 1985.

Alarco, Luis Felipe. *Pensadores peruanos*. Lima: Sociedad Peruana de Filosofía, 1952.

Alcázar, Josefina. *Universidad y financiamiento*. Puebla: Universidad Autónoma de Puebla, 1984.

Alfau Durán, Vetilio. "Documentos para la historia de la filosofía en Santo Domingo," *Anales de la Universidad de Santo Domingo* 15 (1950).

Almeida, Onésimo Teotónio. "Latin American Philosophy? Revisitation of a Recurrent Theme," paper presented at a meeting of the Society for Iberian and Latin American Thought, American Philosophical Association Convention, Eastern Division, December 1984.

———. "Filosofia brasileira versus filosofia no Brasil: Notas de leitura à *Crítica da razão tupiniquim*," *Revista Brasileira de Filosofia* 34 (1985): 400–13.

———. "Brazilian Philosophy and National Thought," *Dictionary of Brazilian Literature*. Ed. Irwin Stein. Westport, Conn.: Greenwood, 1988.

Alzamora Valdéz, Mario. *La filosofía del derecho en el Perú*. Lima, 1968.

Amurrio González, Jesús Julián. *El positivismo en Guatemala*. Guatemala: Universidad de San Carlos, 1970.

Anuario Estadístico. México: Asociación Nacional de Universidades e Institutos de Enseñanza Superior, 1986–88.

ANUIES. Catálogo de carreras: Licenciatura en universidades e institutos tecnológicos, 4 vols. México: Secretaría de Educación Pública, 1986.

Ardao, Arturo. *Espiritualismo y positivismo en el Uruguay*. Buenos Aires: Fondo de Cultura Económica, 1950.

———. "Tendencias filosóficas en el Uruguay del siglo XX," *Cursos y Conferencias* 48 (1950): 27–38.

———. *La filosofía en el Uruguay del siglo XX*. Buenos Aires: Fondo de Cultura Económica, 1956.

———. *Racionalismo y liberalismo en el Uruguay*. Montevideo: Universidad de la República, 1962.

Arico, José. *Marx y América Latina*. México: Alianza, 1980.

Armas Ayala, Alfonso. *Influencias del pensamiento venezolano en la revolución de independencia de Hispanoamérica*. Caracas: Instituto Panamericano de Geografía e Historia, 1970.

Atienza, M. *La filosofía del derecho argentino actual*. Buenos Aires: De Palma, 1984.

Bader, Thomas. "Early Positivistic Thought and Ideological Conflict in Chile," *The Americas* 26 (1970): 376–93.

Bagú, S., *et al. De la historia e historiadores: Homenaje a José Luis Romero.* México: Siglo XXI, 1982.

Balcárcel, José Luis. "Filosofía de la filosofía en Centroamérica," *Revista de Filosofía de la Universidad de Costa Rica* 15 (1977): 197–200.

Balmori, Diana. *Hispanic Immigrants in the Construction Industry.* New York: New York University, Center for Latin American Studies, 1983.

Barradas, Efraín. "La necesaria innovación de Ana Lydia Vega: preámbulo para lectores vírgenes," *Revista Iberoamericana* 51 (1985): 547–56.

Barreto, Tobias. *Vários escritos.* Rio de Janeiro, 1900.

Beltrán, Guerrero. *Introducción al positivismo venezolano.* Caracas: Revista Nacional de Cultura, 1955.

Bendfeldt, Lourdes and Alba Calderón. *Bibliografía filosófica de publicaciones de las Universidades de Costa Rica y San Carlos de Guatemala y de autores guatemaltecos que exhibió la Biblioteca Nacional.* Guatemala: Universidad de San Carlos, 1964.

Benítez, Justo Pastor. "Diagrama de las ideas en el Paraguay," *Revista Dominicana de Filosofía* 2 (1956): 58–62.

Bernal, Martín. *Black Athena: The Afroasiatic Roots of Classical Civilization.* New Brunswick: Rutgers University Press, 1987.

Biagini, Hugo E. "La expresión filosófica latinoamericana," *Latin American Research Review* 14 (1979).

———. *Panorama filosófico argentino.* Buenos Aires: EUDEBA, 1985.

———. "Pensamiento e ideología en la Argentina (1950–1959)," *Ideas en Ciencias Sociales* 6 (1987).

Bianchi, Ana Maria. *Evolução temática da sociologia brasileira.* São Paulo: Fundação Instituto de Pesquisas Econômicas, 1985.

Bibliografía chilena de filosofía: desde fines del siglo XVI hasta el presente. Santiago: La Biblioteca, 1979.

Block, David. "Current Trends in Andean Scholarly Publishing: Ecuador, Peru and Bolivia," *Inter-American Review of Bibliography* 36 (1986): 129–44.

Borges, Jorge Luis. *Evaristo Carriego.* Trans. Norman Thomas Di Giovanni. New York: Dutton, 1984.

Browning, Rufus P. *Protest is not Enough: The Struggle of Blacks and Hispanics for Equality in Urban Politics.* Berkeley: University of California Press, 1984.

Bruce-Novoa, Juan. "Report on El Quinto Festival de Teatros Chicanos," *De Colores* 2.2 (1975): 66–72.

Caño-Guiral, Jesús. *Las ideologías políticas y la filosofía en el Uruguay.* Montevideo: Nuestra Tierra, 1969.

Cárdenas, Horacio. *Resonancias de la filosofía europea en Venezuela.* Caracas: Universidad Central de Venezuela, 1958.

Cardiel Reyes, Raúl. *Retorno a Caso.* México: Universidad Nacional Autónoma de México, 1986.

Cardozo, Efraím. *Apuntes de historia cultural del Paraguay.* Asunción: Colegio de San José, 1963.

Caro Figueroa, G. "Exiliados y proscriptos en la historia argentina," *Todo es Historia,* 246 (1987).

Carrera Andrade, Jorge. *Galería de místicos y de insurgentes: La vida intelectual del Ecuador durante cuatro siglos. 1555–1955.* Quito: Casa de la Cultura Ecuatoriana, 1959.

Carreras en el sistema de educación superior en México. México: Asociación Nacional de Universidades e Institutos de Enseñanza Superior, 1984.

Carrión, Benjamín. "Historia de las ideas en el Ecuador," *Revista de Historia de las Ideas* 1 (1959): 251–63.

Carter, William E. *The Hispanic Room in the Library of Congress.* Washington: Library of Congress, 1984.

Casas, M. G. "Situação atual da filosofia na Argentina," *Revista Portuguesa de Filosofia* 17, 3–4.

Caturelli, A. *La filosofía en la Argentina actual.* Buenos Aires: Sudamericana, 1971.

Cerutti Guldberg, Horacio. "Aproximación a la historiografía del pensamiento ecuatoriano," *Pucará* 1 (1977): 21–48.

———. *Filosofía de la liberación latinoamericana.* México: Fondo de Cultura Económica, 1983.

———. *Hacia una metodología de las ideas (filosóficas) en América Latina.* Guadalajara: Universidad de Guadalajara, 1986.

_____. *Ideologías políticas contemporáneas*. México: Universidad Nacional Autónoma de México, 1986.

Charim, Nizim. "¿Quiénes somos? ICTUS y la creación colectiva," *Tramoya* 12 (July–September 1978): 4–13.

Claps, Manuel Arturo. "Situación actual de la filosofía uruguaya," *Número* 3–4 (1964).

Cobo Borda, Juan Gustavo. *Antología de la poesía hispanoamericana*. México: Fondo de Cultura Económica, 1985.

Cockcroft, James. *Intellectual Precursors of the Mexican Revolution*. Austin: University of Texas Press, 1968.

Cole, John Y. *For Congress and the Nation: A Chronological History of the Library of Congress*. Washington: Library of Congress, 1979.

Conteris, Hiber. "El 'bricolage' como estrategia narrativa del 'inxilio,'" paper presented at the twenty-ninth annual meeting of the Midwest Modern Language Association. Columbus, Ohio, 12–14 November 1987.

Cooper, William. *Francisco Romero's Theory of Value*. Ph.D. dissertation, Baylor University. Waco, Texas, 1966.

Cordero, Armando. *Estudios para la historia de la filosofía en Santo Domingo*. Ciudad Trujillo: Arte y Cine, 1956.

_____. *Panorama de la filosofía en Santo Domingo*, 2 vols. Santo Domingo: Arte y Cine, 1962.

Cosio Villegas, Rafael, *et al. A Compact History of Mexico*. México: El Colegio de México, 1985.

Côtes Guimarães, Aquiles. *O tema na consciência na filosofia brasileira*. São Paulo: Editôra Convívio, 1982.

Crawford, W. R. *A Century of Latin American Thought*. Cambridge: Harvard University Press, 1944.

Cruz Costa, João. *Panorama of the History of Philosophy in Brazil*. Trans. Fred G. Sturm. Washington, D.C.: Pan American Union, 1962.

Cuadernos Americanos, Nueva época 1 (1987): 107–59.

Cueva, Mario de la, *et al. Major Trends in Mexican Philosophy*. Trans. R. M. Caponigri. Notre Dame: University of Notre Dame Press, 1966.

_____. *Estudios de historia de la filosofía en México*, 3rd and 4th eds. México: Universidad Nacional Autónoma de México, 1980, 1985.

Dascal, Marcelo. "Philosophical Analysis in Brazil," in Jorge J. E. Gracia, et al., eds., *Philosophical Analysis in Latin America*. Dordrecht: Reidel, 1984, 277-84.

Davis, H. E. *Latin American Thought: A Historical Introduction*. Baton Rouge: Louisiana State University Press, 1972; 2nd. ed, New York: Free Press, 1974.

Development Associates. *The Demographic and Socioeconomic Characteristics of Hispanic Population in the United States: 1950-1980*. Washington, D.C., 1982.

Díaz Díaz, G. and C. Santos Escudero. *Bibliografía filosófica hispánica*. Madrid: CSIC, 1982.

Diop, Cheikh Anta. *The African Origin of Civilization: Myth or Reality*. Ed. and trans. Mercer Cook. New York: Hill, 1974

"Documento final do II Encontro de Editores de Revistas Científicas," *Dados. Revista de Ciências Sociais* 29.2 (1986): 271-272.

Domínguez Caballero, Diego. "Panamá y la historia de las ideas en Latinoamérica," *Revista de Historia de las Ideas* 1 (1959): 217-35.

———. *Los estudios filosóficos en la Universidad de Panamá*. Panamá: Universidad de Panamá, 1963.

Donoso, José. *The Boom in Spanish American Literature: A Personal History*. Trans. Gregory Kolovakos. New York: Columbia University Press and the Center for Inter-American Relations, 1977.

———. *Historia personal del "boom"*, Appendix I, "El 'boom' doméstico." by María Pilar Serrano. Appendix II, "Diez años después," by José Donoso. Barcelona: Seix Barral, 1983.

Donoso, Ricardo. *Las ideas políticas en Chile*. México: Fondo de Cultura Económica, 1946.

Dorn, Georgette M. "Las colecciones de literatura hispánica en la Biblioteca del Congreso," *Revista Interamericana de Bibliografía* 29 (1979): 337-44.

———. "The Library of Congress and Other Latin American Resources in the Washington Area," *The Americas* 39 (April, 1983): 539-40.

Dussel, Enrique, *Philosophy of Liberation*. Trans. by Aquilina Martínez and Christine Morkovsky. Maryknoll, N.Y.: Orbis Books, 1985. French edition, *Histoire et théologie de la liberation*. Paris: Quvrières, 1974.

_____. *Ethics and the Theology of Liberation.* Maryknoll, N.Y.: Orbis Books, 1978.

Dussel, Enrique and D. Guillot. *Liberación latinoamericana y E. Levinas.* Buenos Aires: Bonum, 1975.

"II Encontro brasileiro de revistas de Educação," *Educação em Debate* 9 (2nd semester, 1986): 136–39.

Escobar, Roberto. *La filosofía en Chile.* Santiago: Universal, 1976.

_____. "El sentido de lo americano en los filósofos chilenos," *Mapocho* 26 (1978): 25–33.

Escobar Valenzuela, Gustavo. *La ilustración en la filosofía latinoamericana.* México: Trillas, 1980.

Estadísticas básicas del sistema educacional nacional. México: Secretaría de Educación Pública, 1986.

Farré, L. and C. Lértora Mendoza. *La filosofía en la Argentina.* Buenos Aires: Docencia, 1981.

Ferré, Rosario. "La cocina de la escritura," in *Sitio a Eros.* México: Joaquín Mortiz, 1986, 13–33.

Fitz, Earl E. *Clarice Lispector.* Boston: Twayne, 1985.

Fornet Betancourt, Raúl and C. Lértora Mendoza. *Ethik in Deutschland und Lateinamerika heute.* Frankfurt: P. Lang, 1987.

Foster, David William, ed. *Sourcebook of Hispanic Culture in the United States.* Chicago: American Library Association, 1982.

_____. "Latin American Documentary Narrative," in *Alternate Voices in the Contemporary Latin American Narrative.* Columbia: University of Missouri Press, 1985.

Franco, Franklin J. *Historia de las ideas políticas en la República Dominicana: Contribución a su estudio.* Santo Domingo: Editorial Nacional, 1981.

Franco, Jean. "Apuntes sobre la crítica feminista y la literatura hispanoamericana," *Hispamérica* 45 (1986): 31–43.

Francovich, Guillermo. *El pensamiento boliviano del siglo XX.* México: Fondo de Cultura Económica, 1956.

_____. *La filosofía en Bolivia.* Buenos Aires: Losada, 1945; 2nd. expanded ed., La Paz: Juventud, 1966.

Fránquiz, José A. "Panorama de la filosofía en Puerto Rico," *Luminar* 7 (1945): 100–17.

Freudenthal, Juan R., and Patricia M. Freudenthal, eds. *Index to Anthologies of Latin American Literature in English Translation*. Boston: G. K. Hall, 1977.

Frondizi, Risieri. "Panorama de la filosofía latinoamericana contemporánea," *Minerva* 1 (1944); reprinted in Jorge J. E. Gracia, ed., *Risieri Frondizi: Ensayos filosóficos*. México: Fondo de Cultura Económica, 1986.

_____. *Ensayos filosóficos*. Ed. Jorge J. E. Gracia. México: Fondo de Cultura Económica, 1986.

Frondizi, Risieri, and Jorge J. E. Gracia, eds. *El hombre y los valores en la filosofía latinoamericana del siglo XX*. México: Fondo de Cultura Económica, 1974; 2nd printing, 1981.

Fuentes, Carlos. *La nueva novela hispanoamericana*. México: Joaquín Mortiz, 1969.

_____. "How I Elected to Write in Spanish," *Ideas '92*. 1.1 (1987): 5–10.

Gann, Lewis H. *The Hispanics in the United States: A History*. Boulder, Col.: Westview Press, 1986.

Gaos, José. *En torno a la filosofía mexicana*. México: Porrúa y Obregón, 1952.

_____. *Historia de nuestra idea del mundo*. 2nd printing. México: Fondo de Cultura Económica, 1983.

García, Ward J. *Comparison of Two Liberation Thinkers*. Doctoral dissertation, De Paul University, 1988.

García Bacca, Juan David. *Antología del pensamiento filosófico en Colombia (1647–1761)*. Bogotá: Imprenta Nacional, 1955.

García Cantú, Gastón. *Años críticos: La UNAM. 1968–1987*. México: Universidad Nacional Autónoma de México, 1987.

García Clark, Rubén. "Información bibliográfica de publicaciones filosóficas de autores radicados en México, aparecidos durante el año de 1985," *Prometeo* 2 (1986).

García Márquez, Gabriel. "The Solitude of Latin America," trans. Marina Castañeda. *New York Times* 6 February 1983, sec. 4: 17.

Garfield, Evelyn Picon. *Women's Voices from Latin America*. Detroit: Wayne State University Press, 1985.

Garibay Gutiérrez, Luis. "Mexico," *International Encyclopedia of Higher Education*. A. Knowles, ed. San Francisco: Jossey-Bass, 1977, vol. 6, 2848–2856.

Garza, Rodolfo de la, ed. *Ignored Voices: Public Opinion Polls and the Latino Community*. Austin: Center for Mexican American Studies, University of Texas, 1987.

Gilreath, James. "Sowerby Revirescent and Revised," *The Papers of the Bibliographical Society of America* 78 (Second Quarter, 1984): 219–20.

Goff, Frederick R. "Jefferson, The Book Collector." *Quarterly Journal of the Library of Congress* 29 (January 1972): 32–47.

Gomes, Roberto. *Crítica de razão tupiniquim*. 6th ed. São Paulo: Cortez Editora, 1983.

Gómez Fuentes, Héctor, and Bruna Benzi Bistolfi. "La publicación periódica: un importante vehículo para la transmisión del conocimiento," *Trilogía* 7 (December 1987): 24–28.

Gómez Martínez, José Luis. "Pensamiento hispanoamericano: una aproximación bibliográfica," *Cuadernos Salmantinos de Filosofía* 8 (1981): 287–400.

———. *Bolivia: un pueblo en busca de su identidad*. La Paz-Cochabamba: Los Amigos del Libro, 1988.

Gómez Robledo, Antonio. *El magisterio filosófico y jurídico de Alonso de la Vera Cruz*. México: Porrúa, 1984.

González, Juliana, *et al. Presencia de Ramón Xirau*. México: Universidad Nacional Autónoma de México, 1986.

González, Juliana, and Carlos Pereyra and Gabriel Vargas Lozano, eds. *Praxis y filosofía: Ensayos en homenaje a Adolfo Sánchez Vázquez*. Mexico: Grijalbo, 1987.

Gracia, Jorge J. E. "Antropología positivista en América Latina," *Cuadernos Americanos* 33 (1974): 93–106.

———. "Importance of the History of Ideas in Latin America," *Journal of the History of Ideas* 36 (1975): 177–84.

———, ed. *Man and His Conduct: Philosophical Essays in Honor of Risieri Frondizi*. San Juan: University of Puerto Rico Press, 1980.

———. "Panorama general de la filosofía latinoamericana actual," in *La filosofía hoy en Alemania y América Latina*, ed. by Héctor V. Ortiz. Córdoba, Argentina: Instituto Goethe de Córdoba, 1984, 169–85.

_____. "Philosophical Analysis in Latin America," *History of Philosophy Quarterly* 1 (1984): 111–22.

_____. "Philosophical Bases of Unbelief in Latin America," in Gordon Stein, ed. *The Encyclopedia of Unbelief*, vol. 2. Buffalo, N.Y.: Prometheus Books, 1985, 385–93.

_____, ed. *Latin America Philosophy in the Twentieth Century*. Buffalo, N.Y.: Prometheus, 1986.

_____. "Religious Skepticism in Latin America," *Free Inquiry* 6 (1986): 30–5.

_____, ed. *Directory of Latin American Philosophers-Repertorio de Filósofos Latinoamericanos*. Buffalo, N.Y.: State University of New York Council on International Studies and Programs, 1988.

_____, ed. *Latin American Philosophy Today*. Double Issue of the *Philosophical Forum* 20 (1988).

_____. "Latin American Philosophy Today," *Philosophical Forum* 20 (1988): 4–32.

_____. "The Impact of Philosophical Analysis in Latin America," *Philosophical Forum* 20 (1988):129–140.

Gracia, Jorge J. E. and Iván Jaksić. "The Problem of Philosophical Identity in Latin America," *Inter American Review of Bibliography* 34 (1984): 53–71.

Gracia, Jorge J. E. and Iván Jaksić, eds. *Filosofía e identidad cultural en América Latina*. Caracas: Monte Avila, 1988.

Gracia, Jorge J. E., and E. Rabossi, E. Villanueva, and M. Dascal, eds. *Philosophical Analysis in Latin America*. Dordrecht: Reidel Pub. Co., 1984. Spanish, more comprehensive edition, *El análisis filosófico en América Latina*. México: Fondo de Cultura Económica, 1985.

Gracia, Jorge J. E., Gary Hoskin and Amy Oliver, eds. *Social Sciences in Latin America*. Special studies, 157. Buffalo, N.Y.: Council on International Studies and Programs, 1989.

Grippa, Adolfo. *As ideias filosóficas no Brasil*. São Paulo: Convívio, 1900.

Guy, Alain. "La filosofía en Costa Rica," *Revista de Filosofía de la Universidad de Costa Rica* 9 (1971): 111–19.

Harris, Marjorie. *Francisco Romero on Problems of Philosophy*. New York: Philosophical Library, 1960.

Harss, Luis, and Barbara Dohmann. *Into the Mainstream*. New York: Harper and Row, 1967.

Hegenberg, Leônidas. "E como vai a lógica no Brasil?" *Convivium* 24 (1986).

Henderson, James D. *Conservative Thought in Twentieth Century Latin America*. Athens, Ohio: University Press, 1988.

Hernández, Enrique. *Positivismo y cientifismo en la Argentina*. Bariloche: Universidad de Comahue, 1975.

Hernández Méndez, Eugenio. *Antología del pensamiento puertorriqueño. 1900–1970*, 2 vols. Hato Rey: Universidad de Puerto Rico, 1975.

Herrera Restrepo, Daniel. *La filosofía en Colombia: Bibliografía 1627–1973*. Cali: Universidad del Valle, 1973.

_____. "El proceso filosófico en Colombia y sus condicionamientos socio-políticos," *Primer Foro Nacional de Filosofía*. Pasto, 1975.

Hodges, Donald Clark. "Philosophy in the Cuban Revolution," in *Marxism, Revolution and Peace*. Ed. H. L. Parsons and J. Sommerville. Amsterdam: Gruner, 1977.

Hountondji, Paulin J. *African Philosophy: Myth and Reality*. Bloomington: Indiana University Press, 1983.

Jackson, Donald. *Thomas Jefferson and the Stony Mountains: Exploring the West from Monticello*. Urbana: University of Illinois Press, 1981.

Jackson, Richard L. *The Black Image in Latin American Literature*. Albuquerque: University of New Mexico Press, 1976.

_____. *Black Writers in Latin America*. Albuquerque: University of New Mexico Press, 1979.

_____. *Black Literature and Humanism in Latin America*. Athens: University of Georgia Press, 1988.

Jaffe, Abram, Ruth M. Cullen, and Thomas D. Boswell, eds. *The Changing Demography of Spanish Americans*. New York: Academic Press, 1980.

Jaguaribe, Hélio. *A filosofia no Brasil*. Rio de Janeiro: ISEB, 1959.

Jaksić, Iván. "Chilean Philosophy under Military Rule," *Occasional Papers in Latin American Studies*, University of California, at Berkeley, 10 (1984).

_____. "Filosofía y gobierno militar en Chile," *Prometeo* 1 (1985): 63–67.

_____. *"Philosophia perennis* en tiempos pretorianos: La filosofía chilena desde 1973," *Cuadernos Americanos* 259 (1985): 59–87.

_____. "La vocación filosófica en Chile," *Cuadernos Americanos, nueva época* 2 (1988): 21–42.

_____. *Academic Rebels in Chile: The Role of Philosophy in Higher Education and Politics.* Albany, N.Y.: State University of New York Press, 1989.

James, George G. M. *Stolen Legacy.* 1954. San Francisco: Richardson, 1985.

Jaramillo Uribe, Jaime. *El pensamiento colombiano en el siglo XIX.* Bogotá: Temis, 1964.

_____. *Entre la historia y la filosofía.* Bogotá: Revista Colombiana, 1968.

_____. *Antología del pensamiento político colombiano.* 2 vols. Bogotá: Talleres Gráficos del Banco de la República, 1970.

Jiménez, José Olivio. *Antología de la poesía hispanoamericana contemporánea: 1914–1970.* Madrid: Alianza, 1971; rev. ed.: 1977.

Jiménez, Mier and Fernando Terán. *El autoritarianismo en el gobierno de la UNAM.* 2nd ed. México: Ediciones de Cultura Popular, 1987.

Jones, Cecil K. "Hispano-Americana in the Library of Congress," *Hispanic American Historical Review* 2 (February 1919): 96–104.

Kempff Mercado, Manfredo. "La filosofía actual en Bolivia," *Notas y Estudios de Filosofía* 3 (1952): 67–70.

Kilgore, William. *Alejandro Korn's Interpretation of Creative Freedom.* Doctoral dissertation, University of Texas, 1958.

Klappenbach, A. "La filosofía en la Argentina actual," *Arbor* 490 (1986).

Kneller, G. F. *The Education of the Mexican Nation.* New York: Octagon, 1973.

Kohn de Beker, Marisa. *Tendencias positivistas en Venezuela.* Caracas: Universidad Central de Venezuela, 1970.

Krause de Koulteniuk, Rosa. *La filosofía de Antonio Caso.* 2nd ed. México: Universidad Nacional Autónoma de México, 1986.

Kusch, Rodolfo. *El pensamiento indígena americano.* México: Cajica, 1970.

————. *Esbozo de una antropología filosófica americana.* San Antonio de Padua: Castañeda, 1978.

Ladusãns, Stanislav. *Rumos da filosofia actual no Brasil em auto-retratos.* São Paulo: Ediçoes Loyola, 1976.

Lagos, Ramiro. *Mujeres poetas de Hispanoamérica.* Bogotá: Centro de Estudios Poéticos Hispanos, 1986.

Larsen, Neil, ed. *The Discourse of Power, Culture, Hegemony and the Authoritarian State in Latin America.* Minneapolis: Institute for the Study of Ideologies and Literature, 1983.

Láscaris, Constantino. *Desarrollo de las ideas filosóficas en Costa Rica.* San José: ECA, 1965.

————. *Historia de las ideas en Centroamérica.* San José: EDUCA, 1970.

————. "Desarrollo de las ideas filosóficas en Costa Rica," *Revista de Filosofía de la Universidad de Costa Rica* 8 (1970): 267–84.

————. "Algunos pensadores centroamericanos," *Revista de Filosofía de la Universidad de Costa Rica* 15 (1977): 281–307.

Lastra, Pedro, and Luis Eyzaguirre. "Catorce poetas hispanoamericanos de hoy," *INTI. Revista de Literatura Hispánica* 18–19 (Providence Coll., Fall 1983–Spring 1984), iii–xvii.

Leia (May 1987). Essays by Juarez Guimarães, Renato Janine Ribeiro, *et al.*

Lértora Mendoza, C. *La enseñanza de la filosofía en tiempos de la colonia.* Buenos Aires: Fecic, 1979.

————. *Bibliografía filosófica argentina.* Buenos Aires: Fecic, 1983.

Lipp, Solomon. *Three Argentine Thinkers.* New York: Philosophical Library, 1969.

————. *Three Chilean Thinkers.* Waterloo: Wilfrid Laurier University Press, 1975.

Liss, Sheldon B. *Roots of Revolution: Radical Thought in Cuba.* Lincoln: University of Nebraska Press, 1987.

Lizcano, Francisco. *Leopoldo Zea: Una filosofía de la historia.* Madrid: Ediciones Cultura Hispánica, 1981.

Lombardo Toledano, Vicente. *Escritos filosóficos.* México: Editorial Nuevo México, 1937.

Luby, Barry, ed. *Anthology of Contemporary Latin American Literature*. New Jersey: Fairleigh Dickinson University Press, 1985.

Luna, José Ramón. *El positivismo en la historia del pensamiento venezolano*. Caracas: Editorial Arte, 1971.

Luzuriaga, Gerardo. "El IV Festival de Manizales, 1971," in Gerardo Luzuriaga, ed., *Popular Theater for Social Change in Latin America: Essays in Spanish and English*. Los Angeles: UCLA Latin American Center Pubs., 1978, 189–200.

MacKenzie, Malcolm Scott. "Emilio Carballido: An Ideational Evolution of His Theatre," Ann Arbor, Michigan, UMI, 1981. 8121001.

MacLeish, Archibald. "The American Experience," in Robert C. Smith, ed., *The Hispanic Foundation in the Library of Congress*. Washington: Government Printing Office, 1939, 3.

Majía Valera, Manuel. *Fuentes para la historia de la filosofía en el Perú*. Lima: Universidad Nacional de San Marcos, 1965.

Malone, Dumas. "Books in Transit: The Library of Congres," in *The Sage of Monticello*. Boston: Little, Brown, 1981, 169–84.

Marrero Navarro, Domingo. "Notas para organizar el estudio de la historia de las ideas en Puerto Rico," *Revista de Historia de las Ideas* 1 (1959): 159–76.

Martí, José. *Our America*. Trans. Elinor Randall, Juan de Onís, and Roslyn Held Foner. New York: Monthly Review Press, 1977.

Martí, Oscar. *The Reaction against Positivism in Latin America*. Doctoral dissertation, City University of New York, 1978.

―――. "Is There a Latin American Philosophy?" *Metaphilosophy* 14 (1983): 39–49.

Martínez, Agustín. "La filosofía en Venezuela: Recopilación bibliográfica," *Semestre de Filosofía* 1 (1977).

Martínez, José Luis. *The Modern Mexican Essay*. Toronto: University of Toronto Press, 1968.

McMurray, George R. *Spanish American Writing Since 1941: A Critical Survey*. New York: Ungar, 1987.

Mearns, David C. *The Story Up To Now: The Library of Congress. 1800–1946*. Washington: Library of Congress, 1946.

Medin, Tziv. *Leopoldo Zea: Ideología, historia y filosofía de América Latina*. México: Universidad Nacional Autónoma de México, 1983.

Mejía, Juan Luis. "Panorama de la industria editorial en Colombia," *Cerlalc. Noticias sobre el Libro* 53 (1987): 1–23.

Merquior, José Guilherme. *The Veil and the Mask: Essays on Culture and Ideology.* London: Routledge & Kegan Paul, 1979.

Mestre Domínguez, José M. *De la filosofía en La Habana.* Havana, Cuba: Ministerio de Educación, 1952.

Millán Albarracín, Juan. *Orígenes del pensamiento social contemporáneo de Bolivia.* La Paz: Universo, 1976.

_____. *Filosofía boliviana del siglo XX.* La Paz: Alcapana, 1981.

Millán, Gonzalo. "Promociones poéticas emergentes: El espíritu del valle," *Posdata* 4 (Concepción, 1985): 2–9.

Miró Quesada, Francisco. *Despertar y proyecto del filosofar latinoamericano.* México: Fondo de Cultura Económica, 1974.

_____. *Proyecto y realización del filosofar latinoamericano.* México: Fondo de Cultura Económica, 1981.

Molina, Enrique. *La filosofía en Chile en la primera mitad del siglo XX.* Santiago: Nascimiento, 1951; 2nd expanded ed., 1953.

_____. *Desarrollo de Chile en la primera mitad del siglo XX.* 2 vols. Santiago: Universidad de Chile, 1952.

Moncada, Alberto. *La americanización de los hispanos.* Barcelona: Plaza y Janés, 1986.

Monleón, José. "Polémica y balance con el teatro colombiano al fondo," *Primer Acto* 203–4 (1984): 9–19.

Monteiro, João Paulo. "A filosofia de Brasil: por um debate planetário," *Expresso*, 25 February 1984.

Moreira Leites, Dante. *O caracter nacional brasileiro: Historia de uma ideologia.* São Paulo: Livraria Pioneira Editora, 1976.

Moreno de los Arcos, Roberto. *La polémica del darwinismo en México: Siglo XIX. Testimonios.* México: Universidad Nacional Autónoma de México, 1984.

_____. *Ensayos de historia de la ciencia y la tecnología en México.* México: Universidad Nacional Autónoma de México, 1986.

Moyano Martin, Dolores. "Hispanic Narrative in the Library of Congress," paper presented at a workshop on Alejo Carpentier. Yale University, New Haven, Conn., 30 March 1979.

Nicol, Eduardo. *El problema de la filosofía hispánica*. Madrid: Tecnos, 1961.

Nuño, Alicia de. *Ideas sociales del positivismo en Venezuela*. Caracas: Universidad Central de Venezuela, 1969.

O'Gorman, Edmundo. *La invención de América*. México: Fondo de Cultura Económica, 1977.

Ornelas Navarro, Carlos. "El estado y las fuerzas democráticas: La lucha por la reforma universitaria," *Foro Universitario* 43 (June 1984): 23–34.

Ortega, Julio. *Antología de la poesía hispanoamericana actual*. México: Siglo XXI, 1987.

Paim, Antônio. *História das idéias filosóficas no Brasil*. São Paulo: Grijalbo, 1967. Many subsequent editions.

_____. *História das ideias filosóficas no Brasil*. 2nd ed. São Paulo: Universidade de Sào Paulo/Editora Grijalbo, 1974.

_____. *O estudo do pensamento filosófico brasileiro*. Rio de Janeiro: Tempo Brasileiro, 1979.

_____. "As opçores da filosofia na universidade," *Revista Brasileira de Filosofia*, no. 125 (1982): 99–107.

_____. "Questões teóricas relacionadas à filosofia brasileira," *Revista Brasileira de Filosofia* 34 (1985): 357–69.

Paladines Escudero, Carlos. *Sentido y trayectoria del pensamiento ecuatoriano. Vol. I: La Modernidad*. México: Universidad Nacional Autónoma de México, 1987.

Parker, C. M. *Francisco Romero's Theory of Man*. Doctoral dissertation, University of Oklahoma, 1973.

Paz, Octavio. *The Labyrinth of Solitude: Life and Thought in Mexico*. Trans. L. Kemp. New York: Grove 1961.

_____. *Sor Juana o las trampas de la fe*. 3rd ed. México: Fondo de Cultura Económica, 1983.

_____. "La literatura escrita en español en los Estados Unidos," *Ideas '92* 1.1 (1987): 11–14.

Pellegrini, Aldo. *Antología de la poesía viva latinoamericana*. Barcelona: Seix Barral, 1966.

Pérez Lindo, Augusto. *Universidad, política y sociedad*. Buenos Aires: EUDEBA, 1985.

Pérez Marchand, Monelisa. "Préambulos para una historia de las ideas en Puerto Rico," *Revista de Historia de las Ideas* 1 (1959): 143–58.

Pescador, Augusto. "La filosofía en Bolivia en el siglo XX," *Cursos y Conferencias* 25 (1956): 61–80, and *Cuadernos de Filosofía* [Concepción] 6 (1977): 93–109.

Pianca, Marina. "El Festival de Quito, 1971" in Gerardo Luzuriaga, ed. *Popular Theater for Social Change in Latin America: Essays in Spanish and English*. Los Angeles: UCLA Latin American Center Pubs., 1978, 201–12.

Piñera Llera, Humberto. *Panorama de la filosofía cubana*. Washington, D.C.: Unión Panamericana, 1960.

Pinheiro Machado, Geraldo. "A filosofia no Brasil," in J. Hirschberger, ed., *História da filosofia contemporânea*. São Paulo: Hender, 1963, 225–312.

Pro, Diego, and C. Jalif, and G. Prada. *Historia del pensamiento filosófico argentino*. Vols. 1 and 3. Mendoza: Universidad de Cuyo, 1973 and 1980.

Proceedings and Addresses of the American Philosophical Association 60 (1986).

Ramis, Pompeyo. *Veinte filósofos venezolanos. 1946–1976*. Mérida: Universidad de los Andes, 1978.

Ramírez, Ignacio. *México en pos de la libertad*. México: PRI, 1986.

Ramos, Samuel. *Profile of Man and Culture in Mexico*. Austin: University of Texas Press, 1975.

Reale, Miguel. *Filosofia em São Paulo*. 2nd ed. São Paulo: Editora da Universidade de São Paulo/Editorial Grijalbo, 1976.

Redmond, Walter and Mauricio Beuchot. *La logica mexicana en el siglo de oro*. México: Universidad Nacional Autónoma de México, 1985.

Report of the Librarian of Congress and Report of the Superintendent of the Library Buildings and Grounds for the Fiscal Year Ending June 30, 1912. Washington: Government Printing Office, 1912.

Revista de Filosofía de la Universidad de Costa Rica 9 (1971).

Reyes, Carlos José. "Teatro e historia," *Conjunto* 61–62 (July–December, 1984), 146–56.

Ribeiro, Alvaro. *O problema da filosofia portuguesa*. Lisboa: Editorial Enquerito, 1943.

Rizk, Beatriz J. "El nuevo teatro en Latinoamérica," *Conjunto* 61–62 (July–December 1984): 11–31.

Rodó, José Enrique. *Ariel.* 1900 (many editions).

Rodríguez Alcalá, H. *Misión y pensamiento de Francisco Romero.* México: Universidad Nacional Autónoma de México, 1959.

Rodríguez Padrón, Jorge. *Antología de poesía hispanoamericana (1915–1980).* Madrid: Espasa-Calpe, 1984.

Roig, Arturo Andrés. *Los krausistas argentinos.* Puebla: Cajica, 1969.

———. *Teoría y crítica del pensamiento latinoamericano.* México: Fondo de Cultura Económica, 1981.

———. *Filosofía, universidad y filósofos en América Latina.* México: Universidad Nacional Autónoma de México, 1981.

———. *Esquemas para una historia de la filosofía ecuatoriana.* Quito: Universidad Católica, 1977; 2nd ed. 1982.

Roig, Arturo, et al. *El pensamiento latinoamericano del siglo XIX.* México: Instituto Panamericano de Geografía e Historia, 1981.

Romanell, Patrick. *The Making of the Mexican Mind.* Notre Dame: University of Notre Dame Press, 1967.

Romero, José Luis. *A History of Argentine Political Thought.* Stanford: Stanford University Press, 1963.

Ross, Waldo. *Crítica a la filosofía cubana de hoy.* Havana, Cuba: Cuadernos de Divulgación Cultural, 1954.

Rovira, María del Carmen. *Eclécticos portugueses del siglo XVIII y algunas de sus influencias en América.* México: Universidad Nacional Autónoma de México, 1979, 1980.

Roy, Joaquín. "Presencia de España en los Estados Unidos: Economía o cultura. Una propuesta para el 92," in *Realidades y posibilidades de las relaciones entre España y América en los ochenta.* Madrid: Instituto de Cooperación Iberoamericana, 1986, 173–97.

Roy, Joaquín, with Clea Sucoff and Manuel Fernández. "Reading and Writing in Spanish in the U.S.," *Hispania* 70 (1987): 830–33.

Salazar Bondy, Augusto. *Philosophy in Peru: A Historical Study.* Washington, D.C.: Unión Panamericana, 1954; 2nd expanded Spanish ed., Lima: Universo, 1967.

_____. *Historia de las ideas en el Perú contemporáneo: El proceso del pensamiento filosófico.* 2 vols. Lima: Moncloa, 1965.

Salmerón, Fernando. *Cuestiones educativas y páginas sobre México.* 2nd ed. Xalapa: Universidad Veracruzana, 1980.

_____. "Tradición filosófica y enseñanza. Notas sobre el caso de México," unpublished, 1987.

Sánchez Reulet, Aníbal. *Contemporary Latin American Philosophy.* Albuquerque: University of New Mexico Press, 1954.

Sánchez Villaseñor, José. *El sistema filosófico de Vasconcelos.* México: Editorial Polis, 1939.

San Juan Cafferty, Pastora and William C. McCready, eds. *Hispanics in the United States: A New Social Agenda.* New Brunswick, N.J.: Transaction Books, 1985.

Sarti, Sergio. *Panorama della filosofia ispanoamericana contemporanea.* Milano: Cisalpino-Goliardica, 1976.

Scannone, Juan. *Teología de la liberación y praxis popular.* Salamanca: Sígueme, 1976.

Schmidt, Henry C. *The Roots of "Lo Mexicano": Self and Society in Mexican Thought. 1900–1934.* College Station, Texas: Texas A&M University Press, 1978.

Schulman, Iván A. and Evelyn Picón-Garfield. *Las entrañas del vacío. Ensayos sobre la modernidad hispanoamerica.* México: Cuadernos Americanos, 1984.

Schutte, Ofelia. "Toward an Understanding of Latin American Philosophy: Reflections on the Formation of a Cultural Identity," *Philosophy Today* 31 (1987): 21–34.

_____. "Nietzsche, Mariátegui, and Socialism: A Case of 'Nietzschean Marxism' in Peru?" *Social Theory and Practice,* forthcoming 1989.

Schwartzmann, Félix. "La Philosophie au Chili," in Raymond Klibanski, ed., *La Philosophie Contemporaine.* Florence: La Nuova Editrice, 1971.

Seoane, Ana. "Primer Festival Latinoamericano de Teatro, Córdoba–1984," *Conjunto* 64 (April–June 1985): 130–41.

Sepich, Juan. *Latinoamérica.* Mendoza: Universidad de Cuyo, 1987.

Shank, Theodore and Adele Edling. "Chicano and Latin American Alternative Theater," in Gerardo Luzuriaga, ed. *Popular Theater for Social*

Change in Latin America: Essays in Spanish and English. Los Angeles: UCLA Latin American Center Pubs., 1978, 213–33.

Shaw, Bradley A. *Latin American Literature in English Translation: An Annotated Bibliography.* New York: New York University Press, 1976.

———. *Latin American Literature in English 1975–1978.* New York: Center for Inter-American Relations, 1979.

Sierra Mejía, Rubén. "Temas y corrientes de la filosofía colombiana en el siglo XX," in *Ensayos filosóficos.* Bogotá: Instituto Colombiano de Cultura, 1978, 99–126.

———. "Sobre el arte de citar," *Revista Aleph* 63 (October–December 1987): 3–9.

Silén, Iván. *Los paraguas amarillos. Los poetas latinos en Nueva York.* New Hampshire–Binghamton, N.Y.: Ediciones del Norte/Bilingual Press, 1983.

Soler, Ricaurte. *El positivismo argentino.* Panamá: Imprenta Nacional, 1959.

———. *Formas ideológicas de la nación panameña.* Panamá: Treas, 1963; 2nd ed., 1964.

Souza, Francisco Martins de. "O problema do conhecimento em Miguel Reale e o diálogo com Husserl," *Ciências Humanas* 18–19 (1981).

Sowerby, Millicent, comp. *Catalogue of the Library of Thomas Jefferson.* Washington: Library of Congress, 1952.

———. "La biblioteca de Thomas Jefferson," *Revista Interamericana de Bibliografía* 8 (1958): 116–19.

Stabb, Martin S. *In Quest of Identity: Patterns in the Spanish American Essay of Ideas. 1860–1960.* Chapel Hill: University of North Carolina Press, 1967.

Stein, Ernildo. "A filosofia no Brasil," in H. Ortiz, ed., *La filosofía hoy en Alemania y América Latina.* Córdoba, Argentina: Instituto Goethe, 1984, 238–47.

Stoetzer, O. C. *The Scholastic Roots of the Spanish American Revolution.* New York: Fordham University, 1979.

Strategy Research Corporation. *U.S. Hispanic Market.* Miami, Fla., 1984.

Terán, O. *José Ingenieros.* México: Siglo XXI, 1979.

———. *Discutir Mariátegui.* Puebla: Universidad Autónoma de Puebla, 1985.

_____. *En busca de la ideología argentina*. Buenos Aires: Catálogos, 1986.

Torchia Estrada, Carlos. *La filosofía en la Argentina*. Washington, D.C.: Unión Panamericana, 1961.

_____. Philosophy section corresponding to several years, Humanities volume of the *Handbook of Latin American Studies*. Gainesville: University of Florida Press.

_____. *Alejandro Korn: Profesión y vocación*. México: Universidad Nacional Autónoma de México, 1986.

Trabulse, Elías. *El círculo roto*. Lecturas Mexicanas 54. México: Fondo de Cultura Económica, 1984.

UNESCO World Guide to Higher Education. New York: Bowkers, 1980.

UNESCO Statistical Yearbook. 1984. New York: United Nations Educational and Social Committee, 1984.

United States Library of Congress. *Hispanic Foundation*. Departmental and Divisional Manuals, No. 12. Washington: Library of Congress, 1950.

Valenzuela, Luisa. "La mala palabra," *Revista Iberoamericana* 51 (1985): 489–91.

Valle, Rafael Heliodoro. *Historia de las ideas contemporáneas en Centroamérica*. México: Fondo de Cultura Económica, 1960.

Van der Karr, J. *José Ingenieros*. New York: Vantage, 1977.

Van Sertima, Ivan. *They Came Before Columbus: The African Presence in Ancient America*. New York: Random House, 1976.

Vargas Lozano, Gabriel. "Notas sobre la función actual de la filosofía en México (la década de los setenta)," *Dialéctica* 9 (1980).

_____. "Corrientes actuales de la filosofía en México," *Prometeo* 3 (1987): 45–54.

Vasconcelos, José. *The Cosmic Race*. Trans. Didier T. Jaen. Los Angeles: California State University, 1979.

_____. *La raza cósmica*. 6th ed. México: Espasa-Calpe, 1981.

Vázquez, Juan Adolfo. *Antología filosófica argentina*. Buenos Aires: EUDEBA, 1965.

Vega, Ana Lydia. *Encancaranublado*. Río Piedras, Puerto Rico: Antillana, 1983.

_____. *Pasión de historia y otras historias de pasión*. Buenos Aires: Ediciones de la Flor, 1987.

Vega, Ana Lydia, and Carmen Lugo Filippi. *Vírgenes y mártires*. Río Piedras, Puerto Rico: Antillana, 1981.

Vélez Correa, Jaime. "Proceso de la filosofía en Colombia," *Anales de la Universidad de Antioquía* 36 (1960): 869–1012.

Vera y Cuspines, Margarita. *El pensamiento filosófico de Vasconcelos*. México: Extemporáneos, 1979, 1985.

Vidal Muñoz, Santiago. "Filosofía en Chile," *Cuadernos de Filosofía* 6 (1977): 19–44.

Villegas, Abelardo. *La filosofía de lo mexicano*. México: Fondo de Cultura Económica, 1960.

――――. *México en el horizonte liberal*. México: Fondo de Cultura Económica, 1983.

――――. *Autognosis: El pensamiento mexicano en el siglo XX*. México: Instituto Panamericano de Geografía e Historia, 1985.

Villegas, Juan. *Antología de la nueva poesía femenina chilena*. Santiago de Chile: La Noria, 1985.

Villoro, Luis. "La filosofía en México en los 80," in *Perfil de México en 1980*. México: Siglo XXI, 1970.

Virasoro, M. A. "Filosofía," in *Argentina, 1930–1960*. Buenos Aires: Sur, 1961.

Vita, Luis Washington. *Panorama da filosofia no Brasil*. Porto Alegre: 1968.

Vitier, Medardo. *Las ideas en Cuba*, 2 vols. Havana, Cuba: Trópico, 1938.

――――. *La filosofía en Cuba*. México: Fondo de Cultura Económica, 1948.

――――. "Cincuenta años de estudio de la filosofía en Cuba," *Cursos y Conferencias* 25 (1956): 130–32.

――――. *Las ideas y la filosofía en Cuba*. Havana, Cuba: Editorial Ciencias Sociales, 1970.

Walsh, María Elena. *A la madre. Poemas elegidos por María Elena Walsh*. Buenos Aires: Sudamericana, 1981.

Weinberg, Gregorio. "Aspectos del vaciamiento de la universidad argentina durante los recientes regímenes miliares," *Cuadernos Americanos*, nueva época 6 (November–December 1987): 204–15.

Weinstein, M. *The Polarity of Mexican Thought*. University Park, PA: The Pennsylvania State University, 1976.

Wilkie, James, and Adam Perkal. *Statistical Abstracts of Latin America.* Los Angeles: University of California, Los Angeles, 1982.

Wilson, Douglas L. "Jefferson's Library," in Merrill D. Peterson, ed., *Thomas Jefferson: A Biography.* New York: Scribner's, 1986, 169–86.

Woll, Allen L. "The Philosophy of History in Nineteenth Century Chile: The Lastarria-Bello Controversy," *History and Theory* 13 (1974): 273–90.

Yamuni, Vera. *José Gaos. El hombre y su pensamiento.* México: Universidad Nacional Autónoma de México, 1980.

Yankelovich, Skelly and White, Inc. *Spanish USA: A Study of the Hispanic Market in the United States: Origins, Characteristics and Life-style. Marketing and Media Behavior.* New York, 1981.

Zalazar, Daniel. *Freedom and Creation in the Essays of A. Korn.* Doctoral dissertation, University of Pittsburgh, 1969.

Zan, Julio de. "El problema de la identidad nacional del hombre argentino," *Megafón* 8 (1978).

Zea, Leopoldo. *El positivismo en México: Apogeo y decadencia del positivismo en México.* México: El Colegio de México, 1944.

————. *En torno a una filosofía americana.* México: El Colegio de México, 1945.

————. *Positivism in Mexico.* Trans. J. Schulte. Austin: University of Texas Press, 1974.

————. *Filosofía de la historia americana.* México: Fondo de Cultura Económica, 1978.

————. *Simón Bolívar.* México: Edicol, 1980.

————. *Latinoaméroca en la encrucijada de la historia.* México: Universidad Nacional Autónoma de México, 1981.

————. *Sentido de la difusión cultural latinoamericana.* México: Universidad Nacional Autónoma de México, 1981.

————. *América como autodescubrimiento.* Bogotá: Publicaciones de la Universidad Central, 1986.

————, ed. *América Latina en sus ideas.* México: UNESCO–Siglo XXI, 1986.

————. *Discurso de la marginación y la barbarie.* Barcelona: Antropos, 1988.

Contributors

ONÉSIMO TEOTÓNIO ALMEIDA was born in the Azores, Portugal. He earned his Ph.D. degree at Brown University in 1980. Almeida is associate professor in the Center for Portuguese and Brazilian Studies, Brown University. His publications include: "Filosofia portuguesa – Alguns equívocos," *Cultura-História/Filosofia* 4 (1985); "Mannheim's Dual Conception of Ideology: A Critical Look," *Ideologies & Literature*, 2nd Cycle 4, 17 (1983); *A questão da literatura açorinan* (Angra: Secretaria Regional da Educação e Cultura, 1983); and *The Labyrinth of Ideology*, forthcoming. Professor Almeida's book on Fernando Pessoa's Mensagem, *Uma tentativa de reinterpretacão* (Angra: SREC, 1987) won the Roberto de Mesquita Award from the Axorean Secretariat of Education and Culture.

HUGO EDGARDO BIAGINI was born in Argentina. He earned his Ph.D. degree at the Universidad de la Plata, Argentina. Biagini is Profesor Titular of the Universidad de Belgrano. His publications include: *Cómo fue la generación del 80* (Buenos Aires, 1980); *Educación y progreso* (Buenos Aires, 1983); *Panorama filosófico argentino* (Buenos Aires, 1987); and *El movimiento positivista argentino* (Buenos Aires, in press).

MIREYA CAMURATI was born in Argentina, 1934. She earned her Ph.D. degree at the University of Pittsburgh in 1970. Camurati is professor of Spanish American Literature and director of the Spanish graduate program at the State University of New York at Buffalo. Her publications include: *Poesía y poética de Vicente Huidobro* (Buenos Aires, 1980); *Enfoques* (Lexington, Mass., 1980); *La fábula en Hispanoamérica* (México, 1978); *Ideas y motivos* (Lexington, Mass., 1975); and "Adolfo Bioy Casares," essay for *Scribner's Latin-American Writers* (in press).

EMILIO CARBALLIDO was born in Mexico in 1925. He earned his M.A. degree in English and Theater Arts at the Universidad Nacional de México. Playwright, critic, director, and teacher, Carballido is the most prolific contemporary Mexican dramatist. His awards include: Rockefeller Foundation grantee in New York, Fellow for two years at the Centro Mexicano de Escritores, *El Nacional's* Prize (1954), "Drama Festival of Mexico City" Prize (1955), *Heraldo* Prize (1967), and Critics and Journalists Society Award (1977). *Rosalba y los llaveros* (1950), *El día que se soltaron los leones* (1963), and *Yo también hablo de la rosa* (1966) are among his better-known plays.

HIBER CONTERIS was born in Uruguay in 1933, and studied in Buenos Aires and Paris. Conteris is currently visiting professor of Spanish American Literature at the University of Wisconsin. His awards include: *Letras de Oro* First Prize in Short Story (1986) and Casa de las Américas Prize (1988). His publications include: *Virginia en Flashback* (Montevideo, 1966); *El diez por ciento de vida* (Barcelona, 1986); *La Diana en el crepúsculo* (Barcelona, 1987); *El Icono Bizantino* (Madrid, 1987); and *Información sobre la Ruta 1* (Barcelona, 1988).

GEORGETTE M. DORN was born in Hungary, and raised in Spain and Argentina. She took her Ph.D. in history at Georgetown University in 1981. Dorn is head of the Hispanic Reading Room and the specialist in Hispanic culture at the Library of Congress, and adjunct professor at Georgetown University. Her awards include: grants from the Washington, D.C. Endowment for the Humanities, and the Organization of American States. Her publications include: *The Archive of Hispanic Literature on Tape*, with Francisco Aguilera (Washington, 1974); *A Report on the Indian Tribes of Texas by José Francisco Ruiz*, translator (New Haven, 1971); "Hilario Ascasubi," "Florencio Sánchez," in *Scribner's Latin-American Writers* (in press); "Bibliographies on Women," *Latina Sourcebook* (1988); and "Las colecciones de literatura hispánica en la Biblioteca del Congreso," *Revista Interamericana de Bibliografía* (1979).

ROSEMARY GEISDORFER FEAL was born in the United States in 1955. She earned her Ph.D. degree at the State University of New York at Buffalo in 1984. Geisdorfer Feal is assistant professor of Spanish at the University of Rochester. Her awards include a Mellon Postdoctoral Fellowship. Her publications include: *Novel Lives: The Fictional Autobiographies of Guillermo Cabrera Infante and Mario Vargas Llosa* (Chapel Hill, N.C.: 1986); "Patriarchism and Racism: The Case of *Cumboto*," *Afro-Hispanic Review* 2 (1983); "Autobiography and the Identity Game in Cabrera Infante's *La Habana para un infante difunto*," *Folio* 16 (1984); "Veiled Portraits: Donoso's Interartistic Dialogue in *El jardín de* *al lado,"* *Modern Language Notes* 103 (1988); and "La ficción como tema: La trilogía dramática de Mario Vargas Llosa," *Texto Crítico* 36–37 (1988).

JAIME GIORDANO was born in Chile in 1937. He received his Profesor de Estado en Español degree at the Universidad de Chile in 1961. Giordano is professor of Spanish at the State University of New York at Stony Brook. His publications include: *La edad del ensueño: Sobre la imaginación poética de Rubén Darío* (Santiago de Chile, 1971); *La edad de la náusea (sobre narrativa hispanoamericana contemporánea)* (Santiago de Chile, 1985); *Dioses, antidioses . . . (ensayos críticos sobre poesía hispanoamericana)* (Santiago de Chile, 1987); *Marzo* (Santiago de Chile, 1984); and *Sobre los ángeles* (Santiago de Chile, 1985).

JORGE J. E. GRACIA was born in Cuba in 1942. He received his Ph.D. degree at the University of Toronto in 1971. Gracia is a professor in the Department of Philosophy, State University of New York at Buffalo and has held a Canada Council Fellowship, a National Endowment for the Humanities Fellowship, and a New York Council for the Humanities Grant. His publications include: ed., *Latin American Philosophy in the Twentieth Century* (Buffalo, 1986); ed., *Philosophical Analysis in Latin America*, with others (Dordrecht, 1984; Spanish version, Mexico, 1985); ed., *Man and His Conduct: Philosophical Essays in Honor of Risieri Frondizi* (San Juan, PR, 1980); ed., *Latin American Philosophy Today*, double issue of the *Philosophical Forum* (New York, 1988); and ed., *Directory of Latin American Philosophers — Repertorio de Filósofos Latinoamericanos* (Buffalo, 1988).

JOSÉ KOZER was born in Cuba in 1940. He has lived in New York since 1960. His Ph.D. equivalency is from Queens College. Kozer is associate professor of Spanish at Queens College, City University of New York. His awards include: Cintas Fellowship (1964) and Julio Tovar Poetry Prize (1974). His publications include: *El carillón de los muertos* (Buenos Aires, 1987); *La garza sin sombras* (Barcelona, 1985); *Bajo este cien* (México, 1983); *Jarrón de las abreviaturas* (México, 1980); and *La rueca de los semblantes* (León, 1980).

OSCAR MARTÍ was born in Cuba in 1941. His Ph.D. degree is from the City University of New York. Martí is associate director of the University of California at Los Angeles French Revolution and Latin American Program; he has been a fellow at the Institute for American Cultures at UCLA and a Fulbright Fellow. His publications include: *The Gabino Barreda Centennial Issue of Aztlán* (Los Angeles, 1983); *Un manual de lógica* (Mexico, 1988); "The Positivist Utopias," *Utopian Dreams*; "El futuro del pasado: La universidad norteamericana y el resto del futuro," *Cuadernos Americanos*; "Is There a Latin American Philosophy?" *Metaphilosophy* 14

(1983); and "La filosofía latinoamericana: posibilidades y preferencias," *Anuario Latinoamerica* 15 (1982).

VINCENT PELOSO was born in the United States in 1938. He received his Ph.D. degree at the University of Arizona in 1969. Peloso is associate professor of the Department of History, Howard University and has held a Woodrow Wilson Fellowship and a Fulbright Fellowship. His publications include: "Transformación de la sociedad campesina, articulación y subdesarrollo en las haciendas algodoneras peruanas: el valle de Pisco, 1883-1925," *Allpanchis Phuturinga* (1983); "Cotton Planters, the State and Rural Labor Policy. Origins of the Peruvian *República Aristocrática*, 1895-1908," *The Americas* (October, 1983); "Succulence and Sustenance: Region, Class and Diet in Nineteenth Century Peru," in J. Super and T. C. Wright, eds., *Food, Politics and Society in Latin America* (University of Nebraska, 1985); "Juan Esquivel, A Tenant in the Pisco Valley, Peru, 1895-1920," in W. Beezley and J. Ewell, eds., *The Human Tradition in Latin America. The Twentieth Century* (Wilmington, 1987); and "Il controlo congressionale, interesi provinciale e il sistema elettorale nel'ottocento peruviano," *Quaderni Storici* (October, 1988).

CELSO RODRÍGUEZ was born in Argentina in 1929. He received his Ph.D. degree in history from the University of Massachusetts in 1974. Rodríguez is editor of *Inter-American Review of Bibliography*, and senior specialist, Program of Development of Latin American Archives at the Department of Cultural Affairs, Organization of American States. His publications include: *Lencinas y Cantoni. El populismo cuyano en tiempos de Yrigoyen* (Buenos Aires, 1979); "Algunas reflexiones sobre el Sistema Nacional de Archivos," *Boletín del Sistema Nacional de Archivos* 6 (México 1984); "Bibliografía norteamericana reciente: *The American Archivist*, 1981-1983," *Anuario Interamericano de Archivos* 9-10 (Córdoba, Argentina, 1984); "Archivos y educación," in César Gutiérrez Muñoz and Rolf Nagel, eds. *Textos para el estudio archivístico. Materiales de Trabajo* (Lima and Bonn, 1986); and "Si nosotros no apoyábamos al Archivo Nacional ¿quién lo iba a hacer?" in *De archivos y archivistas. Homenaje a Aurelio Tanodi* (Washington, 1987).

JOAQUÍN ROY was born in Spain in 1943. His Ph.D. degree is from Georgetown University. Roy is professor in the Department of Spanish and director of the Latin Anerican Studies Program, University of Miami; director of the Spanish Literary Contest *Letras de Oro*; and editor of *Ideas '92*. His publications include: *Catalunya a Cuba* (Barcelona, 1987); *Josep Conangla i Fontanilles. La constitució de l'Havana y altres escrits* (Barcelona, 1986); *ALA: literatura y periodismo* (Madrid, 1986); *Lecturas de prensa* (New York, 1982); and *Julio Cortázar ante su sociedad* (Barcelona, 1974).

TERESA CAJIAO SALAS was born in Chile in 1927. She received her Ph.D. degree at Case Western Reserve University in 1969. Salas is professor at the State University College at Buffalo and has held a Visiting Professor Research Grant at the State University of New York at Buffalo and a Fulbright Fellowship. Her publications include: *Asedios a la poesía de Nicomedes Santa Cruz* (Quito, 1982); *El teatro de hoy en Costa Rica* (San José de Costa Rica, 1973); and *Temas y símbolos en la obra de Luis Alberto Heiremans* (Santiago de Chile, 1970).

IAN ISIDORE SMART was born in Trinidad and Tobago in 1944. He received his Ph.D. degree at University of California at Los Angeles in 1975. Smart is professor of Spanish in the Department of Romance Languages, Howard University. His publications include: *Central American Writers of West Indian Origin: A New Hispanic Literature* (Washington, D.C., 1984); *Short Stories by Cubena*, trans., introduction and notes (Washington, D.C., 1987); "The African Heritage in Spanish Caribbean Literature," *The Western Journal of Black Studies* 5 (1981): 23–31; "The Cuban *Son*: One of Africa's Contributions to Contemporary Caribbean Poetics," *Journal of African and Comparative Literature* 1 (1981): 14–29; and "*Mulatez* and the Image of the Black *Mujer Nueva* in Guillén's Poetry," *Kentucky Romance Quarterly* 29 (1982): 379–390.

FRED GILLETTE STURM was born in the United States in 1925. He received his Ph.D. at Columbia University in 1961. Sturm is professor and chair of the Department of Philosophy, University of New Mexico. His publications include: *Existence in Search of Essence: The Philosophy of Spirit of Raimundo de Farias Brito* (1962); *O significado atual de Farias Brito* (Univ. Ceara, 1963); *Fuentes bibliográficas de la filosofía latinoamericana* (Washington, D.C.: Pan American Union, 1967); "The Philosophical Ambiance of Brasilian Independence," (1971); and "Dependence and Originality in Latin America," (1978).

MARGARITA VARGAS was born in the United States in 1956. She earned her Ph.D. degree at the University of Kansas in 1985. Vargas is assistant professor of Spanish in the Department of Modern Languages, State University of New York at Buffalo, has held the Lilly Endowment Fellowship, a UUP New Faculty Development Award, a Fulbright-Hays Fellowship, and was a finalist in the *Letras de Oro* literary competition. Her publications include: "Las novelas de los Contemporáneos como 'textos de goce,'" *Hispania* 69 (1986): 40–44; "Reality versus Illusion: A Structural Analysis of *Madame Bovary*," *Chiméres* 17 (1984): 39–53; trans., Juan García Ponce's "The Night," *Fiction* 7 and 8 (1985): 63–91; trans., Inés Arredondo's "The Shunammite," *Mundus Artium* (1985): 36–45; and trans., Inés Arredondo's "Mariana," *Fiction* (1981): 156–64.

ANA LYDIA VEGA was born in Puerto Rico in 1946. She received her doctorate at the Université de Provence, Aix-Marseille in 1978. Vega teaches French at the University of Puerto Rico, Río Piedras. Her awards include: Casa de las Américas Prize (1982) and Juan Rulfo International Prize (1984). Her publications include: *Vírgenes y mártires*, with Carmen Lugo Filippi (Río Piedras, 1981); *Encancaranublado y otros cuentos de naufragio* (Río Piedras, 1983); *Pasión de historia y otras historias de pasión* (Buenos Aires, 1987); and co-writer, script for *La Gran Fiesta*, directed by Marcos Zurinaga (1986).

Index

The index records proper names primarily, although a few terms and subjects referring to the philosophy section have also been included. It does not cover the bibliographies on pages 54–63, 204–212, 237–259, or the biographical sketches of the contributors at the end of the volume.